Date Due

CLASS AND HIERARCHY: THE SOCIAL MEANING OF OCCUPATIONS

CLASS AND HIERARCHY: THE SOCIAL MEANING OF OCCUPATIONS

Anthony P.M. Coxon
and
Charles L. Jones

ST. MARTIN'S PRESS NEW YORK

First published in the United States of America 1979.

ISBN 0–312–14256–0

Library of Congress Cataloging in Publication Data

Coxon, Anthony Peter Macmillan.
  Class and hierarchy.

  Bibliography: p.
  Includes indexes.
  1. Great Britain – Occupation – Social aspects.
2. Occupational prestige – Great Britain
3. Occupational mobility – Great Britain.
4. Social classes – Great Britain. I. Jones,
Charles L. II. Title.
HT690. G7C69 1979 301. 44'4'0941 78-11081
ISBN 0–312–14256–0

Contents

List of Figures

List of Tables

Preface

Systems of invidious social distinction between occupations pervade all societies, and many different reasons are given to justify or attack them. Some aspects of social inequality are so obvious that they need no pointing out, and everyone understands and knows their significance. But throughout the greater part of society, other social distinctions are much less visible and are based upon more subtle criteria. It is of no concern to most of us that the face-worker in a colliery is much more highly esteemed than the surface-worker, even if we are aware of the distinction. Equally peripheral to most of us is the difference between a diocesan and a suffragan bishop. Yet in their own fields, such distinctions can assume enormous importance, which all of us become aware of when strikes occur as a result of demarcation disputes or income differentials.

We often talk about these differences under the rubrics of 'social class' and 'occupational hierarchies'. And despite our reluctance to refer, at least in public, to such taboo topics they pervade a surprising amount of our conversation. Class is not simply an obsession of sociologists. Yet whilst we know a great deal about the differences which social class makes in many areas, we know relatively little about how people actually conceive their social world and how social class fits into these conceptions.

Our own interest in occupations sprang originally from a number of disparate concerns, which we have outlined in the Preface to *The Images of Occupational Prestige*. But we should like to emphasise once again that whilst our research focus is almost entirely upon the so-called subjective aspects of social stratification (a description we ourselves have used), we do not wish to give the impression that we are dismissive, unconcerned or unaware of what is usually termed the 'objective' aspects of class. Far from it; we are very conscious of 'the substance and structural sources of inequality, irrespective of how people react to the experience of inequality' (Westergaard and Resler 1975: 2), and we concur with Thompson when he asserts (Thompson 1968: 9):

> I emphasise that [class] is a historical phenomenon. I do not see class as a 'structure', nor even as a 'category', but as something which in fact happens . . . in human relationships. . . . The finest meshed sociological net cannot give us a pure specimen of class, any more than it can give us one of deference or of love.

The point remains, however, that many people *do* see class as a category, and people *do* react to their experiences of inequality. It is our contention that it serves no useful purpose to preserve the misleading distinction between 'subjective' and 'objective' aspects of class, especially if the former is thought of as simply derivative of the latter. Unless people's views of their world are to be ruled out *a priori* as irrelevant, then we think it instructive to entertain the hypothesis that these views — 'theories' of their world — are not generically different from those which we as sociologists hold.

We have also gone on record as expressing the view that studies of social mobility are bound to be restricted and can do scant justice to its multi-faceted complexity when the 'structure' or space through which the mobility occurs is related only contingently, if at all, to the conceptions which the people have of their situation (Coxon and Jones 1975a:14 *et seq.*) Of course a sociologist is at liberty to use his own category system as a basis for analysis, and it may well be that it is a very useful one. But we shall also need to know, in Goldthorpe's words (Goldthorpe 1972:382),

> how cognitive maps of occupations are generated. But I think, first of all, one must know what they are, and the extent to which they vary between social groups and categories.

And we shall certainly need to know this before the experience of social mobility can be adequately analysed.

We locate our work, then, straightforwardly in the area of social stratification, and its utility must be judged in terms of the extent to which it causes others, as it has us, to question the adequacy of many of the foundations upon which that study is based. And since most of the currently contentious areas in the political and economic arena are concerned with inequalities, differentials and conceptions of just allocation of resources, — all topics with relevance to subjective aspects of social stratification — we hope our work will also contribute to these wider debates.

We also recognise that our work cross-cuts a whole set of other familiar, even homely, conventional divides — cognitive/positivist, interpretative/ structural — and that our methodology is eclectic, adapting the rigour and systematic nature of the one approach to the fluidity, complexity and constructive nature of the other. Marginal men are rarely popular, but by criss-crossing the established polarities they can often contribute to the cohesion of the discipline as well as to the richer understanding of the subject-matter. That at least is our hope, and it has sustained us through the changes and chances of the research process.

ACKNOWLEDGEMENTS

The research reported in this volume was made possible by the second of two grants made by the (U.K.) Social Science Research Council from September 1973 to December 1975 (HR1883/2: 'Sociological aspects of subjective occupational structure'). We gratefully acknowledge this support. We again thank our research staff who bore the brunt of most of the exacting inter-viewing and of much of the data-analysis work. A large number of people have had to cope with the often illegible and complicated written versions of this volume, and turn it into readable typescript. We are particularly grateful to May Fraser in Edinburgh, who stayed with us as secretary throughout the project, and to Myrtle Robins, who bore the brunt of typing most of the final version. Our thanks are also due to Margaret Simpson and Jacquie Markie in Cardiff and to Jackie Tucker, Shirley McGill and Michele Cholette in Hamilton, Ontario, for their secretarial help.

Our grateful acknowledgements are also due to our collaborators and colleagues who have been associated with this second part of the research: Mike Burton, Lillian Brudner and Doug White of the School of Social Sciences at the University of California at Irvine; Bob Blackburn, Sandy Stewart and Ken Prandy of the Department of Applied Economics, Cambridge; and to Frank Bechhofer, Scott Boorman, Tom Burns, Aaron Cicourel, Peter Davies, Tom Fararo, Moshe Hartman, Eddie Laumann, Ken Macdonald, Noel Parry, Phil Stone, and Harrison White, who at various times and in many different ways have helped us and offered perceptive critical comment. Throughout the Project, Doug Carroll of Bell Laboratories, Jim Lingoes of the University of Michigan and Eddie Roskam of the Catholic University of Nijmegen have constantly assisted us in the scaling area; we owe them an especial debt of thanks.

ORGANISATION OF THE TEXT

As in *The Images of Occupational Prestige*, we have relegated a good deal of the technical material to separate appendixes which are to found in the third volume (*Measurement and Meanings: Techniques and Methods of Studying Occupational Cognition*). In that volume we include technical appendixes referring to chapters in the first two volumes of this research work. In order to make cross-reference easier, we have prefaced technical appendixes referring to chapters in our first book by the letter 'T', and appendixes referring to chapters in this book by the letter 'U'. Thus the reference 'see T3.5' means that the fifth technical appendix referring to chapter three of the first book should be consulted, and the reference 'see U3.5' means that the fifth appendix referring to chapter three of this book should be consulted. In this way a one-to-one relationship is kept between the chapters of the first two volumes and the contents of the third.

As in the previous book, the authorship is truly joint and, as always in our publications, the order of authors is simply alphabetical. However, we established overall responsibility for analysis of the empirically-based material at an early stage; Coxon was primarily responsible for the analysis reported in Chapters 2-4 and Jones for the analysis reported in Chapter 5.

A.P.M.C
C.L.J.

Cardiff, Wales
and Hamilton, Ontario

1 The Social Meaning of Occupations

No-one has directly encountered an 'occupation'. Why, then, do we speak of
'occupational cognition' and of 'perception of class' as if occupations or social
classes were perceived as directly as chairs, stones or colours? In actual fact we
do not even perceive stones in any simple, direct, manner. Rather, we actively
construct mental models of our world, which form the structure in which we
locate, and neglect, information, make comparisons and organise our
perceptions. This account of cognition, which stresses that knowledge is an
interpretative and a constructive process, contrasts sharply with the longer-
established view of perception emanating from the British empiricists and best
expressed by Hume. In this tradition, perception was viewed as an essentially
passive process involving two distinct *genera*: impressions and ideas.
Impressions − 'lively perceptions' − impinge directly from the physical and
social environment, and are causally prior to ideas. It is ideas which form the
raw material of cognition, and are thought of as being exact *replicas* of
impressions. The epistemology developed on this basis need not detain us, but
its central assumption (that mental processes operate in a straight forward way
upon virtual copies of an external reality) passed almost unchanged into
Freudianism and subsequently into the work of many social theorists. [1]

More recently, cognitive scientists have insisted that when we recall
information about the world, a process of *re*-construction is involved:

> What is the information . . . on which re-construction is based? The only
> plausible possibility is that it consists of traces of *prior processes of
> construction*. There are no stored copies of finished mental events . . . but
> only traces of earlier constructive activity. Recall in words . . . is a new
> verbal synthesis which may be based on information from a number of
> sources, including not only traces of earlier verbalization, but perhaps
> visual images and other constructions as well. (Neisser 1967:285)

But when cognition refers to abstract social and symbolic entities, a double
process of abstraction is involved. When we perceive a table, we certainly
respond in a direct manner to external stimuli, but in 'cognising an occupation'
this is not the case (except perhaps to the extent that individuals present visual
clues to their occupation, such as the clerical collar or the union badge). In
the case of symbolic entities, we operate upon a *conception* which involves
reference to a wider range of information, meanings and interpretations than

is the case with direct perception.[2] In brief, then, the conception that someone has of an occupation or of a social class refers to the knowledge which he
has of it, the beliefs he holds about it and the meaning or significance which
such information has for him.

Usually we gain access to conceptions by means of language. When we
communicate with others we select concepts (which are component aspects of
our model of the world) and these are reinterpreted by the hearer in terms of
his model. In many cases, the receiver's interpretation will be very close to the
speaker's intended meaning, and social scientists have usually assumed that
individuals who share a common culture, background and social situation will
have largely coincident conceptions and models of the world.

These points are basic to anthropology, psychology and sociology, and they
are discussed in a wide variety of theoretical guises such as social memory,
social identity, folk taxonomies, images of society, *verstehen*, structure of the
social world, social sterotypes and subjective culture. Yet despite a good deal
of theoretical and philosophical speculation, and selected anecdotal accounts
which consist of edited verbal transcripts of subjects responding to an
interviewer's leading questions, we know little indeed about the structure of
such conceptions of the occupational world, or about the ways in which (and
the extent to which) they are socially shared.

1.1   SOCIAL SEMANTICS

The questions we have posed closely parallel those which psycholinguists and
computer scientists ask when they investigate meaning, except that we are
additionally concerned with its *social context.* The reason for the overlap is
simply that these disciplines − together with artificial intelligence[3] − have
attempted to represent belief systems and 'stocks of knowledge' in the process
of modelling human thought and language (see Schank and Colby 1973). In
so doing, they have shed much light on issues which also arise in sociological
contexts. The common, and most basic, problem is how to represent cognitive
structures, such as conceptions of the occupational world.

> What are the primitive symbols or concepts, how are they related, how are
> they to be concatenated and constructed into larger knowledge structures,
> and how is this 'information file' to be accessed, searched and utilized in
> solving the mundane problems of daily living. (Anderson and Bower 1973: 15

Summarising an immense amount of work on problem-solving procedures in
artifical intelligence, Amarel (1968:135) comments that choice of appropriate
representations is capable of having spectacular effects in problem solving
efficiency. It behoves us, therefore, to pay especial attention to the
representational aspects of occupational conceptions.

It is often useful to think of 'occupational meaning' as a collection of images and concepts, which represents the accumulated knowledge which individuals have of their (occupational) world. In this context, a 'concept' is a cognitive structure consisting of a set of components embedded in complex relationships to each other (Kiss, 1972:3). In the case of occupational concepts, the basic components will often be the occupational titles themselves, such as 'Diplomat in the U.S. Foreign Service', 'Joiner', or 'Combing-jobber' — (although the obvious differences which exist in the extent to which a title is specified indicates that they are not the simplest elements). The network of relationships linking the components into more complex entities such as social classes can be thought of as representing a wide range of non-logical relations — associative links, attributes, plans[4] — as well as the more well-known logical ones of negation, conjunction, inclusion and implication.

The subject-predicate link is fundamental to these more complex relationships, and is the basic structure which we choose for representing meaning. As well as having a long philosophical history, it is used as a basic feature in virtually all recent work relevant to modelling belief systems.[5] The process of occupational predication consequently features as a central organising feature in the research reported here.

In its simplest form, predication 'combines a topic and comment on that topic' (Miller 1967:26), and is illustrated in a sentence such as 'Doctors are well paid'. Logically, the predicate — in this case, that of being well paid — asserts something about the subject (Doctors). Predication can be made as complex as desired. For example it can be extended to assert a relationship ('Doctors are higher paid than Bus Drivers') and to permit predication of predication ('the proposition that Miners deserve more pay has never been seriously questioned'). It therefore allows the representation of sentences such as 'the Miners' pay rise was justifiable' and 'Managers' higher education gives them access to more prestigious and well-paid positions than Clerks'. In the latter case an earlier sentence ('nominalisation') represented here by 'the Miners' pay rise', becomes a topic for further comment. This recursive process of predication can be continued indefinitely and produces the rich complexity and combinational productivity distinguishing human from animal communication. In such a manner, the meaning of occupational terms can be encoded as 'deeply' as necessary. The components and relations at one level can be viewed in turn as concepts in their own right, each having their own internal structure, and they can also serve as topics for further comment.

How complex are the 'subjective models of the occupational world', which we seek to represent, and how may they be investigated? The brief answer to the first question is 'as complex as necessary'. It is entirely arbitrary to set boundaries around purely occupational knowledge and beliefs, and the degree of complexity will be determined by the purposes of analysis. The effect of social structure itself upon people's conceptions of occupations has usually been taken to be rather simple and undifferentiated, but there is surprisingly little detailed and *systematic* information about the nature of occupational belief systems. The attempt to model such systems in detail would be a major research endeavour in its own right, but was unfortunately outside the allowed resources of our project. We therefore restrict ourselves here to the more fundamental, manageable and tractable task of investigating the general organising principles which inderlie subjective occupational structures and the content and form of occupational predication.

1.2   MEANING AND SEMANTIC STRUCTURE

Despite the obvious need for subtle and formally-rich representations of people's belief systems, there are limits to their complexity. There are

> sharp human cognitive limitations in the face of transient, unfamiliar, noisy and competitive information . . . From sensation to perception to decision-making, there are constraints and pressures toward oversimplification and misjudgment. (Abelson 1973:288)

Some of these tendencies have been mentioned earlier, especially the predilection for simple, linear, end-anchored cognitive orderings, but there are many other types of limitation:

> the amount of information and number of discriminations which a person can usually make in terms of a simple property is severely restricted (Miller 1956; Simon 1969:39 *et seq.*);

> the type of composition rule used to combine information into overall impressions of either social objects or of individuals is usually very crude (Warr and Smith 1970; Yntema and Torgerson 1961);

> the number of categories which can be used if new material is to be well assimilated is rather small (Mandler 1957, cited in Abelson 1973).

It might be argued that these limitations are the result of emotion rather than cognition. This is often true — strong emotional involvement certainly acts as a spur to systematic distortion in social perception but, as Abelson goes on to point out,

> there are plenty of 'cold' cognitive factors which produce inaccurate world-views, and it is important to understand how these cognitive factors operate in their own right (p.258).

How, then can the salient characteristics of occupational cognition be investiged? Virtually every empirical study has recognised that in asking subjects to report upon some aspect of their conception of social stratification — for example, overall imagery, relative prestige, class boundaries and other discontinuities in social stratification, and labels given to social groupings – a request is also being made for information about the meanings which occupational terminology has for the subject. But although considerable attention has been paid to the broad features of the process whereby common meanings are established in social interaction, few procedures for investigating social meaning on a systematic basis have been used.

The only procedure which has been widely used is the semantic differential, which is a method for investigating the connotative meaning of concepts (Osgood, Suci and Tannenbaum 1957; Snider and Osgood 1969). Because of its extensive use as a means of 'measuring meaning' and its apparent suitability for investigating occupational cognition, the semantic differential deserves particular consideration. In this tradition, the meaning of a term or concept (such as 'motherhood', 'accountant', 'myself') is investigated by asking the subject to rate the concept in terms of a number of bi-polar rating scales, like 'dirty-clean', 'sour-sweet', 'good-bad'. The inter-correlation between the scales, aggregated over both subjects and concepts, are then factor-analysed in order to reduce the 'semantic space' to a few general dimensions of variation. The semantic differential has enjoyed considerable popularity, and has been used to some effect in occupational studies to investigate such matters as the signification of the ambiguous term 'general standing' used so extensively in the study of occupational prestige (Gusfield and Schwartz 1963), and the connotation of occupations considered in occupational choice (Coxon 1971). Indeed, Osgood's basic set of 620 concepts used in a massive intercultural study of connotative meaning (Osgood *et al.* 1975:422-52) includes between twenty and thirty occupational titles (are 'prostitute', 'gypsy', 'student' *occupational* titles?). But despite its popularity, the semantic differential suffers from a number of defects which make it ill-adapted to the fine-grained investigation of cognitive structures:

(i) It precommits the user to a restricted type of affective meaning, and also to some dubious psycholinguistic assumptions (Anderson 1969; Brown 1958; Carroll 1959; Deese 1965).

(ii) The stability of the much-heralded general factors of Evaluation, Potency and Activity proves to be friable, susceptible to fracture and recomposition depending on the domain of words or concepts involved (Miller 1967; Heise 1969).

(iii) The bipolar form of rating scales used in semantic differential research can only represent contrasting attributes, yet many qualities which appear in occupational thinking are single properties which have no natural contrast or antonym at all (see Green and Goldfried 1965).

(iv) The methods conventionally used to analyse semantic differential data are ill-designed to detect and represent concept-scale interaction

(that is, the extent to which the relation between the rating scales
changes according to the context or concept involved:Gulliksen 1958;
Bynner and Romney 1972; Levy 1972; Jones 1972; Coxon 1972).
Yet this phenomenon appears repeatedly in empirical studies[6]

These last two defects severely restrict the utility of the semantic differential
for the analysis of predication. Indeed, Osgood himself has developed a quite
different procedure which he terms 'semantic interaction' (Osgood 1970) to
investigate the ways in which semantic features of *combination* of words are
organised.

Despite the inadequacies of Osgood's semantic differential technique, the
most usual mode of analysis of cognitive structures still consists of investigating
their semantic characteristics. Indeed the terms 'cognitive' and 'semantic'
could well be used interchangeably in many recent psycholinguistic and
anthropological studies (Transgaard 1972, Smith *et al.* 1974). The reasons for
this virtual interchangeability are not hard to discern, because the rules which
underlie the *formation* of predicated relationships are very similar to
grammatical syntax, whilst the rules which underlie the *interpretation* of the
components of predication provide, in effect, the semantics of cognitive
systems. Not surprisingly, therefore, linguistic and psychological resources have
been increasingly used to analyse occupational thinking and communication.

There are a number of reasons why the semantic mode of analysis has
dominated such research, perhaps at the expense of the syntactic element. The
first is that in terms of human social *performance* (rather than competence),
meaning can often be communicated effectively with a syntax that is severely
degenerate, whilst syntactically acceptable but semantically degenerate
utterances (such as Chomsky's famous example 'Colorless green ideas sleep
furiously') are obviously ill-adapted to facilitating communication[7] Another
important reason is that the rules which govern occupational predication (i.e
how occupational belief systems are generated and transformed) are far more
complex than the rules which govern its interpretation.

At present we are at the stage of preliminary investigation, not of
explanation, of conceptions of social stratification; and we do not wish to
prejudice the latter by imposing what may turn out to be entirely ill-founded
'syntactic' constraints on our investigation. But when we turn to linguistics
for help, we find that whilst there is an extremely powerful body of theory
concerned with syntax, there is virtually no generally accepted established
theory of semantics.[8]

None the less, we insist that it is the *semantic* analysis of the occupational
lexicon and the predication process which is central to a study of occupational
cognition. We shall therefore be studying an abstracted and simplified seg-
ment of naturally-occuring language and we shall limit ourselves to a rudiment-
ary syntax. The vocabulary of this language, the occupational titles and
terms which enter into comments about them, itself expresses social
structure:

the vocabulary of a particular language will reflect the distinctions and
equivalences which are of importance in the culture of the society in which
the language operates. (Lyons 1968:55)

We shall want to investigate what these 'distributions and equivalences' are
and how they differ between occupational subcultures. In so doing we shall
also encounter in an entirely unprovoked way the conceptions of class and
social hierarchy which also inform our subjects' thinking.

1.3   THE EXPLORATION OF OCCUPATIONAL MEANING

The data analysed in our first book were elicited using techniques which are
often used in sociology (and in other disciplines) to obtain information about
'images of society'. This led us to concentrate first upon establishing a
representation — a cognitive map — of occupational names and then interpret
its significance in the subjects' own terms. The next step consisted of
examining the bases of occupational prestige (since this concept has played
such a central role in sociological accounts of social stratification and mobility)
and then we tried to understand the significance of occupational prestige in
the subjects' own thinking, against the backcloth of their occupational
cognition.

One of the more surprising results was that whilst we were able to establish,
contrary to the received wisdom, that there were socially systematic differences
in both the cognition and evaluation of occupational titles, the form of these
differences was by no means simple. Occupational membership *by itself* seems
to generate rather uninteresting differences. (None the less, the differences
between social classes continue to be important in the analyses reported in this
volume,[9] and we do not underestimate their importance.) Several
explanations could be made of this finding. We have already suggested (Coxon
and Jones 1974a:156) that the stage at which a person finds himself or herself
in their occupational life history is more important than their current job in
explaining such differences, and membership of an organised occupational
community is also a well-known factor in producing notably high degrees of
consensus about what are deemed acceptable opinions, orientations and life-
styles. A third important explanation lies in the social situation itself.
Occupational thinking and expression does not take place *in vacuo*, and there
is no warrant for believing that information elicited in the unusual context of
a social research interview will accurately reflect its use in a natural social
setting. Indeed, there is plenty of evidence that people consistently select what
they want to communicate by reference to the person(s) they are talking to.
However, the artificiality of the research interview does not, we think,
invalidate our methods of enquiry any more than it does any other methods.
But if a sociological account chooses to ignore subjects' accounts of
stratification, then it may not legitimately claim any privileged methodological

status for its own account. Sociologists accounts are not, we believe, *generically* different from those of their subjects, however much more useful, accurate or wide-ranging they may be. And this further implies that if a sociological account does exclude the subjects' conceptions of his social world, then it may not surreptitiously reimport cognitive assumptions into the explanation.

METHODS OF INQUIRY

In this volume we shift emphasis to three tasks which are more complex, are cognitively more taxing and take longer to complete than those used in our earlier book. These tasks we refer to as Free sorting (Chapter 2), Hierarchy-construction (Chapters 3 and 4) and Sentence-frame belief systems (Chapter 5) and produce considerably more verbal information than those used hitherto. They also yield quite different information about occupational meaning and about class and hierarchy.

We intend this last sentence to bear both a narrow and an extended interpretation. The first task (free sorting) leads to the production by each individual of a set of classes of occupations, and the second method (agglomerative clustering) produces a separate hierarchy for each subject. Now it would clearly be foolish to *equate* such a set of classes with the notion of 'social class' as used by sociologists, and the hierarchies which our subjects produce also bear little direct relation to the normal sociological use of the term 'hierarchy', which is usually used simply to mean a social ordering. But there are important parallels and similarities. Social classes are, on any account, a social partitioning of jobs and/or people on some specific basis or set bases. It will therefore be instructive to enquire whether, and in what ways, social class terminology occurs naturally whilst subjects form their classifications and construct their hierarchies. The third new task (sentence-frame substitution) is adapted from linguistics and cognitive anthropology, and is designed to elicit the ways in which beliefs about occupations relate to each other. In its original linguistic context it was a technique used to test the semantic equivalence or synonymy of words. In our adaptation the task consists of the subject selecting a number of belief statements (in fact, nominalisations) such as *'Doctors* are highly esteemed in the community', or *'Building site labourers* have no real career before them', and go on to substitute other occupation names. The subject is now asked to say to what extent he thinks the statement (with the new occupation substituted) is true. We then examine the extent to which one occupational belief is believed to entail, exclude or contrast with another, and we thus build up a picture of the social basis of the subjects' theories of social stratification, which also incidentally reveals the extent of their concern with social class and hierarchy.

1.4 SUBJECTS AND OBJECTS

In this volume we also shift emphasis in the ways in which the subjects and objects of judgements are chosen. (Full technical details are contained in Chapter U1 in our third book.)

SUBJECTS

In the second half of the Project, we moved towards a mode of selecting subjects which was based more directly upon naturally-recurring occupations than was the design used earlier.

There were good methodological and financial reasons for not relying upon a probability sample of all economically active males in Edinburgh, but we did want to keep broadly within the fourfold occupational typology defined in terms of Educational Requirements and Job Requirements (I:67), which we had used in the first part of the research. We decided therefore to select two adjacent areas (enumeration districts or 'census tracts') which differed basically in terms of their social class composition (i.e. the Professional *v.* the Working class contrast implied by Quadrants A and B *v.* C and D). It was a simple matter to identify likely areas from Census records, but it was rather more difficult to find a working-class district which contained a representative number of people-oriented and non-people-oriented working class occupations. [10] On the other hand there was much less difficulty (at least in Edinburgh) in identifying areas which had high concentrations of people-oriented and non-people-oriented professional occupations. [11] After considerable experimentation, we found that if suitable subjects were to be selected in a systematic manner, it would first be necessary to complete a full and accurate census of all separate dwellings in the two areas, and then 'screen' each dwellings by finding out the occupation of all economically active males living therein. A pool of 370 potential subjects were identified in this manner (193 holding a professional occupation typical of Quadrants A and B, and 177 holding a working class occupation typical of Quadrants C and D). In total, a sample of 107 of these men served as our subjects in the tasks reported in this second volume. (The detailed composition of the subsample who completed a particular task is described at the start of each chapter, and in the associated technical appendixes.)

Most of the effort, expense and ingenuity expended in this 'combing' operation involved the search for potential members of Quadrants C and D, and especially of those who had people-oriented working-class jobs. Their very rarity is, of course, an interesting comment on the social structure, since Quadrant C involved an uncommon combination of characteristics. To be involved in a people-oriented occupation usually implies a high educational level and professional status.

OBJECTS

Judging by the set of 16 occupational titles used throughout the tasks of the
first volume, we might justly be accused of selection bias and of nominalism —
of selection bias because analysis was almost completely restricted to a single
set of 16 stimuli, and of nominalism because the objects of judgement
consisted without exception of the names of occupations. But what, it may
be asked, are the objections to selection-bias and nominalism of this sort? If
a social investigation restricts attention to a single *sample* of the universe of
content (such as one set of occupational titles) (and much research is thus
limited) the researcher can never be sure about the extent to which the results
he obtains are due to the idiosyncratic composition of the sample with which
he is operating. Of course, the notion of drawing, or even defining, a sample
in the strict sense in such circumstances is usually impossible or technically
unrealistic — although we did experiment with sampling from the United
Kingdom Registrar General's *Classification of Occupations* and from the
Classification and Dictionary of Occupational Titles (CODOT) of the
Department of Employment, with interesting but unproductive results (see
Coxon and Jones 1976).

The traditional objection to nominalism is that the meaning of a concept
is not exhausted (nor even sucessfully defined) simply by naming its referents.
In this case, the question is whether one can be sure that people mean the
same thing when using the same occupational label. In functional terms, the
answer is very probably 'yes'. In a task not reported here, we first selected
the CODOT definitions of a set of occupations. Each definition consists of a
number of characteristics describing what the job actually involves. Thus, a
'Chartered Accountant' is defined (in part) in the following way:

Prepares financial statements
May audit the accounts of companies
Advises on new issues of share capital
Advises on taxation problems.

The characteristics of the selected set of occupations were then randomised
(so the subject was presented with a jumbled set of characteristics). There
were various differing versions of the task, but two were of especial relevance
to our present question. In the first version, the subject was provided with the
list of occupation names to which the characteristics referred, and was asked
to match characteristics to occupations. In the second version he was not
provided with a list of the occupations, but was asked to group the
characteristics as he wished and then name the resulting groups by an
occupational title. The significant finding about the first version was that
almost everyone was able to match an occupational title to its characteristics,
at least so long as the number of occupations chosen did not make the task
too taxing. But we do not wish to press this argument too strongly. We have

already pointed out (I:67-8) that comments made about two of the basic set of 16 titles showed that there existed widespread misinformation ('Civil Servant, Executive Grade' was often interpreted in fact to refer to an administrative-grade civil servant), or lack of information (the title 'Qualified Actuary' was unfamiliar to a goodly number of subjects, especially those in manual jobs). Other researchers' evidence confirms this impression: cf. Reiss's (1961: 16-17) famous example of the 'nuclear physicist' which was unknown to a half of a national sample, and was correctly described — even partially— by only a fifth of the sample.

Clearly, selection-bias and nominalism pose similar problems and we decided to approach their solution in two ways: by varying the composition of the set of occupations used in the tasks, and by including both predicates *and* titles (sometimes together) among the objects to be judged. (Once again, full details are contained at the beginning of each chapter and in the associated technical appendixes of the third book.)

1.5. ORGANISATION OF THE BOOK

The material reported in this volume originates in the second half of the Project of Occupational Cognition, which we entitled 'Sociological aspects of subjective occupational structures' in order to reflect the main shift in emphasis discussed at the beginning of this chapter. The methods and data we present by no means comprise the full range of methods developed and types of data which we collected; those interested in our failures or concerned to learn from our experiences and mistakes are referred to other sources.[12] In Chapter 2, we examine how people classify and categorise their occupational environment, by looking at the ways in which they form occupational classes, how similar their contents are, and what meanings are ascribed to them. In Chapter 3 the structural characteristics of the hierarchies data are investigated, and it is here that it first becomes obvious that the strategies which subjects use in producing their data are an important and integral part of their interpretation. In addition, since the other tasks (with the exception of sentence-frame substitution) can be though of as special cases of hierarchy-construction, interesting sidelight is thrown on their meaning and their cognitive assumptions. In Chapter 4 attention is directed to the verbal narratives elicited from the subjects when they are constructing their hierarchies. Although the editing process has removed some important linguistic and paralinguistic information, a number of coherent themes emerge as especially salient in subject's judgements. It also turns out that the specific and generalising phases of hierarchy-construction elicit rather different types of semantic information, and it is against this background that the language of class is analysed.

Chapter 5 represents our most ambitious endeavour: to investigate the extent of social communality between occupational belief systems. Sentence-frame substitution provided another important non-directive context for examining how people naturally use the language of social class. This task also allows us to investigate the nature of the rules which people bring into operation whilst making their occupational judgements.

In the final chapter we summarise the main conclusions of this second part of the research, and consider what the sociological consequences of these findings are. In our opinion, they are far-reaching enough to make sociologists approach the analysis of social class and hierarchies in a quite different, and more cautious, manner than they typically have done in the past.

2 Occupational Categorisation: Groups and Classes

How do people categorise their occupational environment? The anthropologist might interpret the question as analogous to the ethnographic problem of how to describe an alien culture. How does one set about discovering the elements which are significant in a given culture, and the principles by which people organise their experience? Because of the fact that the culturally-shared 'mental codes' or 'internal representations' by which experience is structured are undoubtedly mapped in language, the question therefore reduces in part to how people *name* things in their environment, and how these names are classed and related together in terms of the properties they share (Parsons and Shils, 1962:126; Tyler, 1969:6, D'Andrade 1971, D'Andrade *et al.* 1972)

The processes whereby things are named and categorised are also of basic semantic interest, and it is for this reason that the study of subjective belief systems is often referred to as 'ethnosemantics'. Put most simply, our concern is with the ways in which people divide up and classify their occupational world. But there is no need whatever to identify cultural distinctions and categorisations with occupational ranking or grading exercises, though this has been a well-nigh universal practice on the part of sociologists. Instead we shall want to concentrate, first, on what cultural boundaries exist between occupations and how they shift. We shall also want to examine the terms and attributes which people use to name the resulting categories, and which provide the criteria and bases on which their classifications are made. (If we neglect to do so, the pigeon-holes of a categorisation will be known, but their rationale, significance and relevance will remain a 'semantic mystery', as Hymes (1964) puts it.) Finally, we shall once again be concerned with the extent to which such characteristics of occupational classification are socially shared.

Now it happens that the conventional interview technique, as used by sociologists, is not a particularly good way of finding out about the ways in which people divide up the world. Talking to people about what they think of the class structure is no doubt very interesting, and may often throw up nuggets of fascinating information. But if the sociologist is to place his interviewees in one or other category on the basis of their images of society, he must have some defensible, and explicit, way of comparing them one with another. The burden of this chapter is to suggest that a very simple, flexible method of fieldwork — and one that many interviewees appear to find meaningful and enjoyable – can lead to a rigorous and empirically-grounded methodology for comparing individuals in terms of the way they divide up the world.

2.1 METHODS

The method of free sorting was chosen to provide information, of a fairly simple sort, about some of these elementary properties. In this method, the subjects are given a standard set of 'objects', and asked to sort them into *as many or as few* groups[1] as they wish. Each of the groups then contains objects which go naturally together in the estimation of the subject (we used the words 'group them in any way that seems natural to you' in the instructions He is encouraged to rearrange, break and remake clusters until an arrangement is reached which satisfies him. The purpose of this is to gain some insight into the rules which he is using to produce the sorting.

Free sorting is akin to several other methods used to analyse occupational characteristics. In particular, it is obviously very similar to *constrained* sorting, and it resembles rating ('grading') and ranking tests in some respects, but it differs from these methods in that the number of categories (classes) is deliberately left open for the subject to choose, and no particular order or scale is assumed to relate the categories. (This latter characteristic is of considerable importance, for it is circular to argue, as is sometimes done in occupational grading studies, that occupational perceptions or evaluations show independent evidence of a particular structure when the same structure is assumed in the data collection procedure itself.) Moreover, our use of the method of free grouping differs from conventional usage in three important wa

(i)   subjects are asked to verbalise their thoughts as they perform the task. The resulting protocols provide important information on how the subject construes the task, and upon certain features of it – for instance, whether he is aware of using multiple criteria, whether other sortings are recognised as legitimate, whether criteria stated at the start of the task are in fact evident in the process of sorting;

(ii) at the end of the task, they are asked to name and describe the groups they have produced. Such information is particularly important when interpreting their data; in effect, the group of objects thus named forms an extensive definition of the concept used to describe it (ways of obviating the apparent nominalism implied in this last sentence are described shortly);

(iii) *having finished the task*, the subject is then asked whether the groups are in any particular 'arrangements'. (Often, such an arrangement was evident from the spatial positioning of the groups.) Note that the word 'order' is *not* used, although a number of subjects interpreted 'arrangement' in this way (the data of subjects who did specify an ordering in their groups have been analysed in part in section 4.2 in our first book: in this chapter such information is ignored).

NAMES OF OCCUPATIONS AND KINDS OF PEOPLE

The method of sorting was developed and used at a later stage of the Project than the methods of pairwise similarities and rankings described in the first volume. In this earlier stage we had assembled a fairly extensive collection of occupational predicates, and were therefore in a position to use both occupational names and predicates in the sorting task. But it was not immediately clear how the free sorting of *predicates* could be used to yield information directly relevant to the analysis of occupational categorisation. A useful lead was provided by de Soto's (1968) discussion of the cognition of social orderings. He argues that conceptual 'good figures', such as end-anchored single linear orderings, exercise a very systematic and pervasive, even distorting, effect in social perception, and may frequently serve as an 'intellectual trap' for social scientists engaged in analysing subjects' conceptions of social stratification. De Soto comments:

Many respondents stubbornly speak of society as composed of *different kinds of people* rather than different ranks, and it is not to the credit of the social scientist than he insists on transforming their simple grouping into a ranking (p. 538, emphasis added).

TABLE 2.1   Occupational titles used in free-sorting task

Occupational Title*	Abbreviation	Occupational Title*	Abbreviation
1 Chartered Accountant	CA	17 Civil Engineer	CE
2 Secondary School Teacher	SST	18 Photographer	PHT
3 Garage Mechanic	GM	19 Building Site Labourer	BSL
4 Barman	BM	20 Restaurant Cook	RCK
5 Statistician	ST	21 Airline Pilot	AP
6 Social Worker	SW	22 Actor	A
7 Carpenter	C	23 Railway Engine Driver	RED
8 Ambulance Driver	AD	24 Postman	PO
9 Computer Programmer	CPR	25 Geologist	GEO
10 Minister of Religion	MOR	26 Sales Manager	SMG
11 Plumber	PL	27 Trawler Deckhand	TDH
12 Male Psychiatric Nurse	MPN	28 Taxi Driver	TDR
13 Bank Clerk	BCK	29 Eye Surgeon	ESG
14 Primary School Teacher	PST	30 Journalist	JN
15 Unskilled Machine Operator in a factory assembly line	UMO	31 Laboratory Technician	LT
16 Policeman	PM	32 Bus Conductor	BCR

(*set LABLO8)

This comment accorded well with our experience and we therefore decided to make use of the common tendency to speak in terms of 'kinds of people' in order to provide a natural context for judging 'occupational predicates'.

We therefore used *two* sets of 'objects' in the free sorting task — a set of 32 occupational titles and a set of 50 occupational descriptions in the form of brief sentences, usually beginning with the word 'they'. Each set (with the abbreviated forms of labels used) is specified in Tables 2.1 and 2.2, and more detailed technical information is presented in the third volume of our report.

TABLE 2.2   Occupational predicate descriptions used in free-sorting task

	Statements about occupations*	*Abbreviation*
1	They would receive very little public support if they went on *strike*	STRIKE
2	They work very long *hours*	HOURS
3	They are involved in *managing* people as part of their work	MANAGE
4	They spend a lot of time at work *clock*-watching	CLOCK-W
5	They are often *self-employed*	S-EMP
6	They have mainly *phys*ical skills	PHYS
7	They provide a *service* to the community	SERVE
8	They have their job organised as a *closed* shop	CLOSED
9	They have served their *appr*enticeships to become tradesmen	APPR
10	They have *irreg*ular hours	IRREG
11	They have to have a high standard of *acad*emic education	ACAD
12	They often *switch* their jobs	SWITCH
13	They earn a lot of their salary by working *overtime*	OTIME1
14	They often encourage their *sons* to go into the same work as themselves	SONS
15	They have a lot of fringe benefits and *'perks'* in their job	PERKS
16	*Most* people have thought of being one at some time in their lives	MOST
17	They get paid *overtime* for work they do out of normal hours	OTIME2
18	They usually do their work dressed in ordinary *casual* clothes	CASUAL
19	They have a strong *trade union*	TU
20	They often take the *day off* from work	DAYOFF
21	*Any*one with average intelligence could do the job for which they are paid	ANY
22	They often work at *weekends*	WKENDS
23	They are almost always *men*	MEN
24	They are *paid by the week*	PAYWK
25	They have to *clock in* and out of work with a time-card	CLOCKIN

Statements about occupations*	Abbreviations
26 You expect them to be over *30* years old	30
27 They regard themselves as *pro*fessionals	PROF
28 They have to undertake a long arduous *train*ing for their job	TRAIN
29 They are involved in *help*ing other people	HELP
30 They have a *boring* repetitive job	BORING
31 They are paid by the *month*	MONTH
32 They earn a great deal of *money*	MONEY
33 They have a high *social standing* in the community	STATUS
34 They are not paid regularly, but earn *fees* for what they do	FEES
35 They often *move* into some other line of work after a few years	MOVE
36 They have often had experience of working in *various* lines of work	VARIOUS
37 They tend to be active in the affairs of their local *community*	CTY
38 They earn a lot when *young*, but their incomes don't rise much after that	YOUNG
39 They are paid by the *hour*	HOUR
40 They build up relationships with other *people* as part of their job	PEOPLE
41 They work in a very *spec*ialised field	SPEC
42 They are required to have high *educ*ational qualifications	EDUC
43 Society could not continue to *exist* without them	ESSE
44 *No special training* is required to be one	N-TRAIN
45 They do not earn much at first, but do have high incomes *later* on	LATER
46 They are mostly *younger* than 30	YOUNGER
47 They have to be physically *fit* to do their job	FIT
48 They have a *secure* job	SECURE
49 They have to pass difficult *exam*inations	EXAM
50 They have a tradition of *solidarity* with each other	SOLIDY

(* set LABL36)

METHODS AND SUBJECTS

The subjects who performed the free sorting task were chosen in approximately equal numbers to represent the four 'points of view' of the Project typology. The subjects were obtained for the most part by means of the 'combing procedure' described in the third volume. One disadvantage of this method of selection was that since it was based upon a naturally occurring population, very few single occupations are represented by more than a handful of members. Consequently it is not usually possible to perform any extensive analysis of their data in terms of occupational allegiance *per se.*

Three distinct types of sorting are analysed in this chapter. The three variants are as follows:

TYPE A: 71 subjects sorted the 32 *occupational titles* listed in Table 2.1. (The occupational membership and quadrant assignment of these subjects is given in U2.1.)

TYPE B: A further 60 subjects sorted the 50 *occupational descriptions,* or predicates which are listed in Table 2.2.

TYPE C: Having completed the sorting of the 50 *occupational descriptions,* 41 of the subjects of Type B were then *also* given the set of 32 *occupational titles* used in Type A. The idea was that the occupational titles could be used as instances of the groups which they had just formed. Subjects were therefore asked to allocate each occupational title to the 'occupational description group' to which it was thought most naturally to belong. Information was thus obtained on the extent to which the descriptions of the groups they had formed were sufficiently general to cover new occupational instances. It also indicated how 'robust' (in the sense of being stable under small changes) the subject's classification is.

SUBJECTS

The occupational membership and quadrant assignment of these subjects is given in U2.2. (Because the last two types of sorting were developed towards the end of the research, quadrant membership is not as evenly distributed as would have been desirable, and an interviewer's report on a type A free-sorting is reproduced in U2.3).

2.2 STRUCTURAL CHARACTERISTICS OF INDIVIDUAL SORTINGS

The method of sorting provides direct information on three parameters which are recognised to be important characteristics of a subject's classification of the occupational world, namely:

(i)   the number of divisions ('classes') they make;
(ii)   the relative size of the constituent groups;
(iii)   the actual composition of the groups, including the bases or criteria used in forming the groups.

The first two characteristics are closely connected, and will be discussed together.

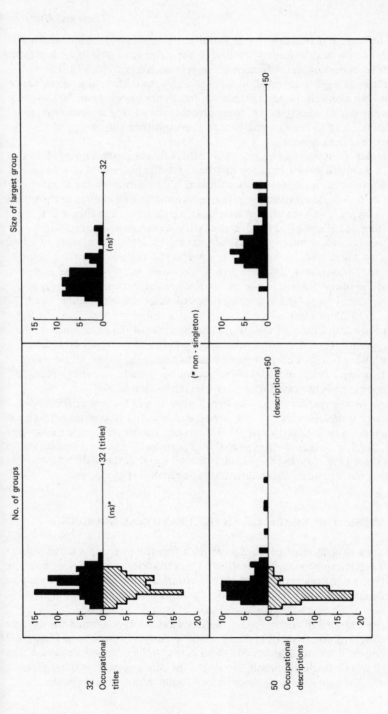

Figure 2.1 Characteristics of sortings

It might seem reasonable to suppose that the number of groups which a person forms would be directly related to the number of objects he is presente with. If so, more concrete domains of objects are likely to lead to the production of a relatively small number of categories. There is some evidence for this. For example, groupings made of nouns are usually found to be fewer than groupings of adjectives. On these grounds the sorting of occupational titles should lead to fewer, more compact, groups than the sorting of occupational descriptions.

In terms of the number of groups formed, this assumption does not in fact hold. In comparing the frequency distributions, the number of groups of occupational descriptions which are formed is very similar to the number of groups of occupational titles, despite the considerable difference in the numbe of cards sorted. (This result, and later ones, are illustrated in Figure 2.1 and are further described in U2.4.) The similarity is even more marked when singletons (groups consisting of one object) are ignored: *the number of 'classes formed by the subjects is virtually the same for both types of sorting despite their different linguistic structure and the fact that one set is half as large again as the other.* Moreover, the number of groups formed is markedly smalle than the number reported in investigations of other domains (Miller 1969: 170 Anglin 1970:21 *et seq.*).

But the compactness of the groups (in the sense of the dominance of the largest group) does differ quite substantially between the types of sorting. Even allowing for the different size of the two sets, the largest single group of occupational descriptions which an individual form is on average considerably larger than is the case for occupational titles (see U2.4).

These two properties — the number of groups, and the size of the largest one — are not independent of each other, and it would be convenient to have some simple way of describing both properties together in a single measure of 'shape'. Such a measure — the 'height' of a partition — has been developed for this purpose (Johnson 1968:2-4), and we shall use it as the main way of analysing the structural characteristics of occupational groupings.

LUMPINESS: THE 'SHAPE' OF AN OCCUPATIONAL GROUPING

There are a large number of ways in which a person can group a set of objects. A useful start can be made in describing this variation by considering how the 'height' of a partition is measured, and illustrating it by reference to a simple example involving the sorting of six occupations — *A*ccountant, *B*anker, *C*arpenter, *D*octor, *E*lectrician, *F*ireman.

At one extreme of sorting styles there is what has been termed the 'lumper' (cf. Arabie and Boorman 1973:153), whose sorting is illustrated in Figure 2.2 The 'lumper' does not discriminate at all between the occupations, and assigns them all to one single, common, group. At the other extreme is the 'splitter' (Figure 2.2B) who does not recognise any communality at all between the

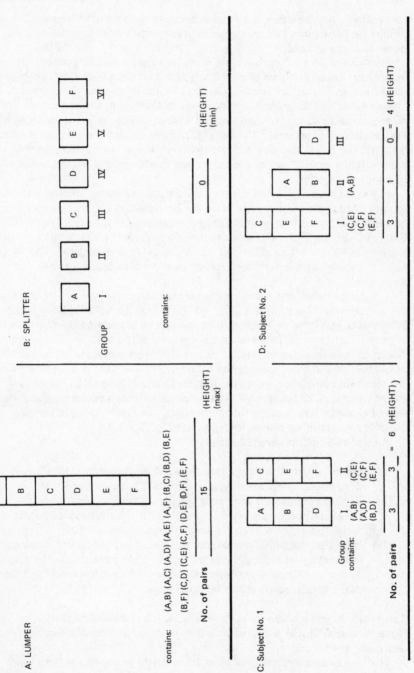

Figure 2.2 Height of a partition

occupations, and therefore assigns each occupation to a separate group. (Whilst these two types rarely appear in practice they possess considerable theoretical importance.)

The 'height' of a subject's sorting provides a simple measure of the 'lumpiness' or compactness of a grouping and it involves both the number and size of the constituent groups. It is defined by the number of the *pairs* of objects in each of his groups, summed over all the groups he has formed. The more compact a sorting is (composed of a small number of groups each with a large number of elements) the more pairs there are and the greater the 'height'. The height measure is therefore a measure of the co-occurrence of pairs within a subject's set of groups, or as a measure of the aggregativeness of a subject's sorting.

For example, Subject 1 of Figure 2.2C divides the six occupations into two groups, (ABD) and (CEF), perhaps on the grounds that the first group are 'professionals', whilst the second group are 'trades'. On the other hand, Subject 2 (Figure 2.2D) divides them into three groups: (AB), 'dealing with money', (CEF), 'working with their hands', and (D), as a singleton. The height of these two subjects' sortings are simply calculated as 6 and 4 respectively.

The height measure has some intuitively attractive properties – the 'lumper' has a maximum 'height' of $n(n-1)/2 = 15$, whereas the 'splitter' has a minimum height of 0, and these two cases can be thought of as defining the two ends of a 'height' continuum referred to as the 'lumper-splitter axis' by Arabie and Boorman. In comparing sortings of different sizes, it is a simple matter to normalise 'height' by expressing the actual number of pairs as a fraction of the maximum possible – i.e. of the lumper's sorting. When thus normalised, the measure may be interpreted as the probability that a randomly-chosen pair of elements will occur in the same group. The height measure for *all possible sortings* of six elements is illustrated in Figure 2.3.

A number of points should be made:

(i)   Several different sortings have the same height value. Hence 'height' does not uniquely identify a sorting, only some properties of it.

(ii) By using pairs as the basic unit, singletons are excluded, whereas large groups contribute substantially to the height measure. Hence 'height' strongly reflects tendencies towards 'lumping'.

(iii) Both the number of groups and also the size of the largest subgroup in a sorting are ordinally related to the height measure. As the number of groups increases, the height decreases, whereas the height increases as the biggest single group becomes larger.

This simple height measure thus provides a useful, if somewhat gross, characterisation of the 'shape' of a sorting, or of the *way* in which subjects demarcate their social world.

The frequency distribution of normalised height measures for both types

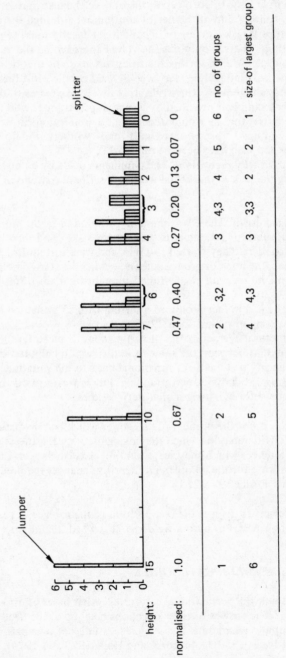

Figure 2.3 Height ('lumpiness') of partitions of a set of 6 elements

of sorting is given in U2.4C. In both types, the bulk of the distribution is fairly close to the 'splitter' end of the height continuum, although there is a tendency for the type B task (sorting of occupational descriptions) to produce more 'lumpy' sortings. There is only one individual approaching the 'lumper'. He is a post-office clerk, who in sorting the titles was insistent that he only wished to recognise 'salaried people' and 'weekly-paid people'. But there are a number of individuals whose sorting style strongly approximates to the 'lumper'. A further example is provided by a general practitioner who announced at the outset that he would divide the 50 description cards 'virtually into two groups — the "professionals" and "workers who do boring and repetitive jobs and who have become militant" '.

'Splitters' are also easily recognised. The comments made by an interviewer after administering the task to one social worker describe the situation graphically:

> We did get bogged down. There was the table, covered in cards, most of which were the 'subjective statements that people make', and therefore didn't belong together. They started as a pile, and were sorted through again and again in the faint hope of grouping them. . .when he started he said, 'This will take me hours', and at one time I thought we'd never finish.

Half an hour later he had in fact produced a sorting with a normalised height value of 0.05, consisting of no less than 29 groups.

None of the structural characteristics of sorting considered so far differs to any significant extent between the subjects in different quadrants: there does not seem to be any systematic occupational basis to the variation, the literature on 'images of society' notwithstanding. But as Westergaard comments in his critique of conventional 'images of society' studies:

> The real question is not the number of categories which people distinguish, but the nature of the relations which they recognise between them; and the basis of the differences which they see. Counting class labels is an easy and misleading substitute for the complex and sensitive analysis required. (Westergaard and Resler 1975:253)

It is even more relevant to inspect the composition of the categories to which people are attaching labels, but before we do so, it is worth taking up Westergaard's point.

RELATIONSHIPS BETWEEN CATEGORIES

What relationships link the occupational categories? What bases of differentiation are recognised? The answer to these questions takes us to the heart of the debate about 'occupational grading' in sociological studies of occupational mobility (Hall and Jones 1950, Goldthorpe and Hope 1972 and 1974), and to the analysis of 'models of the social order' (Goldthorpe *et al.* 1969, Bulmer 1975).

Virtually without exception, grading studies seek to link sociologically-based conceptions about the social order to popular evaluations of occupations. It is important to recognise that the usual sequence of investigation is from the sociologist's *a priori* assumption that occupations are ordered to its empirical endorsement by the subjects. Having required people to rank or rate occupations such grading studies cannot, of course, provide any evidence of whether such ordering naturally exists in subjects' thinking, and the conventional ordering or 'scale' of occupations obtained from the date is simply an averaged representation of the individual judgement. In such studies we simply do not know how or even whether the sociological scales relate in any systematic way to the conceptions of the occupational structure which the subjects use in everyday encounters, nor does this issue normally disturb the sociologists concerned. (This is not to say that notions of ordering do not occur in occupational cognition, only that the link between the sociological scale and the subject's conception is far from clear.)

Two-fifths of the subjects mentioned that their groups of occupational titles were arrayed in some order, or could be thus arrayed, but less than one-eighth of those sorting the occupational descriptions did so. This provides some indication of the extent to which 'occupational grading' naturally features in some subjects' conceptions of the occupational structure.

Those who *did* recognise an ordering were then asked about its basis, or they spontaneously provided one. Their data have already been analysed in our first volume (section 4.2), and the ordering characteristics will not be discussed further here.

The verbal descriptions which subjects give have a familiar ring: 'skill', 'educational qualifications', 'training and ability', 'status', 'salary and pay', 'importance to the community', which are a fair sampling from the predicates elicited from the subjects in other tasks. Even with such relatively small numbers, it is possible to recognise some aspects of the 'models' described by Goldthorpe *et al.* (1969:146-8). A fairly common expressed basis is 'money': those mentioning it are predominantly working class, and they tend to form fewer occupational groupings than their fellows. But there the resemblance ends; the content of the sortings often tells a different story. Indeed, it can be misleading to take subjects' expressed basis at face value. Some people insist that salary was the basis of their grouping, but never refer to it in the process of sortings, whilst others avow intially that a criterion such as 'class' has no place in their thinking, and then proceed to use it liberally.

2.3 COMPARING THE COMPOSITION OF OCCUPATIONAL CATEGORIES

Let us now begin to analyse differences in the *composition* of the groups which subjects make. We begin by taking a pair of individuals at a time, and examining the extent to which they sort occupations into the same categories. The distance between individual sortings will be defined, and then scaled to represent the extent and nature of individual differences in the composition of occupational groupings. (In this section, we shall continue to ignore the name and description which a person gives to his groups; we shall investigate similarity in denotation before turning in the next section to similarity in connotation.)

PAIRWISE COMPARISON OF SORTINGS

How can the composition of the groups of two individuals be compared and their similarity measured? Since the groups in a sorting are not usually ordered, other characteristics have to be used. A commonly used approach, and one which has affinities with the height measure discussed above, it to base a measure of similarity upon the extent to which individuals sort objects (occupations) into the same group.

Let us return to the example given in Figure 2.3 above in order to illustrate the basic ideas. The sorting of 'Subject 1' consists of two groups: (ABD) and (CEF). The sorting of 'Subject 2' consists of the three groups: (D), (AB) and (CEF) (the order is entirely arbitrary). Clearly both subjects agree in grouping C, E and F together as a single group, and they also agree that A and B go together. However, they disagree on occupation D: it is a separate single group for Subject 2 and is part of the (AB) group for Subject 1.

It is helpful to start by arranging these data as a table (matrix) where each row refers to a group of the first subject, and the colums refer to each of the second subject's groups. The entries in row i and column j of the table refer simply to the occupations which occur in group i of Subject 1, and group j of Subject 2: This table is often referred to as the intersection matrix, Z, and it plays a crucial role in the development of measures of similarity in sorting (Boorman and Arabie 1972:231-2).

| | SUBJECT 2's GROUPS: | | |
SUBJECT 1's GROUPS:	I= (D)	II= (AB)	III= (CEF)
I = (ABD)	D	AB	–
II = (CEF)	–	–	CEF

INTERSECTION MATRIX BETWEEN TWO SORTINGS

The significance of the entries of the intersection matrix is that, *taken together,* they provide a sorting which is finer than that of both subjects, *but it is one from which both their sortings can be built up.* In the above example, the sorting corresponding to the intersection matrix is simply:

which has a 'height' of 4, and is incidentally equivalent to Subject 2's sorting, though it will not normally be so.In the case of two identical sortings, the matrix will contain exactly the same groups which each of the subjects have. Where, by contrast, the lumper meets the splitter, the inter-section matrix will turn into one long row (or column) with one occupation in each cell.

DISTANCES BETWEEN SORTINGS

Following Kendall's idea (Kendall 1962:4 *et seq.*) of counting the number of inversions in two rank-orderings to measure ordinal correlation, and Kemeny's idea (Kemeny and Snell 1972:9 *et seq.*) of examining the number of changes necessary to turn one rank-ordering into another Boorman and Arabie (1972) have integrated a family of distance measures for sortings based upon the simple idea of seeing how many moves, or reallocations, are necessary to change one sorting into another. (See also Mirkin 1975 for a related approach.) Each reallocation will produce a different sorting, but each one is related to its predecessor and successor by being one 'move' away. A suitable distance measure between sortings X and Y is defined as *the minimum number of simple moves necessary to transform sorting X into sorting Y.* In the case of very similar or proximate sortings, few moves will be necessary, but for highly dissimilar or distant ones, a large number will be needed. There is, however one important snag: there are different ways of defining such an 'elemental move', each of which defines a different measure.

Following their earlier work, Arabie and Boorman (1973) extended their scheme to encompass various other types of measures (see U2.5). Most of these are not particularly relevant to our purposes for a variety of reasons, and are not discussed further here. But one measure is particularly simple. This has been dubbed 'pairbonds', and it is a simple extension of the height measure discussed above. Once again, the extreme cases of the lumper and splitter play a crucial role, and both the number and composition of the subject's groups is of central importance.

In the pairbonds distance measure, when two sortings are compared, attention is focused upon the number of *pairs* common between both the sortings. Consider the following two sortings:

Subject S: (A)   (BCD)   (EF)   (height = 4)
Subject T: (ACD)   (BF)   (E)   (height = 4)

The intersection matrix Z , is:

		I (ACD)	II (BF)	III (E)
I	(A)	A	–	–
Subject S: II (BCD)	CD	B	–
III	(EF)	–	F	E

Subject T:

(Height (Z) = 1)

This shows that only one pair ('pairbond') of occupations (C and D) is common
to both subjects – i.e. there is obviously very little overlap or consensus between
the sortings of S and T in terms of their common pairwise linkage of objects.
The pairbonds measure of dissimilarity between S and T consists simply of
the number of pairs which are either only in S or only in T, and it also has been
shown to be a metric. In the above example, the pairbonds measure can also
be represented as a Venn diagram (see Figure 2.4). There are 15 pairs in a set

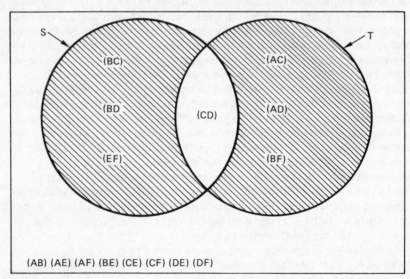

PAIRBONDS (S,T)
= h(S) + h(T) - 2h(S∩T)
= 6

Figure 2.4 Distance between two sortings

of 6 elements; 8 of these occur neither in S's nor in T's sorting, and only one (CD) occurs in both. The pairs (BC), (BD), and (EF) occur *only* in S's sorting and the pairs (AC) (AD) and (BF) occur *only* in T's sorting. The pairbonds measure is easily calculated from such a diagram, and consists of the number of pairs of objects (occupations) assigned to the same category by one, but not the other, subject (i.e. those pairs appearing within the hatched area). In this case, pairbonds (S,T) = 6. The numerical value is easily calculated from the intersection matrix:

$$\text{Pairbonds (S, T)} = \text{height (S)} + \text{height (T)} - 2 \times \text{height (S} \cap \text{T)}$$
$$= \quad 4 \quad + \quad 4 \quad - 2 \times \quad 1$$
$$= \quad 6$$

As in the case of the simple height measure, pairbonds can be normed between 0 and 1.

In the case where two sortings are identical, pairbonds is zero, and where they are maximally different (i.e. Lumper *v.* Splitter), pairbonds is equal to the total number of pairs: $(n(n-1)/2)$.

EXAMPLES OF PAIRS OF SORTINGS

In order to illustrate differences in invidual sortings, three examples are chosen which show differing degrees of similarity. In the first example, two very 'lumpy' sortings are compared. Each of the individuals concerned (a chartered accountant and a décor adviser) produces a dichotomy, based on related criteria, which are incidentally similar to those traditionally used by sociologists when they analyse occupational prestige.

When forming his sorting, the accountant spoke little about what he was doing; he simply named the groups in terms of whether or not the occupations required education beyond formal school-leaving age. The décor adviser by contrast consistently used salary level, and when asked whether this was the sole basis which he used in making his sorting, he replied: 'Uh huh, that's what life is, it's the pay packet at the end of the month; it always will be, you'll never change that. That's my opinion.'

The sortings of these two subjects are presented in Table 2.3. They both agree in allocating all but three titles: the Male Nurse, Policeman and Bank Clerk. These three occupations are considered 'not to require further education' by the accountant, but are considered to be 'capable of earning high salaries' by the décor adviser. The pairbonds distance value is 87 (out of a possible 496), giving a normalised value of .18.[2]

The second example, presented in Table 2.4, provides an instance of reasonable agreement in the sortings, this time of occupational *descriptions,* by two subjects who use fairly similar class terminology to label their groups. Both the shop salesman and the motor mechanic use common class names for describing three of the groups of 'types of people' that they formed,

TABLE 2.3   Example of strong agreement in sorting

| | G 292 (Chartered accountant) | |
Y 035 (Decor adviser)	*A: Further education not required*	*B: Formal education required*
I: *Low potential salary*	GM RCK BM RED C PO AD TDH PL TDR UMO BC PHT BSL	
II: *High potential salary*	MPN BCK PM	CA A SST GEO ST SMG SW ESG CPR JN MOR LT PST CE AP

n = 32 occupational titles

TABLE 2.4   Moderate agreement in sorting

| | Y249 (Motor Mechanic)** | | |
	A: Middle Class	*B: Average and Lower working class*	*C: Upper class*
Y260: Shop salesman * 1. *Upper Class*	S-emp	Men; Wkends	Closed; Acad; Perks; Dayoff; 30; Train; Month; Money; Status; Spec; Educ; Later; Exam
2. *Skilled Classes*	Strike	Appr.	Sons; Casual; Fees

	Y249 (Motor Mechanic)		
	A: Middle Class	*B: Average and Lower working class*	*C: Upper class*
3. *The Devoted*	Serve; Irreg; Help; Cty; Younger; People	Hours; Move Various; Esse; Solidy	Manage; Most; Prof; Secure
4. *Working Class*	Fit	Clock-w, Phys; Switch; Otime 1; Otime 2; T.U.; Any; Paywk; Clockin; Boring; Young; Hour; N-train	

n = 50 occupational descriptions

*Y260's descriptions: groups in order, 'not of social structure, I don't like using class terms', but of 'wealth'.
1. ' . . . better paid, more intelligent, executive-type jobs . . . what do you say — intelligentsia — the sort that become M.P.s.'
2. ' . . . the backbone class — very important to society. Some elements of this group are highly paid, but many skills are not reflected in wages.'
3. ' . . . believe in what they're doing. All necessary jobs; someone has to do them. They have dealings with people in every other group or class; they are the law, the system, the police, the National Health — that sort of thing.'
4. ' . . . the majority group, the " people" if you like . . . after as much as they can get at once — they look for a job immediately.'

**Y249's descriptions: groups in no particular order.
A. 'A small middle group of trustworthy types . . . people who are not in it for money.'
B. ' . . . composed of the "doers". They are responsible for the real work that gets done in society.'
C. ' . . . the bosses and professionals, in it for what they can get out of it.'

to which the salesman appends a fourth group which he calls 'the devoted'. Both sortings are, again, similar in their lumpiness. It can be seen that they agree to a considerable extent in their specification of both 'upper class' and 'working', and the salesman's 'devoted' group and the motor mechanic's 'middle class' overlap to some extent. In this case, the pairbonds distance value is 380 out of a possible 1225 (normalised .50).

The third example is presented in Table 2.5. Here, a splitter (an episcopalian rector whose sorting has a height value of 33) meets a moderate lumper (a quantity surveyor, whose sorting has a height value of 119) and their strong disagreement is reflected in a totally fragmented intersection matrix. This is indicated in the high normalised pairbonds distance value of .94 between the two sortings; they are almost totally dissimilar.

TABLE 2.5   Slight agreement in sorting

C297 Episcopalian Priest	S061 Partner in firm of Quantity Surveyors			
	A *University or equivalent careers*	B *Skilled*	C *Trades, or equivalent training*	D *Unskilled*
1. Lab. work	GEO	—	LT	—
2. 'Public stomachs'	—	—	RCK	BM
3. Education	SST	PST	—	—
4. Figures and mathematics	ST	CPR	—	—
5. Help people in trouble	MOR	SW	PM MPN	UMO*
6. (Related to all by delivering mail)	—	—	—	PO
7. Deal with engines	—	—	AD GM	TDR
8. Deal with building houses	CE	—	C PL	BSL
9. Travel	AP	—	TDH RED	BC
10. Entertaining, publications	—	JN A	PHT	—
11. Deal with figures	CA	BCK	—	—
12. (involved with any†)	ESG	—	—	—
13. (I don't respond to him at all)	—	SMG	—	—

n = 32 occupational titles

* 'When in hospital, the UMO is being helped by the nurse'
† ' . . . if there's anything wrong with their eyesight'

The rector is not a good generaliser, and he seems to look for common semantic components between occupations at a very low level. As a result, there is virtually no connection between his groups, a fact which he himself recognises. The quantity surveyor, by contrast, uses one single general basis which he terms 'the degree of training and ability', and his arrangement gives rise to a simple ordering. This suggests that the 'Lumper-Splitter' axis is concerned not only with (content-free) structural aspects of sorting styles, but may also indicate the level of semantic generality at which the subject is operating.

ANALYSING INDIVIDUAL DIFFERENCES

To what extent do pairs of sortings differ? Is there any systematic social basis to these differences? Several measures of sorting distances were calculated for all pairs of individual, but only the results for pairbonds, and normalised pairbonds are reported here (see Figure 2.5 and U2.6).

Pairbonds
In the case of both the titles and the descriptions, the distribution of pairwise distances occupies the lower half of the possible range of values. In general, occupational sortings tend to be quite similar in composition when compared to each other. There do not appear to be any major breaks in the distribution, which would signal radically distinct conceptions.

Normalised Pairbonds
When the individual height values are taken into account in calculating the distance measure (as in this measure) the picture changes. First, the distributions for both titles and descriptions become much more alike, and the distances between individuals are now considerably greater. When the different *styles* of sorting are taken into account, then, individuals differ to a greater extent in terms of the content of their sortings.

If occupational membership *per se* produces a more homogeneous image of the occupational structure, as many anthropologists and sociologists have argued, then we may expect that the differences between individuals from the same occupation (or the same occupational quadrant) will be smaller than the differences between individuals from different quadrants. (The small numbers of subjects from specific occupations precludes a test at the level of occupations.) In order to test this hypothesis, the quadrant membership of each subject was identified, and this information was used to allocate each pairwise distance measure to the appropriate cell of the quadrant table. The basic tabulations are presented in U2.7.

A number of propositions gain some support from these data:

the differences displayed by 'middle class' (Quadrants I and II) subjects when sorting occupational titles are considerable, whereas 'working class' (Quadrants III and IV) subjects produce much more similar sortings of occupational descriptions;

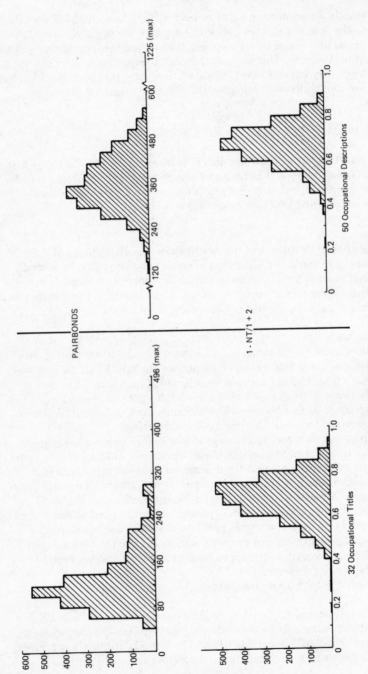

Figure 2.5 Pairwise distance distributions

it is definitely *not* the case that there is greater consensus within 'classes' than between them. At best, consensus is slightly higher only for Quadrant IV subjects, i.e. the lower status, non-people-oriented, 'working class', subjects;
the three distance measures give results which resemble each other to a tolerable degree, but the differences between the sortings of titles and descriptions are substantial.

Whatever the source of variation in conceptions of the occupational world, then (at least with respect to these structural aspects of sorting behaviour) it does not seem to be related in any simple manner to the type of occupation of the subject.

If occupational membership fails to reveal consistent patterns of structural difference, are there none the less (types) of subjects who produce very similar sortings? The pairbonds distances between the 71 subjects who sorted the 32 occupational titles were scaled by the non-metric distance model. The results are presented in Figure 2.6. and the technical details are given in U2.8.

A word of caution is in order before this configuration is interpreted. Arabie and Boorman (1973:163) have shown that multidimensional scaling of many of the height-based distance measures between sortings produces a *contour* representation of the information. In the case of pairbonds, the scaling of individual sortings maps into a set of concentric circles, centred upon the 'splitter'. Each circle links the sortings of the subjects who have the same degree of lumpiness, or height, and the radial distance of the circles from the splitter (at the centre) is in proportion to the height value of the sorting concerned. Consequently, if the MDS map were to be interpreted in terms of clustering or *linear* proximity of individual points then this crucial height information is entirely lost, and any inference drawn will be in error.

In Figure 2.6 the MDS solution to the pairbonds distances is presented, with some of this structural information superimposed. Each of the 71 individual sortings is represented as a point, and (most of) the points are labelled with a number which represents its height. The individuals with the highest and lowest height values (an episcopalian rector and a post-office clerk respectively) act as representatives of the 'Splitter' and the 'Lumper' types respectively, and their points are joined to form the 'Lumper-Splitter axis'. Because the 71 sortings are only a very small fraction of the number of *possible* sortings of 32 occupational titles, we should not expect an easily discernible structure of concentric circles, but it is surprisingly easy to recognise such structure when points with similar height values are joined. In the figure, the circles are drawn for height values in the 90s and in the 100s, and arcs of other recognisable circles are also drawn in. (The structure around the Splitter is rather confused, as we would expect, since a large number of sortings congregate here.)

On inspection there seem to be fairly significant breaks in the height contours after the upper 110s (and, to a lesser extent, in the upper 70s).

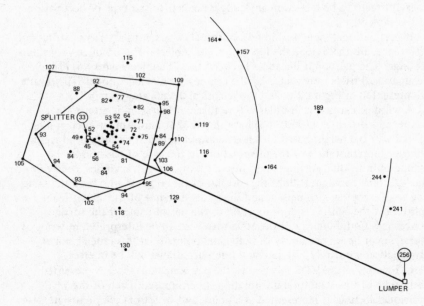

Figure 2.6 2-D Scaling of PAIRBONDS distances between sortings of occupational titles

Those prone to lumping (whose sortings consist of a small number of fairly large groups) are, if anything, drawn unrepresentatively from professional people. But such structural characteristics of sorting do not seem to be associated in any systematic way with occupational membership, and what evidence there is suggests that 'working class' subjects are *least* prone to produce few, strongly demarked classes of occupations.

2.4   COLLECTIVE REPRESENTATION OF OCCUPATIONAL GROUPINGS

From these results, it would seem that the subjects' sortings refer to a common conceptual basis, and so we now turn to the problem of inferring a 'collective representation', and examining the meanings which are ascribed to the occupational groups.

The basic data for analysis are given in the matrix of co-occurrences, (which gives the frequency with which pairs of occupational titles (or descriptions) appear in the subjects' groupings. Cluster analysis is then used to arrive at an acceptable collective grouping. We shall first try to identify the groups which go to make up the individual sortings, by using the verbal material as a basis for the semantic analysis, and when this has been done for both titles and descriptions, it will be possible to see whether they give rise to similar categorisations of the occupational structure.

CLUSTERING SCHEMES

The matrix of co-occurrences for occupational titles is presented in U2.9. If there were total unanimity about sorting, then the entries in this matrix would all be zero or N (the number of subjects), and it would be a simple matter to recover the (single) collective representation simply by inspecting the matrix. In fact, there are some pairs of occupations which no one puts together (e.g. Eye Surgeon and Barman) and which must therefore appear in different groups in any collective representation. On the other hand, there are no occupations which everyone puts together, although there are some which come close to unanimity (all but eight of the 71 subjects put Plumber and Carpenter into the same group, for example). If we were to relax the criterion of unanimity (by decreasing the frequency of co-occurrence which counted as basic agreement that two objects belong together) each value would give rise to a separate sorting (because of the symmetry and transitivity of the sorting operation), and if this is done then there will no longer be a single collective representation but rather a family of groupings at decreasing levels of generality. The only point of ambiguity then comes in deciding on the most appropriate value to represent 'high agreement'.[3]

A similar procedure is implemented by Johnson's hierarchical clustering schemes (HCS), and we shall use that method to analyse the co-occurrence data.[4]

For our purposes, the hierarchical property of the analysis is not of central importance; we wish simply to arrive at an acceptable and representative clustering. What the hierarchical level probably represents in these data is the extent to which subjects group occupations in accordance with their 'shared presuppositions'. Miller (1969) argues that much of the sorting data he analyses can be explained by assuming that subjects pay attention to presupposition rather than to assertion — briefly, an assertion is the part of a proposition that can be denied, whilst a presupposition is the implicit part not affected by denial; thus, to deny that someone is a *mother* is not to deny that she is a *woman* (presupposition) but only that she has children (assertion), cf. Perfetti 1972:253. One these grounds, it would be

foolish to accept a clustering at too general a level (which will be based upon
a low frequency of occurrence and will run the risk of conflating dissimilar
sets of presuppositions). We can, however, ensure a certain congruity with
the subjects' own groups by requiring that clusterings be based upon the
judgements of at least half of the subjects, and that the number of groups
conform approximately to the average (namely six non-singleton groups of
occupational titles, and five occupational descriptions, see U2.4).

OCCUPATIONAL TITLES

The hierarchical clustering analysis of co-occurrences between occupational
titles is presented in Figure 2.7. Since HCS representations are more stable at
the highest level of similarity, it is best to concentrate attention on the initial
clusterings. At these levels, the two methods produce rather similar results —
the first five clusters being with the same pairs, and in the same order:
(Carpenter-Plumber); (Unskilled Machine Operator-Building Site Labourer);
(Secondary-Primary School Teachers); (Postman-Bank Clerk) and (Civil
Engineer-Geologist).

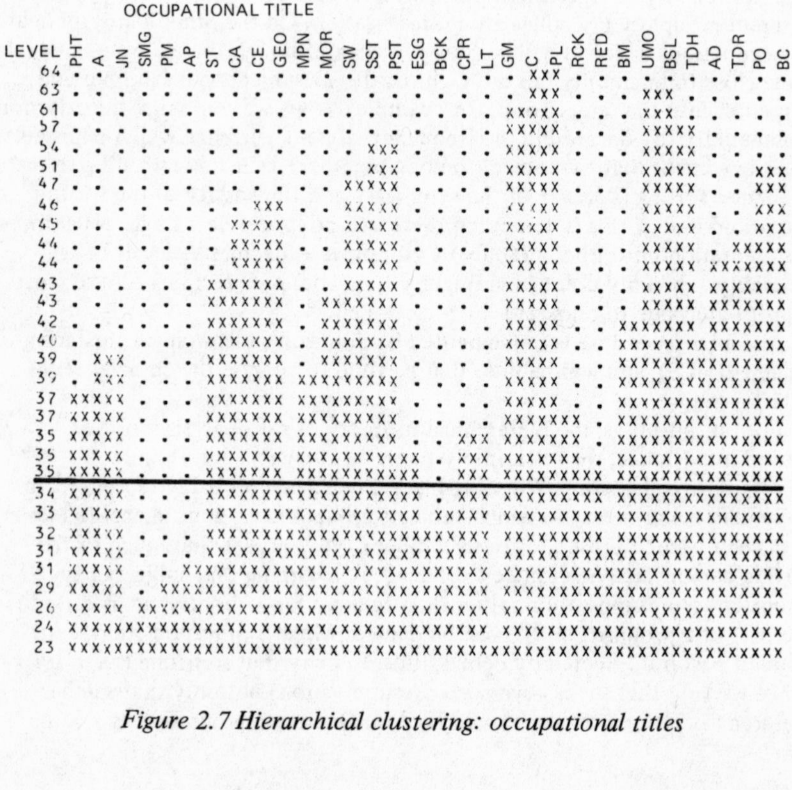

OCCUPATIONAL TITLE

```
LEVEL  P  A  J  S  P  A  S  C  C  G  M  M  S  S  P  E  B  C  L  G  C  P  R  R  B  U  B  T  A  T  P  B
       H     N  M  M  P  T  A  E  E  P  O  W  S  S  S  C  P  T  M     L  C  E  M  M  S  D  D  D  O  C
       T        G              O  N  R     T  T  G  K  R              K  D     O  L  H     R
   64  .  .  .  .  .  .  .  .  .  .  .  .  .  .  .  .  .  .  .  . XXX .  .  . XXX .  .  .  .  .
   63  .  .  .  .  .  .  .  .  .  .  .  .  .  .  .  .  .  .  .  . XXX .  .  . XXX .  .  .  .  .
   61  .  .  .  .  .  .  .  .  .  .  .  .  .  .  .  .  .  .  . XXXXX .  . XXX .  .  .  .  .
   57  .  .  .  .  .  .  .  .  .  .  .  .  .  .  .  .  .  .  . XXXXX .  . XXXXX .  .  .  .
   54  .  .  .  .  .  .  .  .  .  .  . XXX .  .  .  .  .  . XXXXX .  . XXXXX .  .  .  .
   51  .  .  .  .  .  .  .  .  .  .  . XXX .  .  .  .  .  . XXXXX .  . XXXXX .  . XXX
   47  .  .  .  .  .  .  .  .  .  . XXXXX .  .  .  .  .  . XXXXX .  . XXXXX .  . XXX
   46  .  .  .  .  .  .  . XXX .  . XXXXX .  .  .  .  . XXXXX .  . XXXXX .  . XXX
   45  .  .  .  .  .  . XXXXX .  . XXXXX .  .  .  .  . XXXXX .  . XXXXX .  . XXX
   44  .  .  .  .  .  . XXXXX .  . XXXXX .  .  .  .  . XXXXX .  . XXXXX , XXXXX
   44  .  .  .  .  .  . XXXXX .  . XXXXX .  .  .  .  . XXXXX .  . XXXXX XXXXXX
   43  .  .  .  .  . XXXXXXX .  . XXXXX .  .  .  .  . XXXXX .  .  . XXXXX XXXXXXX
   43  .  .  .  .  . XXXXXXX . XXXXXXX .  .  .  .  . XXXXX .  .  . XXXXX XXXXXXX
   42  .  .  .  .  . XXXXXXX . XXXXXXX .  .  .  .  . XXXXX .  . XXXXXXX XXXXXXX
   40  .  .  .  .  . XXXXXXX . XXXXXXX .  .  .  .  . XXXXX .  . XXXXXXXXXXXXXXX
   39  . XXX .  .  . XXXXXXX . XXXXXXX .  .  .  .  . XXXXX .  . XXXXXXXXXXXXXXX
   39  . XXX .  .  . XXXXXXX XXXXXXXX .  .  .  .  . XXXXX .  . XXXXXXXXXXXXXXX
   37  XXXXX .  .  . XXXXXXX XXXXXXXX .  .  .  . XXXXX .  . XXXXXXXXXXXXXXX
   37  XXXXX .  .  . XXXXXXX XXXXXXXX .  .  .  . XXXXXXX . XXXXXXXXXXXXXXX
   35  XXXXX .  .  . XXXXXXX XXXXXXXX .  . XXX XXXXXXX . XXXXXXXXXXXXXXX
   35  XXXXX .  .  . XXXXXXX XXXXXXXXXX . XXX XXXXXXX . XXXXXXXXXXXXXXX
   35  XXXXX .  .  . XXXXXXX XXXXXXXXXX . XXX XXXXXXXXX XXXXXXXXXXXXXXX
───────────────────────────────────────────────────────────────────────────────
   34  XXXXX .  .  . XXXXXXXXXXXXXXXXX . XXX XXXXXXXXX XXXXXXXXXXXXXXX
   33  XXXXX .  .  . XXXXXXXXXXXXXXXXX XXXXX XXXXXXXXX XXXXXXXXXXXXXXX
   32  XXXXX .  .  . XXXXXXXXXXXXXXXXXXXXX XXXXXXXXX XXXXXXXXXXXXXXXXXX
   31  XXXXX .  .  . XXXXXXXXXXXXXXXXXXXXX XXXXXXXXXXXXXXXXXXXXXXXXXX
   31  XXXXX .  . XXXXXXXXXXXXXXXXXXXXXXX XXXXXXXXXXXXXXXXXXXXXXXXXX
   29  XXXXX . XXXXXXXXXXXXXXXXXXXXXXXXXX XXXXXXXXXXXXXXXXXXXXXXXXXX
   26  XXXXX XXXXXXXXXXXXXXXXXXXXXXXXXXXX XXXXXXXXXXXXXXXXXXXXXXXXXX
   24  XXXXXXXXXXXXXXXXXXXXXXXXXXXXXXXXXX XXXXXXXXXXXXXXXXXXXXXXXXXX
   23  XXXXXXXXXXXXXXXXXXXXXXXXXXXXXXXXXXXXXXXXXXXXXXXXXXXXXXXXXXXXXX
```

Figure 2.7 Hierarchical clustering: occupational titles

2.5 INTERPRETATION OF THE AGGREGATE OCCUPATIONAL GROUPINGS

The clusterings which results from the HCS analysis at level 35 are easily interpretable, and correspond in a natural way to the groups which the subjects themselves make. Since the subjects provide verbal descriptions of their groups, it is possible to investigate the semantic characteristics of the aggregate sorting. Before doing so, several general comments about the analysis are in order:

(i)   *There is rarely full equivalence of connotative meaning.*
Individuals often give the same name to groups which have slightly different compositions; this is especially true of more general (and larger) groups, such as 'professionals', and 'skilled workers'. Correlatively, groups with the same composition are occasionally given different names.

(ii)   *There is some slight evidence of differential discrimination according to occupational position.*
Some individuals allocate a set of occupational titles to a single group, whilst others will divide the same titles into a number of groups.
      On the whole, members of professions themselves tend to strongly differentiate the 'arty' occupations (group 1 below) from the 'helping professions' (group 6), but many working-class people simply bracket them together without further specification as 'professions'.

(iii)   *There is strong support of de Soto and Albrecht's observation that many respondents 'stubbornly speak of society as composed of different kinds of people rather than different ranks' (1968:538).*
It is notable how frequently phrases such as
> 'people that have . . . '
> 'sort of people who . . . '
> 'type of person who . . . '

occur in descriptions which subjects give to the groups of occupational titles which they form.

In order to interpret the aggregate sorting of occupational titles, the simple method of 'matching' is used. First, the six constituent groups of the 'Level 35' connectedness sorting were listed. Then each subject's sorting was searched to see whether any of these groups occurred. Whenever a perfect (or virtually perfect) match was made the subject's description was noted. These verbal specifications form the basis of the following analysis.

GROUP 1:   *Photographer, Actor, Journalist*
(based on 11 subject matches)

The most common simple *label* is 'Artists', or less favourably, 'arty types'. The *features* usually singled out are flair, creativity, and extroversion ('brilliant and lazy. . .the extroverts and the idle'), together with the need for strong individual aptitudes and orientations ('failure by yourself in these jobs'). Less commonly they are described as 'professionals'.

There are obvious *contrasts* implied in many of the descriptions: people in these occupations are dealing with reality 'at second remove', they are 'individualistic' as opposed to social; their skills are at the opposite pole to the 'technical'. Moreover, they are recognised as occupying an ambiguous, marginal role; they are 'oddballs' mediating between the trades/professions categories.

Evaluations of this group differ, but where expressed they tend to be negative – 'we could do without them without incurring any great loss'.

GROUP 2: (i)   *Statistician, Chartered Accountant*
         (ii) *Civil Engineer, Geologist*
(4 matches)
No one single label is used for this group, and the features cited tend to be rather general descriptive terms rather than taking the form of particularising contrasts: they are 'highly trained', 'require intelligence' and 'are rewarded well in terms of income'. The second group is recognised as being based on scientific skills and there is more than a hint of single-minded motivation ('they knew what they were after, these people').

GROUP 3:   *Minister of Religion, Social Worker, Secondary School Teacher,*
             Eye Surgeon, Male Psychiatric Nurse
(based on 12 matches)
This cluster of occupations is a familiar one, recurring constantly in the literature (Robinson *et al.* 1969:402), and one to which we have referred to in this context (Coxon and Jones 1974 a:142; Coxon 1971:347). Its short title should probably be 'people-oriented occupations' or 'social types' – which are labels actually used by subjects. The most salient common core of meaning is that these occupations 'deal with people' – they are 'helping agencies', which are involved in 'serving the community' (and 'people in need' in particular). This theme is virtually universal in all descriptions. Subsidiary components include the notions of education, welfare, communication and – more rarely – professional status.

Probably the most distinctive characteristic is not so much that they are thought to be well-educated or highly trained as that *individual* qualities are thought of as a prerequisite for them – dedication, beliefs, vocation; these jobs are considered to provide their own intrinsic reward. These two characteristics – service-orientation and intrinsic reward – are so important in the descriptions of this group of occupations that they obscure all other bases of differentiation.

GROUP 4:   *Computer Programmer, Laboratory Technician*
This group did not occur by itself in any subject's sortings.

GROUP 5:   *Garage Mechanic, Carpenter, Plumber, Restaurant Cook, Railway Engine Driver*

(based on 15 matches)

Most of the subjects whose groups matched this one were themselves drawn from broadly 'working class' occupations. One tag was virtually universal — 'Tradesmen', i.e. those who have served their time in an apprenticeship. People in this cluster of occupations are typically thought of as 'working' or 'lower class' people — (such terminology quite naturally occurs in descriptions of this group) and their main attribute is their *manual skill* as opposed to their education. Beyond this, there is little consensus over attributes such as level of pay, extent of dedication and so forth. The evaluative overtones are bland — such jobs are 'useful', but essential to the community, a recognition often brought about, it is thought, by strike action.

GROUP 6   comprises as subset:

  (i)   *Ambulance Driver, Taxi Driver*
  (ii)   *Unskilled Machine Operator, Building Site Labourer, Trawler Deckhand*
  (iii)   *Barman, Postman, Bus Conductor*

(based upon 30 matches of at least one subset)

This is unquestionably the 'unskilled' group (the label given by almost everybody). The most frequent comment is that these jobs are the sort that 'anyone could do', and require very little training. Often enough, they are said to be held by people who left school early, who 'haven't made the grade'. Consequently, they have few qualifications, and there is more than a suspicion that the incumbents are neither bright, dedicated nor ambitious.

The jobs themselves are 'honest-to-goodness', but are often 'boring', 'dirty', and 'unrewarding'. Many people make reference to pay, although not in a consistent manner. Some view the jobs as being highly paid (to compensate for the dead-end nature of the job, it is averred). Others, whose own jobs are closer to this group and who are often more knowledgeable, recognise that although these jobs have a reputation for providing high wages, they are in fact based on low basic rates, but carry considerable overtime opportunities.

The contrasts predominantly involve the *training* factor: these jobs are 'unskilled' as opposed to being 'trades', and involve 'physical' rather than 'intellectual' capabilities.

On the whole, the evaluations of the actual jobs are fairly neutral, but the sort of people who take them up are often subject to considerable disapprobation.

Occasionally, one of the constituent subsets is singled out for special comment. For instance, the first subset is described in terms of the 'driving factor', and the third subset is said to involve the 'sociability factor' — the ability to get on with a wide range of people.

This 'matching' procedure has allowed us to identify a set of occupational groupings which correspond surprisingly well to subjects' own groupings. Moreover, the descriptions which they give make their meaning clear.

Co-occurrence data can also be interpreted quite naturally as defining a distance between the objects concerned, and a family of such measures has been proposed by Burton (1975). (The technical details will be found in U2.10.) In the simplest case (called measure M1) the distance between a pair of objects is the one we have used already, i.e. the frequency with which they were put together in the subjects' sortings. But its simplicity masks two important questions: is not the size of the groupings in which a pair appears important? Does information on pairs which are *not* put together carry any significant information? We have seen above that subjects divide the occupational names and descriptions into different numbers of groups, and the differences in the number used seem to indicate that subjects are operating at differer levels of generality when they do a sorting task. If this is so, should not these differences be compensated for? The next two measures provide variants which take the size of the group into consideration; M2 assumes that objects which occur in large groups are more similar than those which occur in small groups, whilst M3 assumes the reverse — that the finer the gradation or the fewer the constituents of a group are, the more highly similar they are. The final measure, M4 also emphasises finer gradations, but in addition it takes account of the extent to which pairs of objects are sorted into *different* groups.

If the recovery of structure from the sorting task depends upon differential discrimination, then we may expect to find significant differences in the four distance measures when they are calculated for the same set of data[5] Non-metric multidimensional scaling will once again be used to portray this information, and provide a parallel to the hierarchical clustering analysis (technical details of the analysis are contained in U2.11).

The results of the scaling analysis indicate fairly unequivocally that the aggregate co-occurrence data are well fit by a unidimensional solution. In any event, the similarity of the maps produced from scaling the four distance measures is striking. As may be expected, M3 and M4 solutions are very similar indeed, since they both exaggerate fine discriminations. The only non-trivial differences in location between the best and most fitting solutions occur for: *Journalist* (close to the 'Professional' group for one, and within the 'Artists' group in others), *Sales Manager* (close to the 'Professional' group in one) and *Photographer* (close to the 'Working Class' group in one, but within the 'Artist' group in the other). The map based upon M3 is presented in Figure 2.8 with the aggregate groups superimposed upon it. (The one-dimensional solution is virtually identical with a horizontal axis running from Eye Surgeon to Building Site Labourer.) Perhaps the most striking feature of the solution is what might facetiously be termed 'le triage dichotomique': the first dimension separates out two main clusters — 'professional' *v.* 'working class' in the subjects' terminology, which are in turn differentiated into people-oriented/extrinsic reward and skilled/unskilled subgroups; the 'artists' group is simply incongruous with the others.

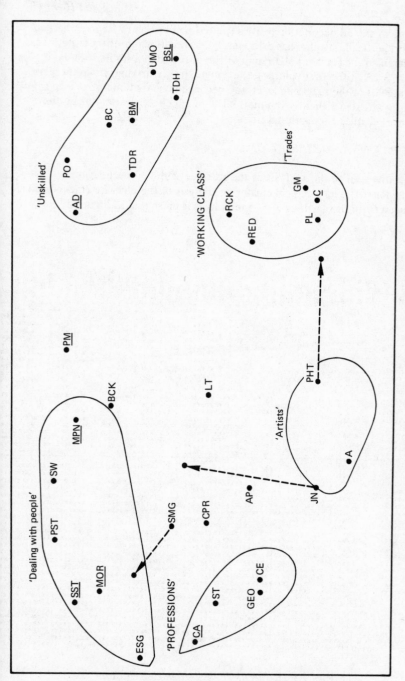

Figure 2.8 MDS analysis of sorting data

Nine of the 32 occupational titles (underlined in Figure 2.8) are marked almost identically by the 'basic 16' set. When the location of these points is compared to the (metric) MDS map of the occupational similarities data (Figure 3.2A in the first volume), the congruence is striking. It would seem that, at least at the aggregate level, the perceived occupational structure is not seriously affected either by the method of data collection used, or by the presence of other occupational titles.

OCCUPATIONAL DESCRIPTIONS

Let us now turn to the analysis of the sortings of the 50 occupational descriptions. The hierarchical clustering analysis of the pairwise co-occurrences produced from the sortings of 66 individuals is presented in Figure 2.9.

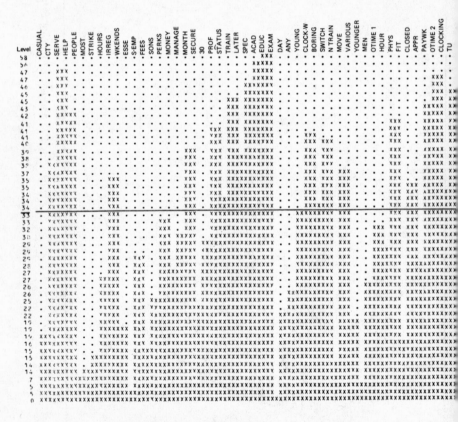

Figure 2.9 Hierarchical clustering: descriptions

In this case, the two clustering methods produce groupings which differ somewhat. The connectedness solution is very 'lumpy', comprising two main clusters sharply dissociated from each other, one centred upon academic, educational, professional and 'people-oriented' characteristics, the other based upon trade-union and manual predicates. The chaining effect is very noticeable in this solution.

The diameter solution, by contrast, is much more fine-grained, consisting of a larger number of smaller groups. But here, too, there are clusters centring upon people-orientation, academic/professional and trade-union/manual characteristics.

In the case of both titles and descriptions the deepest 'cleavage', which radically differentiates the two main 'branches', corresponds clearly to the manual/non-manual or perhaps the working class/middle class dichotomy. Once again, the grouping based upon a co-occurrence of 50 per cent of the cases is used as a baseline for comparing the two solutions. The intersection table is given in Table 2.6. The two solutions are much less alike in the case of occupational descriptions than they were in the case of titles. In large part this is due, as we have seen, to the way in which the diameter solution breaks up the large clusters which characterise the connectedness solution.

NAMING CLUSTERS OF OCCUPATIONAL DESCRIPTIONS

Once again the 'matching' procedure is used to identify the occurrence of the aggregate solution groups in subjects' own sortings. But because of the differences between the solutions, the standard set of groups will have to be defined less stringently.

In all, 66 subjects made sortings of the 50 occupational descriptions (see U2.2) and they were then asked to name and talk about the groups they had formed. Following this, two-thirds of them were then presented with the set of 32 occupational *titles,* and asked to sort them as instances into the groupings they had just made. This process of 'instantiation' provides a crude, but useful, test of the generality of the subject's groupings, and it furnishes useful information for linking titles and descriptions.

GROUP 1: SERVE, HELP, CTY, PEOPLE
(a distinct group in both aggregate clustering schemes)
Identification: based on 31 matches (42 per cent of subjects).
The most common label for Group 1 is 'Social Workers' (note that such verbal descriptions were elicited from subjects before they sorted occupational titles into their groups) and the most salient feature is the service-orientation of such people – they 'help people', 'serve the community', 'work for the benefit of people', they are 'the caring professions'. More than any other, this group is described in evaluative and moral terms: they are trustworthy, dedicated, devoted, respectable ('the great ones', as a social worker unblushingly describes them) and they are socially aware. Somewhat less complimentarily, they are

TABLE 2.6   Intersection Table: diameter and connectedness HCS at level 34: 50 occupational descriptions

DIAMETER HCS	A Younger	B Strike	C Casual	D Esse	E Most	F Hours	G S-Emp	H Irreg, Wkends	I Fees	J Cty Serve, Help People	K Perks, Manage, Sons 30, Money Month, Secure Prof, Status Train, Later Spec, Acad Educ, Exam	L Men, Move	M Various	N Any Otime1, Young Day-off, Phys Fit, Hours Appr, Switch N-train, Clock-w Closed, Boring Paywk, Otime2 Clockin, TU Solidy
I 18. Casual			18											
II 37. Cty 7. Serve 29. Help 40. People										37,07 29,40				
III 16. Most					16									
IV 1. Strike		01												
V 2. Hours						02								
VI 10. Irreg 22. Wkends								10,22						
VII 43. Esse			43											
VIII 5. S-Emp							05							
IX 34. Fees									34					
X 14. Sons											14			
XI 15. Perks											15			
XII 32. Money											32			
XIII 3. Manage											03			
XIV 31. Month 48. Secure											31,48			
XV 26. 30											26			
XVI 27. Prof 33. Status 28. Train 45. Later 41. Spec 11. Acad 42. Educ 49. Exam											27,33,28, 45,41,11, 42,49			
XVII 20. Day off														20
XVIII 21. Any														21
XIX 38. Young														38
XX 4. Clock-W 30. Boring 44. N-train 12. Switch														04,30 44,12
XXI 35. Move 36. Various												35,36		
XXII 46. Younger	46													
XXIII 23. Men												23		
XXIV 13. Otime 1														13
XXV 39. Hour														39
XXVI 6. Phys 47. Fit														06,47
XXVII 8. Closed 9. Appr														08,09
XXVIII 24. Paywk 17. Otime 2 25. Clockin 19. TU 50. Solidy														24,17,25 19,50

CONNECTEDNESS HCS

PAIRBONDS: 98 (normalised. 0.286)
APPROX: 14.

the 'do-gooders', 'the people on the corporation'. The discrepancy between worth and reward is recognised. Although they are 'most vital to society' and do thankless, necessary jobs, they are 'not paid enough', but then 'they're not in it for the money'. They also need to be highly motivated — these are not 'the sort of jobs that lend themselves to glory-seekers'.

Instances

What such people are *never* described as is often as significant as what they *are* described as; the list of such 'negative descriptions' gives a useful gloss upon what is said, and provides information on the contrasts which are implied. To a considerable extent the main contrast is with Groups 3 and 4 below (q.v.) — unlike them, Group 1 people are never described in terms of CLOCK-W, PHYS, APPR, SWITCH, OTIME2, TU, DAYOFF, ANY, CLOCKIN, BORING, YOUNG, and HOUR; theirs are not factory jobs involving manual work or union organisation. But, in contrast to Group 2, neither are they described in terms of EDUC, EXAM, PERKS or MONEY — their jobs are poorly paid, but the jobs are not seen as involving especially long, complex or arduous academic training. Finally, unlike any other group, no one expects these people to be 'almost always men' (MEN), or to be often self-employed (S-EMP).

What occupations do these sort of people have? It will occasion little surprise that even those who were not provided with the standard set of occupational titles spontaneously mentioned the Social Worker, the Minister and the Teacher as examples. The most frequently allocated titles were: Social Worker, Minister of Religion, Male Psychiatric Nurse, Secondary School Teachers, Primary School Teacher, Postman and Policeman.

This group is virtually identical to Group 3 of occupational titles. The core of meaning common to both groups is 'serving the Community', and this is adopted as its label.

GROUP 2: ACAD, PROF, TRAIN, STATUS, SPEC, EDUC, LATER, EXAM (which are common to both aggregate clustering schemes) together with any of: MANAGE, SONS, PERKS, 30, MONTH, MONEY, SECURE, which also occur in Group K of the Connectedness solution (see Table 2.6)
Identification: based on a total of 53 matches (80 per cent of the subjects).

This group is described as 'professional' by almost everyone, and it is often said to include managerial and executive jobs. The term 'professional' is used in two ways — either as a substantive noun, or to qualify a further noun. In its substantive use, the adjectives 'higher' 'established' and 'traditional' typically qualify 'professions', whilst 'middle-class', 'well-respected', 'highly-paid' are used to qualify 'professionals'. When used adjectivally, the term 'professional' is used to designate a category of persons: professional person, people, men, folks, class, group, men. The common substantive form justifies the label 'Professional people' as the best simple description.

The main characteristics of this group is described as their high and prolonged academic training — 'they have had to study hard for their qualifications'. As a result, they achieve 'good jobs', meaning a high level of pay, and deliberately chosen careers in jobs which are 'tough to get into'. They are accorded 'high social standing', they are the 'upper bracket in society' and they form a well-respected elite.

But such high estimation is by no means generally accorded. Such people are often 'in it for what they can get out of it', and are 'wanting as much back as possible for what they've put into it, scrupulously or unscrupulously'. In any event, such a view is held by a number of subjects who are not themselves in higher-status jobs, and it often forms an important basis of distinction between Groups 1 and 2. The former are credited with loftier motives, and latter with greater financial success.

As in Group 1, the 'negative instances' point towards the characteristics of the non-manual groups: Professional people are thought *not* to switch jobs (SWITCH), get overtime pay (OTIME2), or be paid by the week (PAYWK). The jobs they have are not thought to be boring (BORING) or to involve little training (NTRAIN).

Class terminology occurs occasionally. Three subjects term their Group 2 'upper class' (a jobbing heating engineer, a boutique manager and a motor mechanic) and it is also called 'middle' and 'top' class by single subjects.

The instances given of members of this group are, in order, Eye Surgeon, Chartered Accountant, Civil Engineer, Airline Pilot, Geologist, and Statistician.

Group 2 corresponds in a fairly recognisable way to the second Group of occupational titles, and is reasonably dubbed 'Professional People'.

GROUP 3: CLOCK-W, SWITCH, BORING, N-TRAIN
(common to both aggregate clustering schemes)
together with any of: DAYOFF, ANY, YOUNG (which occur close to this group in the Connectedness grouping).
Identification: based on a total of 23 matches (33 per cent of the subjects).

The two key characteristics are being unskilled and being workers, (or labourers). The label 'unskilled workers' is appropriate. The lack of skill means that 'anyone can do their jobs'; they are 'jobs which you take if you can't get anything else' (social worker). There is no job satisfaction, they are menial, boring and repetitive. The single negative instance is that such jobs are *not* secure. What of the incumbents? They are described as casual 'drifters', whose sole motivation is money-making; they are irresponsible and 'are destined to reproduce the children who will be the football crowds of tomorrow' (electronic engineer). Such disapprobation is most marked in comments about this group, and typifies those made by people of very different occupational allegiance.

Class terminology is common. In many cases this group is a subset of a larger group, called simply 'working class', but where this group appears as a separate entity, the epithet used is 'unskilled'.

The instances cited are: Trawler Deckhand, Unskilled Machine Operator, Building Site Labourer, and, to a lesser extent, Bus Conductor, Postman, Bank Clerk and Barman.

This group corresponds almost exactly to the second and third subsets of the sixth group of occupational titles, and is labelled 'unskilled workers'.

GROUP 4: OTIME2, TU, PAYWK, CLOCKIN, SOLIDY
(common to both clustering schemes)
together with any of: CLOSED, APPR: PHYS, FIT: OTIME1, HOUR, which are close to this group in the Connectedness grouping.

Identification: based upon a total of 44 matches (two-thirds of the subjects).

Just as in Group 2, there is a main designation and a subsidiary one. In this group, the most common conception is the skilled factory worker, but time-served trades are also mentioned (especially by those who are themselves tradesmen). 'Skilled workers and Trades' is an adequate appellation.

Features predicated of this group differ more widely than for any other. In part, this is because it covers both the skilled manual and the trades group. The former are described as money-oriented ('after as much money as they can get at once'), and unambitious, whereas the tradesmen are said to display pride in their job, be underpaid and regard themselves as superior. But in part the differences reflect different orientations to the trade union and solidarity descriptions. These two are obviously very central, and affectively-laden, elements of this group of descriptions and they provoke strong reactions. But there are some themes common to both groups: they are 'the doers' as a manager expresses it, 'the backbone of the country', 'responsible for the real work that gets done' as two heating engineers say. Their skills are manual rather than intellectual.

Unlike the Professional People of Group 2 (the main negative reference point) this group are not self-employed, do not receive fees, and are not active in the affairs of the community.

Class terminology, which appears most frequently in connection with this group, is straightforwardly 'working class' and is strongly associated with the Trade Union and Solidarity components. Some reactions were probably uncharacteristically negative because of the miners' strike of 1974, which was in progress during part of the interviewing. But, quite apart from this situational factor, there can be no doubt that such a response is a generally potent factor, as the second of these examples drawn from the interview reports illustrates:

(i) After perhaps 20 minutes he responded, becoming suddenly heated: 'Union-minded tradesmen, first group, O.K.? Characteristics? Bloodymindedness. . .they look after themselves, all right. . .when you've got the wrong type leading, you've got trouble. Take the miners. . .' (An Aircraft fitter)

(ii) No order (to the groups), the subject insisted; and if I seemed to be suggesting during his pauses that he use alternative terms, he would sharply repeat that 'this is a one-class society'. . .The subject took violent exception to the 'tradition of solidarity' description, dismissing it as 'rubbish – straight out of the Communist Party Handbook.' (Fork-truck driver)

The occupational instances cited without prompting included miners (repeatedly), engineers and car workers. The most common standard occupational titles in order of frequency, are: Garage Mechanic, Carpenter, Plumber, Railway Engine Driver, Bus Conductor, Ambulance Driver, Unskilled

Machine Operator. The only titles never appearing in this group are the main professional titles — Chartered Accountant, Statistician, Minister of Religion, Civil Engineer, Airline Pilot, Geologist and Eye Surgeon.

This group corresponds well to the fifth group of occupational titles.

OVERALL GROUPINGS: A COMPARISON

The groups produced from the aggregate clustering analysis of both the occupational titles and the occupational descriptions are remarkably similar, despite the 'looser' structure in the latter case (see Table 2.7).

There were no compelling *a priori* reasons for expecting such a convergent result, and the high degree of similarity indicates just how structured (or stereotyped) occupational judgements are. The results also free us from the suspicion that the constructs which people use in occupational judgement refer only to the *names* of occupations — people clearly operate almost as adeptly, and with similar results, whether the objects of judgement are names or are descriptions of types of people.

In order to portray this similarity, the co-occurrence data (between both descriptions and titles, obtained from the 'type C' subjects) were scaled, using the Z-distance measure (M4) which emphasises fine discriminations and also takes account of the extent to which pairs of objects are sorted into different groups (see U2.10). The resulting two-dimensional map is presented in Figure 2 and technical details are given in U2.12. The map is similar to that for occupational titles alone (Figure 2.8) (and indeed it is even more similar if map based on the same measure are compared). It is very easy to identify the overall groupings and, as expected, both the titles and descriptions fall into the same clusters, with the exception of the 'Artists' group (A).

The MDS solution provides a spatial representation of the group position, so that stimuli which are considered to 'go together' in terms of common characteristics are located close to each other, whereas those differentiated by subjects are separated by a social distance. It is important to pay especial attention to where discontinuities, 'breaks', or empty regions of space appear, which are akin to the 'class boundaries' discussed in the context of status crystallisation (Galtung 1966, Landecker 1960, Lenski 1954, Martin 1954). The major discontinuity once again clearly appears between two main groups: the Professionals and Working Class. Within these two major clusters, differentiation occurs, but not on the same basis. The Professions are distinguished in terms of an extrinsic/intrinsic reward and people/things factor whilst the Working Class group are distinguished in terms of skill. (It could be argued that at a very abstract level both contrasts involve technical skill, although this does not appear naturally as a significant feature in subjects' verbalisations.)

What bedevils an interpretative exercise of this sort is that we do not know whether subjects' verbal descriptions relate to the same level of generality. There is strong internal evidence, as we have seen, to suggest that most of the

TABLE 2.7   Occupational groups: a comparison of components

	32 Occupational titles	82 Occupational descriptions and titles (50 descriptions)	(32 titles as instances)	Brief label
GROUP A	(Group 1) PHT, A, JN			Artists
GROUP B	(Group 5) ST, CA, CE, GEO	(Group 2) ACAD, PROF, TRAIN, STATUS, SPEC, EDUC, LATER, EXAM + (MANAGE, SONS, PERKS, 30, MONTH, MONEY)	ESG, CA, CE, AP,	Professional people
GROUP C	(Group 6) MOR, SN, SST PST, ESG, MPN	(Group 1) SERVE, HELP CTY, PEOPLE	SW, MOR, MPN SST, PST, PO, PM	Serving the community
GROUP D	(Group 9) GM, C, PL, RCK, RED	(Group 4) OTIME 2, TU, PAYWK, SOLIDY + (CLOSED, APPR; PHYS, FIT; OTIME1, HOUR)	GM, C, PL, RED, BC, AD, UMO	Skilled workers and trades
GROUP E	(Group 10) AD, TDR, UMO, BSL, TDH, BM, PO, BC	(Group 3) CLOCKW, SWITCH, BORING, N-TRAIN + (DAYOFF, ANY, YOUNG)	TDH, UMO, BSL, BC, PO, BC	Unskilled workers

predicates elicited from subjects are fairly specific and are at a low level of generality, whilst sociological interpretation usually invokes concepts at a high level of abstractness. It may well be, for instance, that the modest amount of 'class' imagery elicited so far occurs simply because it is by its very nature a generalising concept, as many stratification theorists would argue. If this is

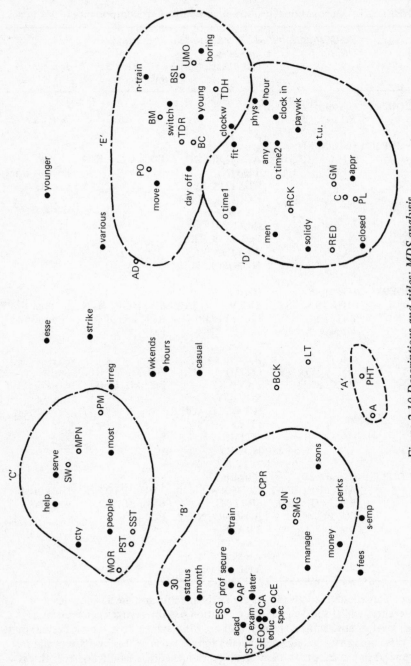

Figure 2.10 Descriptions and titles: MDS analysis

so, then subjects have somehow to be encouraged to relate their conceptions to increasing levels of generality, and yet we have to ensure that these levels are comparable between subjects. This is the strategy we adopt in the next chapter.

2.6 SUMMARY

In this chapter, we have concentrated on investigating:
- (1) the elementary structural properties of the ways in which people differentiate the occupational world;
- (2) how these subjective classifications compare one with another in terms of their content;
- (3) what meaning the groupings have.

The main findings are as follows:

1. ELEMENTARY STRUCTURAL PROPERTIES OF OCCUPATIONAL SORTINGS

- (i) The number of groups formed is markedly smaller than that reported for free-sortings in other domains.
- (ii) It might be thought that the number of groups formed would be a function of the number of objects involved. In fact, it is virtually the same for both occupational names and descriptions (7 ± 2 groups), despite the differences in size and linguistic type.
- (iii) Although there is a considerable amount of variation in the structural properties, they do not appear to differ significantly on a straightforward occupational basis.
- (iv) The most useful overall structural measure is the 'height' of a sorting. Increasing values of 'height' appear to reflect increasing levels of semantic generality in the description which a subject gives of his groups.
- (v) The characteristics which are crucial to a sociological interpretation of subjective occupational classification are the relationship between a subject's categories and the basis he gives for differentiating them. After sorting, subjects were asked about any 'arrangement' (not order) thought to underlie their groups. The tendency to order groups is much more strongly marked in dealings with occupational titles than with occupational descriptions (31 per cent as opposed to 8 per cent). In a fifth of the cases any ordering principle at all was disavowed. The bases elicited correspond well to predicates which were elicited in the pairwise and triadic similarity task. It is concluded that occupational grading studies can be very misleading in so far as they may claim to represent subject's concepts of the occupational world.

2. COMPARING THE CONTENT OF SORTINGS

(i)   There is evidence of considerable differences in the content of sortings, especially when different tendencies toward aggregativeness are taken into account.

(ii)   Broadly speaking, 'working-class' subjects tend to produce more similar groupings than 'middle-class' subjects do.

(iii)   On sociological grounds it would be expected that consensus on the content of groupings will be consistently higher among subjects drawn from the same occupational type (quadrant) than among those from different types. This expectation was not supported.

3. STRUCTURE AND MEANING

(A)   *Occupational Titles*

(i)   In the 'aggregate sorting' of titles there are six significant groupings. The major contrast is made between 'Professionals' and 'Working class', the former subdivided into 'people-oriented' and extrinsically-oriented groups, and the latter into 'Tradesmen' (skilled) and 'unskilled'. In addition, two other marginal groups are discernible: 'Artists' and 'Technicians'.

(ii)   The semantic features characterising the groups are varied, but are strongly dominated by a 'skill' contrast similar to the sociological manual/non-manual distinction (rarely so called by the subjects). Other features are equally salient, but are not as widely applied.

(iii)   Fairly subtle occupational differences are discernible: 'working-class' subjects tend to be less evaluative and more matter-of-fact in their judgements, whilst 'professionals' tend to concentrate upon the personal characteristics expected of the person holding the job.

(B)   *Occupational descriptions*

(i)   The aggregate sortings are not as similar as in the case of titles, reflecting a less well-structured domain. The 'Connectedness' solution consists of two main clusters, sharply dissociated — an academic, and people-oriented, Professional cluster, and one based on trade-union and manual predicates. The 'Diameter' solution subdivides these groups, producing four significant groups, identified as 'Professional people', 'Serving the Community', 'Skilled workers and trades' and 'Unskilled workers'.

(ii)   Many more semantic features are involved in judging occupational descriptions. Of especial note is the strongly evaluative comments evoked by the trade-union descriptions, in part due to the occurrence of a major strike during the period of data collection.

(iii)   Few systematic occupational differences were evident, except that working-class subjects particularly stressed the trades/manual distinction.

(C)   *Comparison of aggregate groupings*

The groups produced from the titles and descriptions were markedly similar, and correspond to a fourfold classification of occupational types. The major distinction is between the Professional and Working Class group, but the professional group is further distinguished in terms of extrinsic/intrinsic reward or people/things factor, whereas the Working Class group is differentiated in terms of skill. Since the overall measure used for scaling incorporates information about both similarity (co-occurrence) and dissimilarity (sorting into different groups) at an individual level, this can be taken as evidence for the cognitive reality of the sociological notion of class-boundaries, although overt class-imagery as such seems rather infrequent.

3 Hierarchies of Occupations

INTRODUCTION

Hierarchy is the best known, and the most prevalent, system of organisation in physical, biological and social systems, and all of us are familiar with the organisational chart, the book index and the family tree. The hierarchy is a serviceable concept, simple in form but also rich enough to facilitate expression of ideas as diverse as span of control, generative grammar, dominance and dependence (Simon 1969, Wilson 1969, Dawkins 1976). As Koestler (1972:233) puts it '[the hierarchy] is at the same time a conceptual tool, a way of thinking, an alternative to the linear chaining of events'.

But we are chiefly interested in the hierarchy as a form of cognitive organisation. As such, it certainly has 'psychological reality'. Experiments designed to investigate the structure of the 'subjective lexicon' have repeatedly led to the conclusion that the most prevalent form of organisation which subjects impose on lists of words (in recall, learning and memorisation) is hierarchical. This structure mirrors the supposition of much semantic theory (Miller 1967, 1969) that, as a particular subject area or topic is elaborated, the concepts activated at one level also evoke categories at a higher level of generality (Mandler 1957, Kiss 1971, Bower *et al.* 1969) and even dimensional scaling has 'recovered' hierarchical word structures of this sort from appropriate data (Young 1971:163 *et seq.*).

Posner (1973:89) points out a further interesting consequence of hierarchical organisation of information—whilst it is an efficient means of storage and recall, given the limitations of short-term memory, it is also intimately linked to stereotyping. In a hierarchical system, the predicates assigned at one level are necessarily an integral part of the description at lower more specific levels, so that if a property is assigned to a general class (as in examples such as 'manual workers are shiftless', 'Civil servants exploit your ignorance') then it will be held to apply to every instance. It is therefore important to know at what level of generality (and to what collectivity) occupational properties are predicated.

A semantic hierarchy, or taxonomy, provides a conceptual framework within which lexical items (in this case, the names of occupations) can be located. What differentiates the taxonomy from the paradigmatic or componential system of organisation is, first, that the semantic markers are organised at different levels of abstractness, in the sense that a higher-level feature is more general, and will include, or 'dominate' the features beneath it in the hierarchy. An instance of this property is provided by Anglin's (1970) schematic representation of the hierarchy of features presumed to underlie the set of words: 'boy, girl, horse, flower, chair, idea'. (This structure is incidentally well recovered from the word-sortings made by adults.)

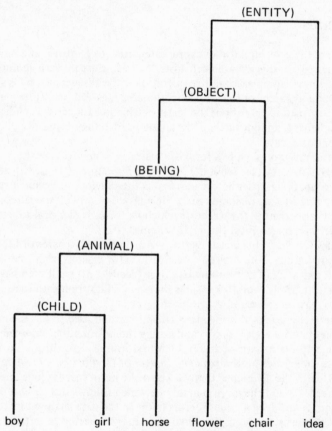

Figure 3.1 Hierarchical tree with organising features (based on Anglin 1970:10)

Each feature is a further specification of the one immediately above it, and is more general than the one directly below it. Thus a 'being' includes animals and children, and is included in the general category of 'objects'. Moreover, in a hierarchy there is no assumption made that a feature must apply to all objects – it applies only to those beneath it in the structure; a 'boy' is an entity, an object, a being, an animal, and a child, whereas a 'flower' is simply an entity, an object, and a being. However, hierarchies will not normally be as neatly nested as this example, and in the case of occupational conceptions we can expect that much less deeply nested structures will emerge, with relatively few instances of levels of inclusion, and most branches joining only at the highest, most abstract level (see for example Burton 1972:69; Burton and Romney 1975:403-4).

3.1 METHODS

But what are these hierarchical semantic categories (or features) and how may they be elicited? In this hierarchical clustering task, the subject is required to perform the most complex cognitive operation so far discussed — he is asked to construct a hierarchical tree of occupational names and, whilst he constructs it he is encouraged to talk about the features which characterise each level. This is, we believe, an innovative undertaking in sociology,[1] and it yields complex and rich data.

The hierarchy task is really a form of clustering which follows the agglomerative strategy (see section 2.2 above). The subject starts with all the separate occupational titles before him and is then invited to begin clustering them according to a set of simple rules. He continues until all the titles are clustered. Consequently, the structure which he forms is identical to what Johnson terms a hierarchical clustering scheme (HCS).

The rules for clustering are straightforward, and simply prevent the subject from joining more than two occupations (or clusters of occupations) together at any step. (The resulting HCS tree (see Fig. 3.1) will then have exactly fifteen 'levels', and this ensures that clusterings from different individuals may be compared at any given level.)

The hierarchy task is also the most general method used so far, incorporating elements from each task but integrating the information obtained. Each time a subject opts to form a cluster, he is performing a cognitive task akin to pairwise similarities judgement (*The Images of Occupational Prestige,* Chapter 3) with the difference that we know the more specific judgement which precedes it and the more general one which follows it. It is also possible for a subject to produce a rank-ordering (akin to the data analysed in Chapter 4 of the earlier book) by 'chaining' i.e. by choosing an initial pair, and then continually adding a single occupation. This strategy occurred very rarely in practice.

The task most obviously similar to hierarchy construction is free sorting, which can be thought of as a hierarchy in which the subject stops the clustering at a particular level. Because the number of groups which a subject forms is allowed to vary, the method of free sorting provides information on the tendency to aggregativeness along the lumper-splitter axis, and, as we have suggested, on the likely level of generality of the final sorting. In the hierarchy task, by contrast, the subject provides *fifteen* sortings, each at a distinct level of generality and each linked to its successor and predecessor by a single allowable move (such as adding an element, starting a cluster, merging clusters). Hence the hierarchies task allows the whole sequence of clustering to be studied, and permits individual sortings to be compared at any level of generality.

Hierarchical clustering is a cognitively taxing task, and we were frankly surprised that subjects performed the task so readily and uncomplainingly. Its complexity is further illustrated by the fact that, on average, it took several minutes longer to cluster the 16 occupations hierarchically than to free-sort twice as many (see section 2.1). On average, subjects took 35 minutes to complete the hierarchy task; no-one took less than 15 minutes, and several people took over an hour to complete it. An example will help to give some substance to this account.

The subject (Y090) is an aircraft fitter, and he took 35 minutes to complete the task. The interviewer comments: 'Although friendly, he warned me at once that I'd picked the wrong man, that he didn't say a word all day at his job, was a bad talker anyway, and that, therefore, how could he possibly think aloud for my benefit? But having said that, his speech proliferated.'

His hierarchical clustering proceeded as follows (see Fig. 3.2):

Step (level)	Action	Subject's comments
1	MTO and C²	'Their social standing's on a similar basis': 'manual workers with the same interests outside work — same standard of drinking habits — they'll go to the public bar, not the lounge': 'football.'
2	AD and LD	Same social standing, again, but quite how it might be described, he didn't know: 'It depends on their social habits.'
3	CA and QA	Their 'professional interest' meant that they 'have a lot in common to talk about — they'll pick up on each other's experiences — court cases and the like.' 'Unlike the Lorry Driver these men learn new tricks every day.'
4	MIN and MPN	Devoted, patient, open-minded and sympathetic.
5	SOL joined to (→) level (3)	(no comment)
6	BM and CT	'Both take a lot of abuse from the public' (he had been a Barman, so he knew); and 'must have a quick answer for everybody' — the Commercial Traveller, especially, was 'two-faced; you know — "yes sir, no sir".'
7	CST and CSE	'All *they* can talk about is their work — they're so tied up in it.' 'Obviously, they're quite

Step		
(level)	*Action*	*Subject's comments*
		brainy to be where they are . . . but . . . narrow-minded, inclined to shut off from things which don't concern them.' Also, 'They ought to pass on more of what they learn.'
8	RP and BSL	'Two of the more lowly jobs in life' – one might think these people had a more restricted outlook on life, but that was untrue: 'they're happy with the simple things in life . . . Well, on reflection, they have to be, since they have no chance of getting on.' They were 'bottom of the grade'.
9	PM → 2	The Policeman joins the drivers (AD and LD) due to their common 'concern with down-to-earth things'. They were always having to 'make up their own minds, make quick decisions'.
10	7 → 5	'All professional men, a lot in common to talk about – their interests will run away from ordinary run-of-the-mill things.'
11	10 → 4	The Male Nurse and the Minister 'follow on closely' from the professionals.
12	6 → 2	'Middle class.' This made level 11 now 'upper class'.
13	8 → 1	'Manual workers – working class – they're actually getting to grips with things, the men in overalls.' Although orders 'came down the tree' (the subject appropriated my word) to them from the upper class, their jobs were 'every bit as important'.
14	13 → 12	No comment
15	14 → 11	No comment

This hierarchical clustering can be represented in a number of ways. Although all of them are equivalent in the information they give, each representation draws attention to slightly different characteristics, or can be read in different ways. Three drawings of this same hierarchy are presented in Figure 3.2.

In the form of a rooted tree (A) the terminal nodes appear at the level at which they are first appended. It is very easy to see the sub-tree structure – in this case it consists chiefly of the three branches he calls 'upper class' rooted at level 11 (see his comment at level 12), 'middle class' (rooted at 12) and 'working class' (rooted at 13). The Taxonomic form (B) by contrast

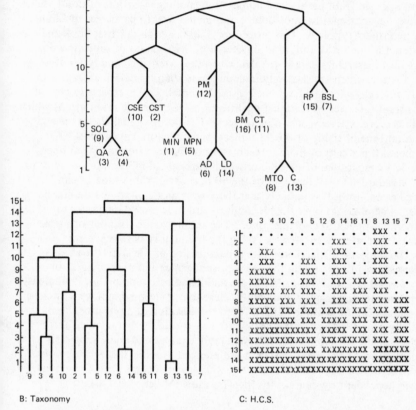

Figure 3.2 Representations of a hierarchy (subject YO 90)

places all terminal nodes at the base, but is otherwise read in the same way as (A). Finally, the HCS representation is read from the top downwards, and the joining of branches is represented by extending the 'XX' bars across the nodes which are clustered.

The same tree can be drawn in slightly different ways. For instance, two branches rooted at the same level can be exchanged at will, so that, for example, the 'middle class' branch, could be drawn to the left of the 'upper class' sub-tree, if so desired. For this reason it is advisable not to pay too much attention to the order in which terminal nodes occur across the page.

SELECTION OF SUBJECTS AND OCCUPATIONAL TITLES

The hierarchies task was being developed and tested during the middle part of the Project, as the shift was being made between sampling professional registers and adopting the 'combing' procedure (a process whereby subjects were selected from particular Enumeration (polling) Districts of Edinburgh, whose occupational composition corresponded well to particular quadrants of the Project typology. This procedure is discussed in our first book and in detail in the third. But, as a consequence, the final set of subjects who provided hierarchies data is unbalanced to the extent that the types of occupation which are relatively uncommon in the population at large also tend to occur with low frequency in the 'sample'. This is especially true of Quadrant C (lower educational qualifications, high people orientation) which here is represented by only nine subjects. The occupational allegiance and quadrant membership of the 93 subjects is detailed in Appendix U3.2. Almost 70 per cent of these subjects went on to do a free sorting either of the 32 occupational titles (nine of which correspond more or less exactly to the standard set used here), or of the 50 occupational predicates — and in some cases, both. It is unlikely that there were any contamination effects (e.g. remembering) since the hierarchical structure would be harder to remember than a free sorting. In order to minimise the risk, the two tasks were deliberately separated by taking the life history between them.

The 'objects' of the hierarchies task consisted of the standard 16 occupational titles used in the pairwise similarities and ranking tasks of Chapters 3 and 4 of our earlier book, and listed below on p.194. Preliminary experimentation made it abundantly clear that sixteen stimuli were as close to the maximum feasible number; even the addition of a few more stimuli usually proved to be too taxing cognitively, considerably extended the length of the interview and understandably exasperated some subjects. Occupational titles were chosen in preference to predicates, because nouns seem to have a more stable character, whereas predicates seem to be much more dependent on context for their meaning (Miller 1967:70).

3.2 STRATEGIES IN FORMING HIERARCHIES

Different styles of construction are clearly evident in the development of hierarchies (see U3.16 for a full discussion). In general, subjects tend to move from one phase to another in a fairly regular way. But the actual branches (sub-trees) are not built up in such a consistent manner: subjects tend rather to act more haphazardly, adding one occupation to one branch, then jumping to another branch, returning perhaps at later stages to making further additions to the initial branch. (This should of course be the case if subjects are taking the notion of 'degree of similarity' at all seriously.)

Let us now return to the general types of hierarchy which are formed. A good example of continuous chaining *and* dichotomy construction is provided by a social worker, whose hierarchy is produced in Fig. 3.3A. The first two pairs took a long time to make, but once he got beyond this stage, the subject continued to use the same basis for constructing the tree, and recognised that he had ended with two groups which were entirely disjoint.

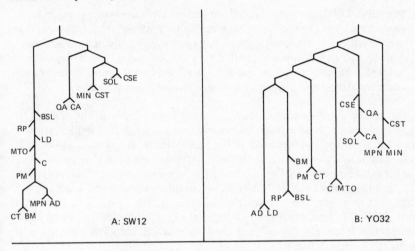

A: SW12

B: YO32

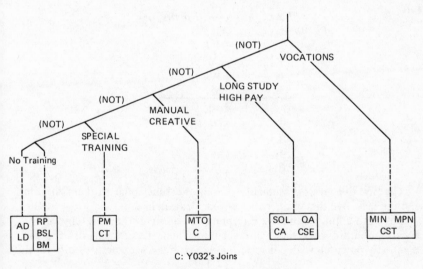

C: YO32's Joins

Figure 3.3 Two subjects' hierarchies

The interviewer comments:

The first pairing was made in terms of functional dependence: 'The barman is involved in terms of what products are stocked . . . and presumably the Commercial Traveller is involved in the stocking.' Attention then shifted to another basis; the Male Psychiatric Nurse and the Ambulance Driver 'work in a medical setting'; they probably have a connection in terms of the Driver being 'involved with psychiatric patients'. These were then joined — itself an unusual choice at such an early stage — in terms of their 'non-academic training'. This basis was then used for the next six steps, completing one group of the dichotomy. At step 10, the new group was formed by a pairing in terms of 'those with academic training' which served for the subsequent steps until the final — and very artificial — joining of the two counterposed groups.

In the case of a self-employed Manufacturing Screen Process Printer (Y032), by contrast, there is an explicit *ordering* process at work (see the interview report in U3.5 and the hierarchy in Fig. 3.3B). He would, he said at the end, 'put them into order starting at the very beginning with the blue-collar workers and building right up to the final white-collar workers'. Given the fact that the subject explicitly admits to producing an order or 'grading', it is important to notice that a number of different criteria or bases are used in its construction. Indeed, there are two ways in which his 'order' can be interpreted. If we take the order as the *level* at which mergings were made, it yields (from the bottom):

Level	Constituents
1	AD,LD
2	RP,BSL
3	C,MTO
4	PM,CT
5	BM
6	MPN,MIN
7	SOL,CA
8	CST
9	QA
10	CSE

The first five levels presumably contain the 'blue-collar workers' in order, and the next five the 'white-collar workers', again in order.

But a more understandable interpretation occurs if the hierarchy-construction process is taken into account. Then, the first part of the sequence is actually taken up with constructing six sub-trees, each defined differently:

Sub-tree	Description (see U3.4)
1 (AD,LD)	Both drive
2 (RP,BSL,BM)	No (specific) training
3 (PM,CT)	Ex-apprentice
4 (C,MTO)	Manual, skilled, manufacturing
5 (SOL,CA,QA,CSE)	University training, initially poorly paid
6 (MPN,MIN,CST)	'Specialised'

Here (as is usually the case) it is the subsequent *joinings* which introduce increasingly abstract and comparative generalisations, and which in this particular case happen to take the form of an ordering. It is at this stage (step 11) that he begins to comment on his own strategy, as if the main task were finished. It is also here that he first begins to use explicitly the terminology of ordering ('Next . . .') and ordering action (putting one set of cards *above* another). Since the task requires the production of increasingly inclusive mergings, he achieves the ordering structure by creating binary oppositions, yielding the 'superordinate structure' between the six subgroups indicated in Figure 3.3C.

These examples make it clear that different forms of structure (dichotomies, groupings, orderings) can be embedded by the subjects in the same hierarchical task, and suggest that it is the 'joining' choices which introduce second-order comparative information. They also alert us to the fact that the level of the information (or step at which a merging occurs) is only approximately related to relative similarity: until the subject has built up his basic groupings or sub-trees, the order of construction is often rather arbitrary: subjects repeatedly comment that a particular merging could equally have come before the previous one. However, once the 'repeated joining stage' has been reached, it is rarely disturbed by the occurrence of a new pairing or a chaining; it is very obvious that at these highest levels the order of the steps *is* significant. In these structural characteristics, none of the differences between quadrants are substantial.

3.3 SIMILARITIES BETWEEN HIERARCHIES

A hierarchy can be thought of as a set of classifications made at a series of levels, each level related to the higher one by inclusion. This fact makes it easy to compare the content of different occupational hierarchies. In the previous chapter (section 2.3) we saw that it was possible to compare the composition of different occupational classifications by looking at the extent to which two subject's groups overlap. The distance between two classifications was then defined, following Arabie and Boorman, in terms of the number of moves necessary to transform the one classification into the other. Because there is more than one way in which a move can be interpreted, this gave rise to a family of measures, from which the pairbonds ('height') distance was selected for our purposes.

The notion of the minimum number of moves needed to transform one structure into another has also been used to compare tree-hierarchies, especially by Boorman and Olivier (1973). The notion had also been developed in a more familiar context by linguists attempting to explain why sentences such as 'he put the book back' and 'he put back the book' mean the same, despite their different structure. In Chomsky's account, each sentence is initially represented as a hierarchy of rules (the 'phrase structure' tree) for rewriting constituents of the grammatical structure of the sentence. The mechanism for moving from one sentence (or tree) to the other is then provided by a set of transformational rules, which are 'rules for rewriting one tree-diagram as another' as Thorne (1972:194) puts it. The same basic idea can be used to represent the difference between subjective hierarchies i.e. by a sequence of rule-governed modifications or 'allowable moves'. Miller and Chomsky, in fact expressly recognised the *general* utility of using the notion of 'the least number of allowable moves' as a measure of dissimilarity for comparing other complex behavioural and cognitive structures:

> A hierarchical organization of behaviour to meet some new situation may be constructed by transforming an organization previously developed in some more familiar situation. The number of transformations involved would provide an obvious measure of the complexity of the transfer from the old to the new situation. (1963:485).

The principles by which these metrics are constructed are fairly straight-forward, although a number of technical problems are encountered in generalising to other types of hierarchies (see U3.5). The basic ideas will be explained by reference to the simple example of comparing the hierarchies S and T given in Figure 3.4. The key to understanding the distance measures is that each level of a hierarchy is considered as a classification, or partition, in its own right. Thus, in Figure 3.4, the trees S and T can be written as follows.

				Level
Tree S:	(ABCDE)	Tree T:	(ABCDE)	4
	(ABCD),E		(ABCD),E	3
	(ABC),D,E		(AC),(BD),E	2
	(AB),C,D,E		(AC),B,D,E	1
	A,B,C,D,E		A,B,C,D,E	0

A number of distance measures (metrics) are available for comparing two partitions (see U3.5). The most natural way of extending these measures to characterize the similarity between two whole trees is first to compare the hierarchies *level by level* in terms of a given measure, and then finally sum over all the levels. Fortunately, the sum of metrics is again a metric (Boorman and Arabie, 1972:32), which guarantees that the resulting 'tree-distance' will itself obey the triangle inequality, and thus be a distance.

Let us compare trees S and T in terms of the pairbonds partition metric discussed in 2.3. At level 0, the lowest point, all the five elements are distinct and therefore at this level S and T are identical, having a zero distance. At level 1, tree S merges A and B, whilst tree T merges A and C; the two partitions are hence: (AB),C,D,E   for S and   (AC),B,D,E   for T. The 'height' of (number of pairs in) both the S and T partitions at this level is 1 in either case, whilst the 'height' of the intersection is zero. Hence:

$$\text{Pairbonds} = h(S) + h(T) - 2 \times (2 \cap T)$$
$$= 1 \quad + 1 \quad - 2 \times 0$$
$$= 2$$

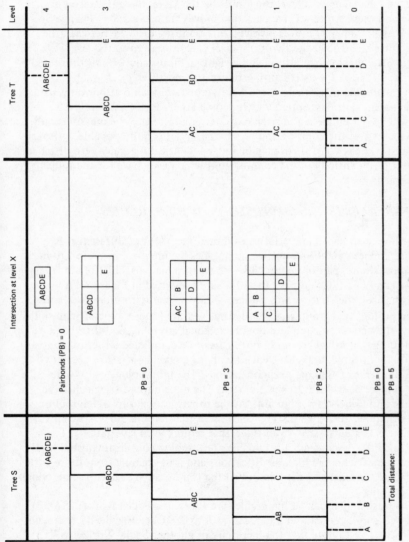

Figure 3.4 Distance between two hierarchies (trees)

That is, it would be necessary to move two *pairs* — namely (AB) and BC) — in order to convert one partition into the other at level one.

At level 2, the most substantial moves are necessary, because at this level the hierarchies are most dissimilar. At level 3, the partitions are in fact the same, and at the highest level they must be the same; there is a zero distance.

Overall then, a total of five pairbond moves are necessary to change S into T; the number of moves involved represent the distance between the hierarchies S and T. (Note that no special weight is given to the level at which differences occur, although a weighting factor could be incorporated without affecting the metric properties of the measures.)

In calculating the distance between two hierarchies, no attention is paid to the meaning or description which people attach to the various levels; this will be our concern at a later stage. At present, since the measures only take account of the composition of a hierarchy, it is quite possible — though unlikely — that two of them may be judged identical (i.e. have zero distance) and yet differ entirely in the connotations which they have for the subjects concerned.

DIFFERENCES IN THE COMPOSITION OF HIERARCHIES

With these provisos in mind, let us examine the extent of differences in the hierarchies data. First, no two hierarchies are identical in composition. The most similar pair of hierarchies — those of a male psychiatric nurse (Y346) and of a horticulturist (S190) — are presented in Figure 3.5A. In both cases, the strategy was similar — they began by forming two 'cores' of the professional group and the medical/welfare (later a type of semi-skilled) group, they go on to complete the professional grouping, and then begin to build up the unskilled group. In both cases, the completed structure consists essentially of three 'branches', each involving a main contrast of greater *v.* lesser amounts of training or qualifications. The terminology used to describe the branches does differ to some extent. The male nurse distinguishes the 'middle and upper class' branch from the other occupations which require 'some training', and then distinguishes those that require 'no as specialised training as at a university' from those that require even less training. The horticulturist, by contrast, uses no class terminology but distinguishes 'the professionals' who had high qualifications and long training from those with only *some* training, and then described the third branch as occupations which are 'just jobs'.

The least similar pair of hierarchies are those of a Social Worker (SWO2) and a self-employed Painter and Decorator (Y089) (see Fig. 3.5B), although it is instructive to note that the hierarchy of another Social Worker (SW12) differs to almost the same extent as the Painter's. But it can also be seen, simply by inspection, that the Social Worker's hierarchy far more obviously resembles those of the most similar pair of subjects. The Painter's hierarchy undoubtedly has some idiosyncratic features, especially the inclusion of

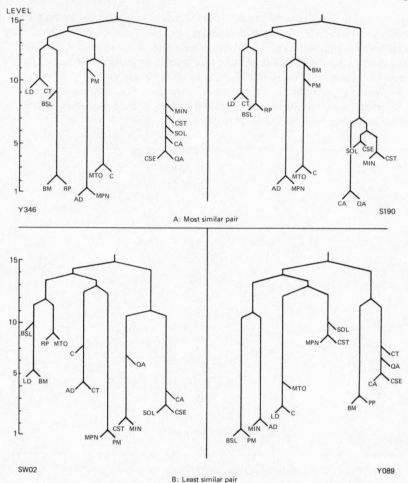

Figure 3.5 Contrasting hierarchies

Country Solicitor with the Male Nurse and the Teacher ('very hard jobs requiring patience'), and the merging of the Barman and Porter with what would normally be described as Professional jobs. In this instance, the connotations he gives are far from favourable: the Accountant and Civil Servant titles are joined at level six on the grounds that they are 'jobs anyone could do, in a sense . . . they don't take much out of you'. The Actuary was next appended with the comment, 'Again, an average person could do it — takes the smallest amount of training', and he stuck to this judgement despite what the interviewer describes as his wife's 'intervention with a strong protest'.

This once again emphasises the point that identical composition by no means implies identical connotation or evaluation! Yet the Painter's hierarchy clearly shares some common features with the other hierarchies, at least at the level of pairs of occupations. His final structure is most unusual in the higher-level descriptions, which differ radically from those normally given.

The range of variation in composition of hierarchies can be represented conveniently by a two-dimensional scaling of the distance measures, which is given in Figure 3.6 (see U3.6 for full details).

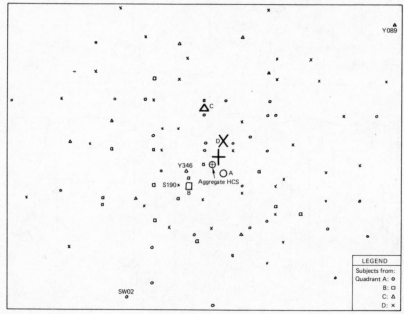

Figure 3.6 Scaling of distances between subjects' hierarchies

On the figure, each individual is symbolised by his quadrant membership. The average location (centroid) of the subjects in each quadrant is separately represented, as is the overall centroid (denoted by a large cross) and the (aggregate) Minimum HCS (see section 3.4 below), denoted by the circled cross. There is little evidence of systematic discontinuities in the space, which would signal distinct types of hierarchy. But there appear to be three regions:
  a fairly compact central group of hierarchies which are close to the most 'typical' subjects (including the centroids of quadrants A, B and D);
  a distinct inner circle of fairly similar points, which include the quadrant C centroid, and
  an outer region of rather unalike points, including the two most different subjects.

There is evidently a goodly amount of individual variation; the immediate question is whether it is systematically linked to occupational (or rather Quadrant) membership. The Quadrant centroids are certainly distinct, but are hardly markedly dissimilar. The analysis of variance reported in U3.7 indicates that, in terms of the scalings based on all three distance measures, the differences between Quadrants could easily have arisen by chance, and we should not, therefore, attach too much importance to the between-quadrant differences. Indeed, as we have seen, the differences among two social workers' hierarchies alone are as substantial as those occurring over the whole group of subjects, and the most similar hierarchies are as likely to be between members from diametrically opposite quadrants. Whatever is causing the variation in the composition of subjective hierarchies, it does not seem to be linked in any substantial way to occupational membership. (This should not be interpreted as meaning that there are no important differences in the way in which members of different occupational groups conceive of occupational hierarchies, only that the hierarchical relations between the occupations, *when entirely divorced from the meaning attached to them,* show no signs of being so determined.)

3.4 AGGREGATED HIERARCHY OF OCCUPATIONS

Since there are apparently no major discontinuities in the 'subject space', we can now go on to produce a representative aggregate hierarchy. For this purpose, the data of the individual subjects are added together, and the averages and dispersions are presented elsewhere (see U3.8 and compare with T3.8).

COMPARISON WITH THE AGGREGATE SIMILARITIES DATA

The pattern of these averaged data is certainly very similar to that of the average pairwise similarities ratings reported in Chapter 3 of our first book, and they correlate in excess of −0.95 (the relationship is negative because the data relate similarities with distances; see U3.9 for details of the relationship). The size of the correlation coefficient is surprisingly similar to that reported between national studies of occupational prestige. It also appears to be impressively large when it is recalled that the subjects involved in making the two kinds of judgement are quite different and that the methods of data collection differ very substantially. But we may legitimately invoke the same argument here as we did in Chapter 4 of the first book (pp. 39 *et seq.*): *such differences as occur are swamped in the massive agreement that also exists.*

In the case of the hierarchies data there are, first, differences in how well the relationship holds among the occupations being judged (see U3.9). For instance, the Commercial Traveller and Ambulance Driver titles fit notably less well than the others. Moreover these differences seem to involve the middle/working class contrast (the former being better accounted for than the latter), and those occupations which are socially visible titles are better fitted than those which are not.

More important differences are evident in how some *pairs* of occupations are judged in the two tasks. Here, the differences are both substantial and systematic:

(i)   *The Ambulance Driver and Lorry Driver are viewed as far more alike, on average, in the similarities than in the hierarchies task.* This may well be due to differences in the methods of data collection. In the pairwise similarities task each subject is required to make a judgement about the Ambulance Driver and the Lorry Driver. Having been brought to their attention in this explicit way, most subjects understandably decide that the driving skills mentioned in both titles are a good basis for judging them to be rather similar. By contrast this property is hardly ever invoked as a ground for similarity in either the free-grouping or the hierarchies data.

(ii)   In the hierarchical data, *the Lorry Driver is repositioned closer to the Unskilled Working Class Group, and the Ambulance Driver is closer to the uniformed 'people-oriented' jobs.*

These changes can easily be seen when the scaling solution (presented in U3.10) is compared with the configuration of Figure 3.2 in the earlier book.

THE AGGREGATED HIERARCHICAL CLUSTERING

It might be thought that since every subject's data exactly specifies a hierarchy, one single unambiguous hierarchy will result when individual hierarchies are added together. In fact, this will not usually be true (see U3.9), although these aggregate data do in fact satisfy the ultra metric inequality very well. When the aggregate data are analysed by Johnson's hierarchical clustering procedure, a particularly clear structure is evident. In Figure 3.7 the minimum and maximum solutions are presented together on the left-hand side, and the rooted tree versions are drawn at the right-hand side for comparison (in this representation, the height of a join is proportional to the average value at which the merger occurred).

There are obvious affinities between the hierarchical clustering of similarities data (see Fig. 3.4 and p. 91 *et seq.* in the first book and the present solution, both in terms of structure and interpretation. All the HCS solutions contain, in some form, the three sub-branches corresponding to what are clearly the most fundamental and salient features of this domain — the 'generic taxa' as Kay (1971:878) terms them — which have been identified repeatedly in this research as the *Professions/Working Class, Skilled/Unskilled* and *People-Oriented/Non-People-Oriented* contrasts. The first appears in both the similarities and hierarchies HCS solutions as the most general level of distinction. The Skilled/Unskilled distinction also occurs as the fundamental

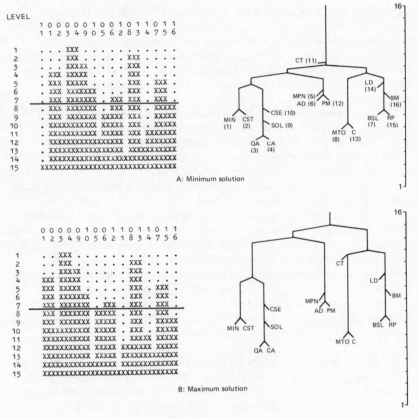

Figure 3.7 HCS of aggregated hierarchies

split in the 'Working Class' branch of both the hierarchies data solutions, but is not so evident in the similarities data solution. Finally, the third 'Extrinsic/Intrinsic reward' factor, which is not clearly present in the similarities data solutions, appears to operate in two ways in the hierarchies data — to distinguish people-oriented *jobs* (Ambulance Driver, Male Psychiatric Nurse), from *the professions,* but then to differentiate the professions in terms of people-orientation.

The hierarchical clustering scheme of the aggregate hierarchies data, then, gives a more internally consistent and cleaner structure than the HCS of the aggregate similarities data, and this structure also corresponds strikingly to the groups isolated in the analysis of the free-sorting data.

3.5 INTERPRETATION OF THE AGGREGATE HIERARCHY

Our task now is to identify segments of the aggregate hierarchy in the judgements which the subjects have made. Because this hierarchy is a simple three-branch structure, it makes sense to start at the most specific (terminal) pair of each branch, and then follow each branch upwards as it becomes more general.[3]

How can the process of tracing and identification proceed? In brief, by comparing subjects' comments or 'incomplete definitions' (as Miller (1972:346) terms them) in order to detect common themes in content or areas of meaning. In so doing we encounter two problems — how different statements are to be recognised as synonymous, and whether it is legitimate for the social scientist to interpret and expand ('gloss') the subject's actual words. Cutting through a complex and contentious methodological debate, let us simply assert that we view it as the researcher's responsibility in these circumstances to use his intuitions and knowledge to put together words which have similar meanings, whether or not such 'glossing' would be recognised by the subject. The attempt to be uncompromisingly literal in such accounts is both unnecessary and doomed to failure (cf. Cicourel 1973: 109 and Barnes and Law 1976:235). In such 'putting together' of incomplete definitions we are looking for more general or abstract concepts — or themes — which inform the subjects' judgements of similarity and difference. Miller, citing Gleitman and Gleitman (1970) gives a very apposite example:

> To be a garbage-man implies that you remove garbage, but to remove garbage does not imply that you are a garbage-man. Thus, a *man who removes garbage* is an incomplete definition of *garbage-man,* incomplete in that the occupational aspect (at least) is missing. (Miller 1972:346)

The organisation of the subjects' incomplete definition into different headings need not, of course, depend simply upon our intuitions. After all, the subjects themselves use a stock of terms and concepts to describe the general characteristics of the groups which they create in performing tasks such as free-sorting. There also exists a number of category-systems developed by linguists and social scientists to describe the content of communication, and these too will be used, as appropriate.

BRANCH ONE: PROFESSIONAL MEN

Consists at the lowest level of:	(QA,CA)	(i)
joined next by:	SOL	(ii)
and then by:	CSE	(iii)
At this point a new sub-branch begins:	(MIN,CST)	(iv)
And finally, the two sub-branches merge:	(((QA,CA)SOL) CSE)	
	(MIN,CST))	(v)

(i) Qualified Actuary and Chartered Accountant

Over half of the subjects begin a sub-branch with this pair, and one-third begin with this branch as their first step. The predicates most used to describe these two occupations will occasion little surprise: both are 'men of figures', as a window-cleaner puts it. The commonly-used bases for judgement are:

their status (mentioned by 32 per cent);

their qualifications and training (mentioned by 40 per cent);

their level of remuneration (mentioned by 12 per cent); and

their financial dealings (mentioned by two-thirds)

The first theme, concerned with professional status, refers to the *symbolic characteristics* of the occupation. It can be specified as follows:[4]

THEME 1: STATUS (1)

Key terms: *Profession*(s) (NOUN.MASS.COLL.ECON.ECON.[5])

chosen-, business-, caring-,

Professional (MODIF.EVAL.ECON.ECON.HUMAN)

– group, – man, – men, – person, – people, – classes, – job

– interests, – qualifications, – standards, – qualities

Status (=STATUS 1: NOUN.ECON.POLIT.THINK.EVALU.MEANS. POWER)

job –

– in community

also (Social) *position, looked up to,* (Social) *scale*

The second theme relates to similar high educational and skill *prerequisites.* It is specified as follows (and see U3.12):

THEME 2: QUALIFICATIONS AND TRAINING (1)

Key terms: *Qualify/ied* (=QUALIFY 2: SUPV.COMN.QUALIF)

– individual, – type of person, – men,

Qualification(s) (=QUALIFY 2)

educational –, professional –, university –, academic –, high –, very high degree of –,

Trained (=TRAIN 4: MODIF.VIRTUE.THINK.EVALU)

highly –

Training (=TRAIN 3: THINK.EVALU.DOCTR.ACAD)

many years –, (very) long –, fairly lengthy –, lot of –, academic –, university –

and

(Well) *educated, University, exams, degree, educational background career structure, expertise, attainment, intelligent*

(tagged in terms of ECON.ACAD or POWER)

The third theme is concerned with high pay – commented on most of all by Business Managers and by those in jobs with similarly high salaries – and indicates the most salient *consequences* of holding the jobs (and see U3.12):

THEME 3: REMUNERATION (1)
Key terms: *Remunerat(ed,-ion)* (does not appear in the dictionary)
                    highly —
                    Salary (NOUN.ECON.THINK.EVALU.MEANS.ECON*)
                    — bracket, — range
                    high —
                    Fees (NOUN.ECON.COMN.FORM.ECON*)
                    exorbitant —
                    Income (INCOME 1: NOUN.ECON.COMN.FORM.ECON*)
                    — bracket, — level,
and   *Standard of living,* (financial) *reward,* well/lowly *paid, earn*
      The fourth most commonly cited theme is a specification of the main
job content of these two occupations (and see U3.12):

THEME 4: JOB CONTENT

SUB-THEME: FINANCIAL DEALINGS
Key terms: *Business* (=BUSINESS 1: NOUN.ECON.DOCTR.ECON*.THINK.EVALU)
                    same —, different —, way of —, line of —, do —
                    — profession/al, — affairs, — environment, — capacity
                    Finance (=FINANCE 1: NOUN.DOCTR.ECON.ECON*.THINK.EVALU)
                    field of —
                    — transactions
                    Money (NOUN.COM.ECON.ECON*.COMNOBJ)
                    administration of —, dealing in —, other people's —
                    Figures (=FIGURE 1: NOUN.COM.COMNFORM)
                    men of —
                    calculation of —, manipulation of —, involved with —,
                    work with —, concerned with — produce —
                    Insurance/Assurance (NOUN.MEANS.ECON.ECON*.THINK.EVALU)
                    life —
and   *Commerce, Commercial, Business, Statistics, Calculations, Tax*
                    affairs, Book-keeping, Economic, Mathematical, Pension(s)
                    (tagged in terms of ECON and/or ECON*)

      In addition to this core of common meaning, there are a number of more
idiosyncratic comments largely concerned with personal characteristics
which are believed to typify the job incumbents — the 'kind of person' they
are likely to be (conventional, precise, mathematically-oriented, willing to
change jobs to improve their pay etc).

(ii) 'Country solicitor' is added to Actuary and Accountant (this branch is
matched exactly by 29 subjects' data)

The addition of Solicitor to the group does two things: the job-specific Financial/Legal Dealings theme decreases dramatically, whilst both the symbolic (Status) theme — now almost exclusively 'professional' — and the consequential (Remuneration) theme become more salient. (The Qualifications theme remains virtually at the same level.)

Emphasis upon the legal characteristics of the jobs is heightened by the inclusion of the Solicitor: the three occupations are now seen as being 'men of affairs': 'non-productive labourers — no, that's nasty . . . they sort out the affairs of others, producing papers, writings, figures, words . . . they're non-material assets to the community.' (gynaecologist)

THEME 4: JOB CONTENT
Key terms: *Affairs* (=AFFAIR 1: NOUN.ACTV.THINK.KNOW)
            — of others
SUB-THEME: LEGAL DEALINGS (Sub-tree ii, iii)
        Legalities (see LEGAL)
        deal with —
        Legal (MODIF.ECON.POLIT.DOCTR.THINK.EVALU.DOCTR.LEGAL)
        — field

In terms of personal characteristics, the same main themes remain and there is a strong impression that the job holders exude a conventional worthiness:

'not high-powered, sensible' (actuary); 'hardly in the mainstream of glamorous events — quiet and comfortable . . . not a dynamic doctor, nor a high-powered QC, or whatever' (social worker)

(iii) 'Civil Servant (Executive)' is added to Actuary, Accountant and Solicitor (based on 26 cases)
No new themes appear with the addition of this single occupation, but several are interpreted somewhat differently (see U3.12). The Status theme now becomes the one most commonly cited, and is identified in straight-forwardly professional terms by the 'middle-class' subjects, but in explicitly class terms ('upper class' or 'upper middle class') by the 'manual' subjects. The most distinctive shift of meaning occurs in the 'job content' theme; these jobs are repeatedly described as involving a high degree of responsibility (by the 'middle class'), or as being a desk job (predominantly by the manual group).

In summary then, the thematic content common to all the subjects is that this group is: a high-status, highly trained and well-paid group of professionals whose jobs are primarily concerned with the economic and legal affairs of others.

But there is disagreement on how they should be identified (as 'upper-class desk jobs' by working-class subjects and as 'highly responsible' by the middle-class ones — a degree of occupational egotism is obvious here), and on how they should be esteemed. The personal characteristics ascribed to the job incumbents differ, but on no obvious social basis and tend to be highly stereotypical — safe, methodical, conventional, a little dull, conservative.

(iv) A new sub-branch is begun, which consists of: Church of Scotland Minister and Comprehensive School Teacher (based on 30 cases)
Most subjects merge 'Church of Scotland Minister' and 'Comprehensive School Teacher' into a single group between steps 4 and 7, and one-third of the subjects begin a branch with this pair.

The same general themes — Status, Qualifications, Remuneration — are as much in evidence here as in Branch One, but the Job-content theme changes to what we have at an earlier point described as the 'Service-orientation'. In the hierarchies task, Service-orientation has two discernible components — an Affiliation theme (Atkinson 1958) concerned with helping people, and an Associative theme, where the emphasis is simply upon interacting with people. For this reason the more general 'people orientation' is chosen as a general descriptive category.

THEME 4: JOB CONTENT

SUB-THEME: PEOPLE-ORIENTATION
Key terms: *Social* (=SOCIAL 1: MODIF.POLIT PØLIT*.HUMAN.THINK.EVALU.
              DOCTR.COLL)
                 — aspect/side
                 — concern
                 — contact
                 — problems
                 — working
              People (=PEOPLE 1: NOUN.HUMAN.COLL.MASS)
                 benefit of other —
                 contact with —
                 deal with —
                 get on with —
                 handle —
                 relating to, in a relationship with —
                 understand —
                 working for —
also   *Community, folk,* (personal) *contact, public, service, society,
              caring* (tagged in terms of HUMAN and COLL)

A second job-content theme, which refers primarily to the Teacher, and by extension to the Minister, refers to the Educative skills of these two occupations and includes an interesting ethical component, concerned particularly with the moral upbringing or shaping of lives.

THEME: JOB CONTENT

SUB-THEME: EDUCATIVE SKILLS

Key terms: *Teacher/s* (NOUN.HUMAN.ACAD.POWER)
             Teach (=TEACH 1: SUPV.COMN.ACAD.POWER)
             Educate (SUPV.ACAD.POWER.ACTV1.STRNG1.COMN)
             (FORMATION)
             Instruction (NOUN.COMN.FORM.ACAD.POWER)
             Responsibility (NOUN.ABS.ABS*.VIRTUE.THINK.EVALU.POWER)
             Form (of lives) (=FORM 2: SUPV.WORK.MAKE)
and   *Standards, influence*
             (tagged in terms of POWER and VIRTUE)

As in the first stage *Job Content* theme(s) dominates the others in the frequency with which it is mentioned, and it does so even more strongly. (see U3.12). By contrast, the *Status* theme is much less salient; it is scarcely mentioned at all by the subjects in manual occupations. Indeed, it is left entirely to the higher status subjects to cite the professional standing of the Minister and the Teacher. The unusual conjunction of high status with low income and the marked differences in evaluation of the Minister's role are discussed in U3.17.

    The academic and educational requirements of these two jobs are considered to be just as exacting as for the first branch and, if anything, more academic in form; and when remuneration is mentioned, it is the lowness of pay which is felt to call for comment, either on the grounds that it is an anomaly (the professional group), or because people who enter the jobs concerned are not motivated by economic gain: 'They (CST and CSM) deal with the greatest aspects of life. Our society is built on an education system; without education we learn nothing . . . I wish I'd stayed at school. The Minister, too, is one of the most important jobs, contributes to the greatest needs of society. *Their low incomes don't matter to them.'* (Electronic engineer; emphasis added)

Finally, the Job Content (themes) of People-Orientation and Educative Role are the major defining characteristics of these two occupations (often described by subjects as 'vocations' in this context), and they are equally cited by both groups of subjects.

(v) The two sub-trees merge, and now include: Qualified Actuary, Chartered Accountant, Country Solicitor, Civil Servant (Executive), Church of Scotland Minister, Comprehensive School Teacher (based on 23 cases).
The specific Job-content theme virtually disappears, whilst the Status and Qualifications themes assume prime importance. These jobs are professional, the incumbents are 'professional people' — so say the middle-class group, almost to a man. The manual group recognise the common status, certainly, but they prefer more overtly status-linked terms: 'middle/upper class',

and even 'toffs' and 'nobs' (the latter, especially in the form 'nab', is a term of Scottish origin to denote 'a person of some wealth or social distinction', OED). But both groups agree overwhelmingly that these men and jobs are academically qualified, or university-trained (the only occasional exception is the Civil Servant, but even though he may not have been to university 'he is a university-type person', as an insurance broker puts it).

The job-content theme at this level is either extremely general 'responsible jobs', 'to do with training', or else refers to the fact that they are 'office jobs' or 'office workers'. Parenthetically, only the manual group use this description and it may well serve as their contrast to the term 'professional' in this context

The pattern of theme-usage for this main branch of occupations is interesting and can best be seen by examining at each level the proportion of subjects who mention a given theme. (This process is illustrated in Fig. 3.8.)

BRANCH TWO: PUBLIC SERVANTS
Consists at the lowest level of: (AD,PM)   (i)
joined by: MPN   (ii)
(This branch merges with Branch One at level 11)

(i) Ambulance Driver and Policeman
These titles tend to be put together either at a relatively early stage, or just before the end of a sorting; the distribution is clearly bimodal, and the break occurs at the 11th stage. That is, subjects tend either to recognise a strong communality between the Ambulance Driver and the Policeman (about 60 per cent), or virtually none at all.

The 27 subjects who begin a branch with these two occupations do so, on average, at the fourth stage, and their data provide the basis for the following analysis.

Job-content references share a number of features and words in common with the People-orientation theme of Branch One, used to describe the Minister and the Teacher, where the 'people' referred to are again thought of as a collectivity rather than individually. The additional feature is now the connotation of submission to authority (the Harvard IV dictionary's SUBM tag) — these occupations are above all in the public *service*.

THEME 4: JOB CONTENT

SUB-THEME: PEOPLE-ORIENTATION (2): PUBLIC SERVICE
Key terms: *People* (specified in People-orientation (1))
          together with:

          Service (=SERVICE 1: NOUN.ECON.ACT.GENRLTY.ECON*.SUMB.
          PSTV*)
          — agencies, — occupations, — jobs, — people
          Servant(s) (NOUN.HUMAN.ECON.ECON*.SUBM)
          public —

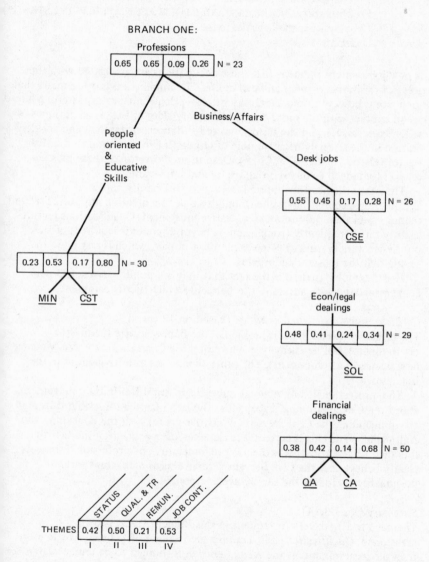

Figure 3.8 Branch One themes

Public (=PUBLIC 1: NOUN.COLL.POLIT.MASS)
         serving the —, concerned with the —, contact with the —
         Community (NOUN.MASS.COLL.POLIT.ECON.AFFIL.PSTV2.STRNG2
         loyalty to the —, service to the —
also   *Citizens*

A new job-content theme is that these occupations are associated with the
areas of crisis, misfortunes and evil in life. The implication is often made that
such work, however important, may be either demeaning or distasteful (they
are in contact with the more 'tragic and seamy sides of life' as an antiques-
seller expresses it), and the terms involved — danger, emergency and accident -
feature in the strongly negative pole of Osgood's Cross-cultural Evaluative
Factor (Osgood *et al.* 1975, Ch. 5). Despite such overtones, these jobs are
repeatedly judged to be essential, useful and important.

The other themes encountered in Branch One hardly appear at all here.
On the most generous assessment, only two people mention any status-related
theme — and then only to make a relative judgement. Qualifications feature
slightly more frequently (some training beyond school is required, of the
on-the-job variety) and as often as mention of pay (which is restricted to
saying that the jobs are underpaid).

For these jobs, then, it is the fact that they are public services (93 per
cent) associated with adversity (26 per cent) which merits comment.

(ii) Male Psychiatric Nurse is added (based on 17 cases)
The effect of this addition is negligible; the Public Service theme still
predominates, but less heavily, followed by the Crisis theme (where 'violence'
now occurs as a component). The other themes are as infrequent as in the
last case.

The 'professional' and 'manual' subjects do not differ in their judgements
about these occupations — except that the latter form a somewhat different
group including the Civil Servant (Executive grade) with the Policeman and
Ambulanceman. This is perfectly reasonable, of course, given the fact that
it is their service role that is seen as predominant. The professional subjects
clearly believe that the Civil Servant's 'service' is of a different sort,
presumably excluding the submissive component.

Summary (see U3.14)
Themes I to III are very infrequent in this Branch; *Status* is scarcely
mentioned, *Qualifications and Training* are thought of as being a little more
than the legal minimum, and *Remuneration* is thought to be unnecessarily
poor. By contrast, the *Job-Content* theme — here a more submissive variant
of people-orientation and concerned primarily with service of the public —
dominates all subjects' comments. A supplementary 'Crisis' theme, concerned
with emergency and danger, is also evident. Finally, a number of subjects
stress, indeed overstate, the virtue they believe the Policeman and the

Ambulance Driver to have, but this high evaluation does not extend to the Psychiatric Nurse. Although the numbers involved are small, and the Branch structure is very simple, citations of Theme 4 (Job Content) decrease, as in Branch One.

BRANCH THREE: MANUAL WORKERS
Consists of two sub-branches

The larger sub-branch begins with:	(BSL,RP)	(i)
joined next by:	BM	(ii)
and then by:	LD	(iii)
The smaller sub-branch consists of:	(MTO,C)	(iv)

(later augmented by CT, but ignored in this analysis)
Finally, the two sub-branches merge: ((((BSL,RP) BM) LD) (MTO,C))   (v)

(i) Building Site Labourer and Railway Porter (based on 39 cases): *'Manual unskilled jobs'*
Of the three general themes, only the Qualifications Theme appears with any frequency in this branch, in the form of specifying the jobs as unskilled. It is a moot point whether in fact 'unskilled' should be included with the other entries in the Qualifications theme. However, the deciding factor would seem to be the fact that *training* (or the lack of it) is a common element to both professional or academic qualifications, and to the distinction between skilled and unskilled manual work.[6]

These two occupations are unequivocally judged to be *un*skilled. This single theme dominates all others, being mentioned explicitly by one half of the subjects.

THEME 2: QUALIFICATIONS (3)

SUB-THEME: (LACK OF) SKILL
Key Terms: *Unskilled* (not tagged as such: see SKILLED)
              − job, − man, − labour
              relatively −, rather −, largely −, basically −
              Skills(s) (=SKILL 1: NOUN.ECON.VIRTUE.PSTV*.THINK.EVALU)
              no −, untrained −, lower degree of −
              Skilled (=SKILL 2: MODIF.EVALU.VIRTUE.PSTV*.THINK.EVALU)
              not all that −, less −

The Job-content theme for these two occupations is clearly that they are *Manual* labouring jobs (See U3.15).

THEME 4: MANUAL LABOUR

SUB-THEME: JOB CONTENT

Key terms: *Manual* (not tagged as such)
                      — jobs, — labour, — labourers, — type
                  Labour(ing) (=LABOR 1: NOUN.COLL.ECON.MASS.ECON*)
                  Physical (MODIF.BODYIND)
                      — job, — lifting,
                      — effort, — strength
and   *Muscle-power, hands*

Status is mentioned by one-fifth; the jobs are either 'working class', or are allocated to the lowest part of a person's grading ('at the bottom of their respective occupations', 'lowest down the scale of occupations', 'lowly jobs, bottom of the grade'). References to *remuneration* concentrate on the fact that such jobs are often well paid, and that this must therefore act as the main motivating force.

A high moral tone of disapprobation is also generally evident, on the lips of working class and professionals alike:

It would be easy to get by without them   (School Principal)
They are useless kinds of person   (Fork truck driver)
Lazy layabouts   (Medical consultant)
People who take up such a job can't do much worse   (Toiletry wholesaler)
Nobody with any goals would ever consider them   (Electronic engineer)

A wry touch is added the same Fork-truck driver:

Yon Porter disappears like snow off a dyke as soon as the train comes in . . . still, it's no' much of a job.

(ii) 'Barman' is added to Railway Porter and Building Site Labourer (based on 26 cases): *'Unskilled jobs'*
Virtually everyone describes these jobs as 'unskilled' — sometimes with a slight qualification (*less* skilled, *fairly, basically* unskilled), and many go on to comment on how casual the work is, involving 'drifters'. Now, only a third mention Qualifications: no formal qualifications/training is required, they say. The few who talk of remuneration cite the additional income to be derived from tipping. Only one person cites a status theme explicitly, but forcefully:

. . . the lowest of the low in my experience. A Building site labourer is ninety per cent of the time totally unskilled, extremely casual and irresponsible . . . there are quite a lot of them in my practice. The Barman's quite often a fly man, not above making a bit of money on the side at the expense of his employer. It's difficult to find an honest Barman . . . Railway porter? It's difficult to find a helpful one (general practitioner).

(iii) 'Lorry Driver' is added (based on 8 cases)
The small number of exact matches preclude any thematic analysis.

(iv) Sub-branch: Machine Tool Operator and Carpenter (based on 58 cases):
'Skilled manual workers: Trades'
There is greater agreement on the fact that this pair form a separate branch
than for any other feature of the aggregate hierarchy. There is equal
unanimity on its description: the jobs are *skilled* and *manual,* and they are
trades. This last term is of considerable importance as it implies the serving
of time ('time-served') as an apprentice, after which the worker becomes an
accredited craftsman. It is also used frequently as a contrast to 'profession',
both here and in common speech. (We had earlier been of the opinion that this
contrast was especially salient among working-class subjects; this does not
appear to be true. For these data at least, such characteristics are equally often
cited by higher-status subjects.) The significant difference seems simply to
be that professional people use the term 'manual' somewhat more frequently,
perhaps as a 'distancing' term.

THEME 4: JOB CONTENT: (Trades)
Key terms: *Trade(s)* (=TRADE 1: NOUN.ECON.THINK.EVALU.DOCTR.ECON*)
               own −, same −, learn a −
              Apprenticeship(s) (not tagged)
              serve on −, do an −, try an −, go through an −
              Craft(s)(man/men) (not tagged)
and   *Apprenticed, Time-served*

Income is rarely mentioned, except by subjects who are themselves in
allied occupations, and status hardly arises, except in the occasional reference
to the 'better working class'. But a laboratory technician was triggered into
making a very illuminating diversion into his conception of class: 'Work with
their hands, semi-skilled, frequent the same pub . . . the same class of people,
left school with the same qualifications . . .' What did he mean by 'class'?
asked the interviewer. 'Everybody finds their own class through their
occupation; they might mix socially, but it's at work that you're on your
own with your mates. Class distinction really exists, especially among the
lower classes.' He paused, then continued: '. . . it's how you feel: we feel
dominated . . . so we are.'

(v) The two branches merge to include *Machine Tool Operator, Carpenter,
Building Site Labourer, Railway Porter, Barman and Lorry Driver* (based
on seven cases)
It would be hazardous to base any analysis on so few cases. It is nevertheless
interesting that the descriptions which are given tally well with the interpretation so far: the common (job content) basis in manual work, and the
differentiation in terms of qualifications − the degree of skill or training:

These are the manual and skilled trades, not professions. They have on-the-job training, rather than professional skills, and they are paid by the week (college of education lecturer).

That's a broad manual type of job, using a lot of degree of skill from one (MTO, C, LD) to very little on the other (BSL,RP,BM) (brewery traffic controller).

Unfortunately, the number of matches at two crucial points in Branch Three are too small to permit the analysis of theme frequency by branch structure, which was so successful in Branch One (see Fig. 3.8). Nonetheless, the interpretation is obvious: the branch as a whole describes Manual Jobs, in contrast to the Professions. The main division is between the Unskilled Jobs and the Skilled Trades. The Remuneration theme is uniformly infrequent in subject's descriptions, perhaps surprisingly in view of the fact that these jobs are also paid by wage rather than by salary. Status terms are used primarily to describe the lowest, least skilled jobs, and consists usually of an undifferentiated 'working class' appellation.

MEANING AND THEMES

Although the four themes occur throughout the subjects' hierarchies, they do not do so in an undifferentiated manner. As we saw in the analysis of Branch One, some themes increase systematically in the local structure (for instance, by level), but others do not. Moreover most themes change meaning, often fairly subtly, in moving from one part of the structure to another — just as the predicates shifted meaning along the 'horseshoe' sequence of occupational similarities (pp. 26-90 of our earlier book).

Let us now examine each theme in its changing context within the aggregate hierarchy, by reference to Figure 3.9.

(a) Status

The status theme is an important and salient one in describing the occupations of Branch One, and is especially prominent in the 'Business' group of occupations. Citations also increase systematically through the branch structure, becoming dominant in the most general judgements. The content is overwhelmingly that of professional status, and class ascription, when it occurs, is of 'middle' or 'upper-middle' class.

In Branch Two, status ascription is rather uncommon, very probably because the occupations concerned occupy an ambiguous position with respect to the main branches, which are more obviously identified.

In Branch Three, status features predominantly in identifying the 'lowest' end of labouring jobs, which are unequivocally described as working class. In the higher levels, and in the skilled sub-branch, it does not feature significantly.

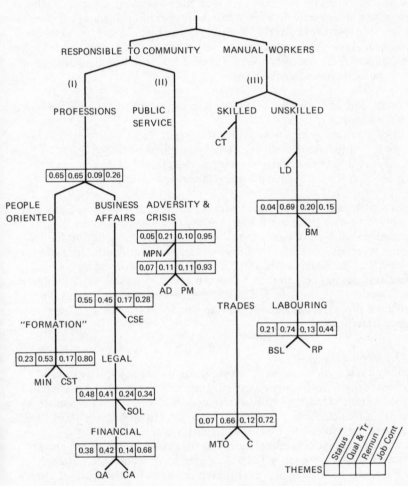

Figure 3.9 Interpreted aggregate hierarchy

(b) Qualifications and training

This theme is most consistently and repeatedly referred to, in all levels and in all branches: it saturates subject's occupational judgements. The main distinctions again come in the differentiation of Branches One and Three. In the Professional branch educational qualifications, and training are uppermost in the judgements: these jobs are educationally certificated and involve full-time training. In the Manual branch, the notion of degree of skill is crucial, with the main divide being on precisely this criterion. (None the less the Skilled Trades are rarely merged with the Professions; there is clearly thought to be a generic difference between types of qualification and training. Despite the reservation of 'skill' for manual occupations and 'training' for professional ones, the usage of these two concepts is none the less strikingly similar (see U3.12, specification of Theme Two), involving the same semantic contexts and distinctions –

> both 'skill' and 'training' are referred to as quantitative attributes (*degree of, amount of*);
> they are finely graded in amounts, (*no, bit of, high*);
> they both feature in comparative judgements (*same, more, less*);
> they are differentiated by type (*specialised, technical, basic*), and
> they both feature in modal contexts (*requires, needs*).

Such regular variation, associated with generic separation, nicely illustrates the point we have made in Chapter 3 of the first volume – that a purely dimensional analysis of occupational judgements is misleading, in that it cannot represent the semantic shifts and categorical discontinuities which are so clearly evident in these data. Equally, of course, a discrete hierarchical analysis is also unlikely to detect important 'locally smooth variations' in the attributes. Clearly, some hybrid model is necessary to capture both types of structural property, and current developments here (Carroll 1976) are highly relevant.

(c) Remuneration

Although it is a constant theme, Remuneration does not appear to vary systematically in its frequency with the branch structure, but the content does. In Branch One, the favoured reference is to salary, and (to a much lesser extent) in Branch Three it is typically to wages. (In both the 'people-oriented' branches, the neutral term 'pay' avoids such specification!)

It is the context of remuneration that the politically important areas of perceived income inequality and wage differentials feature most strongly. As Rainwater (1974:118 *et seq.*) has emphasised in his discussion of images of income levels, the most common way in which people do this is by distinguishing various 'levels of living', each of which has (implicit) consumption patterns, and each of which needs a given range of income for 'getting along'. We have little directly comparable information to offer, but Rainwater's characterisation certainly underlies our subjects' thinking, and his levels correspond reasonably well to the sub-branches of the hierarchy. The subjective – but shared – conceptions of appropriate 'levels of living' serve as a rough yardstick in judging how well different groups are – and should be – rewarded.

In Branch One, the 'Business' professions are almost without exception thought of as being highly rewarded, in part because of the responsibility of the job, but also because of what people outside the jobs think of as the unexciting dullness of the task. By contrast, the 'people-oriented' jobs are thought of (but only by those who accept their social utility) as being considerably underpaid. The same is broadly true of the uniformed public services, except that there is less questioning of their social usefulness (or 'necessity' in this case).

In regard to both 'People-oriented Professions' and the 'Public Services' there is more than a suggestion that a trading relationship exists between the vocational nature of its job – in the form of a moral bonus, as it were – and its financial rewards. By contrast, the occurrence of high wages among Branch Three occupations (at least with benefit of overtime, or tips) is thought of as compensating for the work conditions, and their low public esteem (a view shared equally among professionals and skilled manual workers).

(d) Job content

The substance of the job-content theme changes markedly in the local structure of the tree, and it predominates as a theme in the specified detail at the initial (lowest) levels. It also discriminates most obviously between sub-branches of the hierarchy, and in the case of the Public Services occupations (Branch Two), it is virtually the *only* theme. In terms of frequency of mention, citations decrease systematically as the structure becomes more general. In particular, details of job content form either a dominant or a substantial part of subjects' judgements when they are making initial pairings and (to a lesser extent) when extending the groups by adding new occupations. But they feature to a very limited extent in their more general, abstract, judgements. This is in many ways a comforting fact; if highly specific characteristics did remain salient in the more general judgements, then it would be virtually impossible to generalise from the particular set of occupational titles used, and inference to common structural and evaluative characteristics, which form the basis of any general theory of social stratification, would be impossible.

3.6 SUMMARY

In this chapter we have used the hierarchical clustering task to investigate the different levels of generality at which people make occupational judgements, and to examine the degree of consensus in the composition and naming of parts of the occupational tree. The hierarchies task, which possesses features in common with all the other methods we have used so far, is eminently suited to eliciting both structural and semantic information in a specified context of judgement and at a given level of generality.

The sequence of investigation has been first to examine the strategies which subjects employed in constructing their hierarchies, in order to glean information on the significance of the task and how it was used to indicate relationships between occupations. Secondly, the individual hierarchies were compared to explore the extent and type of variation in their composition. Thirdly, a single 'representative' hierarchy was constructed from the aggregate data. Finally, components of this structure were identified in the subjects' hierarchies and then interpreted by referring to the namings and descriptions which they used.

1. STRATEGIES IN HIERARCHY CONSTRUCTION

The three basic choices open to a subject are *pairing* (of two occupations), *chaining* (of a single occupation to a larger group) and *joining* (already existing groups). A 'strategy' was defined as the sequence of the 15 such choices made by a subject. A large number of distinguishable strategies were found, but they showed a marked similarity in their important structural characteristics. The initial and middle stages in constructing a hierarchy were largely taken up in initiating and extending basic clusters, and the final stage (from the 10th step) concentrated overwhelmingly on joining. Very clearly, the major disjunction occurs here; the later joining stages carry information on the main organising characteristics (such as dichotomisation and ordering), whilst the initial stages carry the job-specific detail.

2. DIFFERENCES IN COMPOSITION

The Boorman-Olivier (1973) pairbonds distance metric, developed for comparing sortings and extended to provide a measure for comparing hierarchies, was used to examine differences in composition. Once again, there is evidence of a very considerable amount of variation, yet some of the greatest variation occurs among subjects from a single occupation. Clearly, whatever it is that produces such variation, it is not obviously linked to occupational membership. (This does not mean that there are no important differences in conceptions of occupational hierarchies, only that the compositional structure, divorced from its connotative meaning, shows no signs of being so determined.)

3. AGGREGATED DATA

(i) Each subject's hierarchy is defined by a set of ultrametric distances, and these were then pooled to obtain an aggregate or 'group' estimate of inter-occupational differences. When compared to the aggregate pairwise similarities data (see p. 75 of the first book), there is a striking likeness (correlating at 0.95). But, as in the case of aggregate occupational rankings (ibid., 129 *et seq.*), important differences which do occur are swamped by the massive agreement that also exists. In this case, important differences occur for example in the positioning of the 'Driver' occupations, indicating the main methodological shortcoming of the pairwise similarities task of prompting responses by bringing titles explicitly to the subject's attention, and then eliciting a common basis which would not normally feature in his repertoire of occupational judgement.

(ii) When analysed by Johnson's HCS procedure, the aggregate data yield a hierarchy which clearly shows three main branches ('generic taxa'), later identified as:

(1) *Professional men* (sub-divided into People-oriented and Men of Figures);
(2) *Public Servants*; and
(3) *Manual workers* (sub-divided into Trades and Unskilled).

(iii) Analysis of the verbal material yielded four major themes present throughout the hierarchical judgements:

(1) *Status* (representing symbolic aspects of occupations);
(2) *Qualifications and Training* (specifying the prerequisites of jobs);
(3) *Remuneration* (the consequential component); and
(4) *Job-content* (the descriptive detail).

4. INTERPRETATION OF THE AGGREGATE HIERARCHY

The aggregate hierarchy was interpreted by matching branches of the aggregate HCS in the subjects' own hierarchies, and then noting the dominant thematic content and its changes in the local structure.

(i) The themes differ considerably in the way in which they vary in the local structure:

Status increases in Branch One (Professions) and decreases in Branch Three (Manual Workers);

Job-content references are universally higher at the lowest (most specific) levels, and decrease systematically;

Qualifications and Training increase in Branch One, and decrease in Branch Three; and

Remuneration displays no systematic variation.

(ii) *Status* references predominate in Branch One, and consist in large part of allusions to their middle class and professional standing. Status references also differentiate the unskilled manual workers from the skilled trades as being unequivocally working class. Status terminology is rarely used in assessing people-oriented jobs, often because it is thought to be incompatible with their vocational nature.

Qualifications and Training. The main contrast is again between Branches One and Three. The Professional group is thought of as having educational certification and full-time training whereas the Manual workers are distinguished in terms of their degree of skill. This theme occurs most frequently of all in these judgements.

Remuneration citations primarily refer to income differentials and how they may be justified. Some occupations are highly paid, it is said, because of

their long training and early deferment of gratification (the professions),
but on the other hand some unskilled manual workers are highly paid to
compensate for what are now termed 'unsocial' hours and conditions. Nor is
evident underpayment necessarily recognised as a legitimate basis for an
increment: clergy are repeatedly cited as grossly underpaid by those who
accept their social utility, but are believed to be in receipt of their just
deserts by others.

Job Content changes rapidly between different sub-groups, and often contains
fortuitous or slender bases of comparison (such as 'driving' or 'preaching at
people', or 'crisis-management'), which do not survive into more general
occupational judgement.

4 Language and Class in Occupational Judgement

INTRODUCTION

The interpretation given to the aggregate hierarchy is bound to be tentative until it can be grounded more directly in subjects' accounts. We therefore need to explore in greater detail the meaning which the subjects ascribe to the categories they use, and the use to which they put them. To do so, attention must be shifted to a number of concerns:

(1) the synthetic characteristics of the language used,

(2) the conceptions and semantic categories used to encode meaning,

(3) the cognitive component, which involves the relation between the symbols and experience, and how such interpretation works (Deese 1969:40),

As sociologists, we shall also be concerned with:

(4) how membership of social groups and the nature of social interaction informs and modifies the ascription of meaning.

But first, we must inspect the source material a little more closely. The most important point is that the hundred or so transcripts of subjects doing the hierarchies task are *edited* versions, and do not represent the *ipsissima verba* of the interviews. Let us recall how the transcripts were obtained. Most interviews were tape-recorded (if the subject gave permission) and the interviewer also kept his own notes of the sequence of steps and the final reasons given for each decision. Following the interview, the interviewer constructed an official report (usually averaging about 300 words; see U3.4) by listening to the tape again and extending his written notes to include significant material which had been missed. The interviewer's comments and glosses hence form part of the official report. (In subsequent analyses, the machine-readable version of this file distinguished between interviewer's comments and the subject's reported words.)

4.1 METHODS

THE FULL AND THE REPORTED TRANSCRIPTS

Since the *reported* transcript, rather than the direct transcription, forms the basis of the analysis, it is important to see how much selectivity took place in editing, and what form it took. This may be done by comparing a full transcription of an interview, and the reported one. (The full transcript and the official report of one such interview are reproduced in U4.1.)

A number of preliminary points should first be made about the full transcript:

(i)   Most of the interview is in silence, and pauses within sentences are often quite extended. (In reconstructing the situation, it would have been especially useful to have a videotape record in order to place the verbal statements in their behavioural contexts; this would have been especially useful where pronouns and demonstratives such as 'he', 'they', 'this one' are used, since they are often accompanied by pointing to particular cards.)

(ii) The syntactic structure is often very degenerate in parts, and this subject utters a surprisingly large number of incomplete sentences. Such incompleteness is a very common phenomenon; in transcribing such material it is extremely difficult *not* to correct the subject's syntax and finish his sentences unwittingly, and both social scientists and typists are also prone to 'cosmetise' the English in the course of transcription.

(iii) This subject's speech possesses a curious mixture of 'extended' and 'restricted' code characteristics (Bernstein 1962). On the one hand, there are a considerable number of sociocentric tags, such as 'y'know' and plural pronouns such as 'we' and 'they' which presuppose a framework of shared experience, whilst on the other hand much of the speech is couched in the first person singular, and contains few exophoric pronouns (which make reference to things which are socially assumed, rather than being explicitly present in the sentence or context concerned). Moreover the density of modifiers (adjectives, adverbs), which usually denotes elaborated code, is surprisingly variable and does not seem to vary by context. In short, the speech in this instance — and in most others, it should be added — contains a curious admixture of both codes. (See Lumby 1976 for a similar observation.)

(iv) The interviewer's role is supportive, and she sticks closely to the guidelines. Her speech is concerned in a large part to give direct, extended or additional instructions, to ensure the 'rules of the game' are adhered to. Her most active contribution is to admit to not listening, and her most passive is when she avoids giving direct help ('strictly speaking, I'm not supposed to help you'). None the less, she does *interact* with the subject, especially in the beginning when he repeatedly asks 'Do you want me to . . .?' (whilst he learns the rules, and at later points when he seeks confirmation of his actions).

(v)   Despite the much-discussed 'one at a time' convention, simultaneous speech occurs fairly frequently, and for the length of several seconds.

(vi) Hesitation phenomena (um, er, mmm) are common and usually signa rather different things. 'Um' tends to be used by this subject before he goes on to specify something further, add a qualification, or simply acts as a marker before a 'thinking pause' (often accompanied by him scanning the layout of the cards). 'Um' is also used interactively as an indication that the speaker intends to continue his sentence. By contrast 'er' is used less frequently, usually to precede a more careful choice of phrase, or in a cautious manner to signify the use of a euphemism or 'touchy' issue, such as class (see the environment 015-020, where it is also accompanied by nervous laughter). This point is taken up below.

If resources and time had permitted, it would have been very profitable and interesting to produce a complete set of full transcripts, and subject them to detailed sociolinguistic analysis. As it is, only a small portion exist in full form, and it is these which must be used to ascertain the differences between the extended and edited forms. We have already seen that the interviewer's contribution is important in understanding the sequence of the subject's comments, and it hence plays a significant role in determining the extent to which background knowledge is assumed, elicited or called upon in an interview; the interview transcript, like any realisation of the spoken word is, to this extent, inherently indexical. Indeed, in this context, Bernstein's two codes simply represent two different *ways* in which background knowledge is signalled or called upon (see Gumperz 1972:23) and the shortened official account, stripped of the communicative framework of the interview, might therefore seem an impoverished vessel for obtaining the information we require on the categories of our subject's occupational thinking. Yet the edited transcripts are not so deficient as they may at first sight seem. First, the extended transcript shows that the interviewers were often successful in eliciting the taken-for-granted in the subject's thoughts. In effect, the interviewer has been trained to be *lacking* in social competence in order to bring out precisely these assumptions. Secondly, the official reports are more selective than interpretative; a comparison of the two forms will confirm this. In producing the abbreviated transcript, the interviewer does not usually add to the content, except to remove hesitations, indulge in occasional paraphrase and tidy up the grammar. For example, in putting the Barman and Commercial Traveller together, the subject actually says that they are 'involved in . . . face to face (laughs) relationships and therefore might need . . . to have perhaps more social skills and er . . . sorry, as unskilled, or rather untrained people.'

In the interviewer's account, 'face to face' has become 'personal', 'may need to have' has become 'may have', and the sequence 'and er . . . sorry' has understandably become 'but' (there is some ambiguity in the spoken version as to whether he said 'sorry, as still rather untrained', or 'sorry as unskilled, or rather untrained'; in any event, his precise meaning is obscure). But the interviewer has in fact missed a number of apparently inconsequential, but relevant pieces of information. For example, the subject goes on to refer explicitly to social class (see 015-020): 'I suppose I am to a certain extent, mm, conditioned by, er . . . slight familiarity with social classes, y'know or categories . . . mm . . . but that doesn't matter (laughs) . . .', but no reference to class appears at this point on the official report. The reason for this omission is understandable; the subject, a lecturer in planning, is referring primarily to the 'skill' component which happens also to be used in the Registrar General's Social Classification, with which he is professionally familiar. He is not really making a full-blown class reference.

CHARACTERISTICS OF THE HA VERBAL CORPUS

The shorter transcripts reporting the performance of the 93 subjects doing the hierarchies task forms the verbal data for analysis, and are referred to subsequently as the HACONS (hierarchies:constructs) file. Interviewers' comments have been removed for the purpose of analysis.

In this file, there are 2365 sentences and a total of 34,176 'tokens' (words and punctuation). Of the tokens 29,548 are words, giving an average of 318 words or 25 sentences per interview transcript.

There are approximately 3238[1] distinct de-inflected words, ranging in frequency from 1253 ('The') to one (e.g. 'adolescents', 'gratuitous', 'sheep', 'yielded', and a fair number of misspelt words). As is usually found with sources of any size, the Zipf-Mandelbrot law (that the relative number of repetitions of a word is inversely proportional to its rank)[2] holds fairly accurately. A list of the 100 most frequent lexemes (root words) is given in U4.2 and the occupation-relevant ones are highlighted in the graph of Figure 4.1. Even so gross a characterisation of talk about occupations has some noteworthy features.

1. PRONOMINAL REFERENCE ·

Since the subject-matter consists of judgements about occupations, pronoun usage is naturally dominated by third-person reference, and especially by 'they' (as subject of the sentence), 'them' (as object) and 'their' (as possessors of a property). The reference is overwhelmingly to the person or people involved, rather than to groups, categories or jobs. Trailing a bad second are the first-person references (especially 'I', referring to the person judging, rather than 'me' or 'mine').

The exophoric use of 'we' is especially interesting: are the implied other(s) the interviewer ? the community at large ? The usage is varied. In a few cases it is purely a matter of idiom ('. . . shall *we* say . . .'), or reflecting usage similar to the royal or episcopal 'we' ('*we* often wonder if *we* sometimes think . . .'). But in the majority of cases the 'we' is clearly communal, either an appeal to a generalised social interest:

'*we* need more teachers . . .' (doctor)
'*we* can get along without ministers' (teacher)

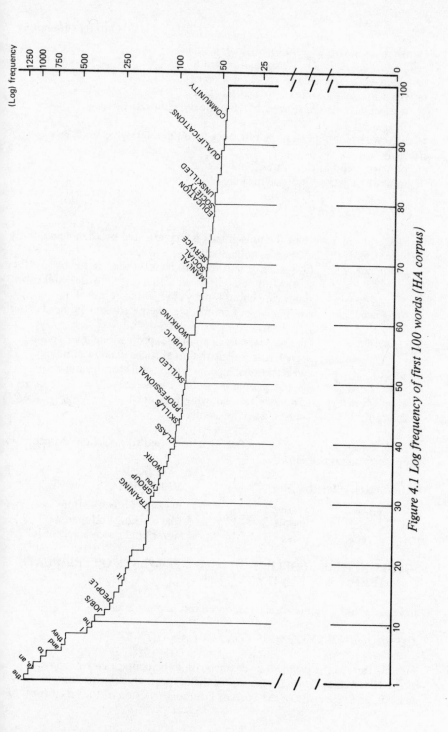

Figure 4.1 Log frequency of first 100 words (HA corpus)

'*we* must have law and order' (draughtsman)
or in a few cases, to a more specialised group:
    'when *we* were students' (social worker)
or (from the wider context) to a social class:
    '*we* feel dominated; so *we* are' (laboratory technician)

In the few remaining cases, the reference is to the interviewer/interviewee pair:
    'now we come to the professionals . . .'
    'now we're getting more semi-skilled . . .'

1. COLLECTIVITIES

The generalising nature of the judgements is well attested by the uncommonly frequent use of the language of collectivities:

people who . . .	(are more or less likely to be interested in the people they work with; look after our welfare; get further education; don't care about money; I regard as responsible)
the group . . .	(of highly paid people; who help people; who need qualifications)
class of . . .	(people working in an office; professional men; public servant), as well as the usual social class terminology
sort of . . .	qualifications; income group; skills for dealing with people; people the public can go to)
type of . . .	(people who; chap who; person who)
kind of . . .	(person who; job; skill)

Indeed, the most frequent syntactical structure used to predicate an occupational property takes the form:

	NOUN PHRASE				VERB PHRASE	
the	{ sort / kind / type }	of	{ person / people / job/s }	who/ which	{ have high qualifications / like working with people / never hold down a decent job }
	GENERALISING TERM		COLLECT-IVITY		PROPERTY OR PREDICATE	

and this is the structure we have adopted in Chapters 2 and 5.

THE INQUIRER SYSTEM OF CONTENT ANALYSIS

We now turn to the problem of characterising the content and meaning of the Hierarchies Constructs data. We shall repeatedly refer to content analysis, and especially to the current Edinburgh version of the latest form of a computer system widely used in content analysis, the General Inquirer (Inquirer III). In the content analysis extensive use is made of the Harvard IV – 3 Psycho-sociological Dictionary.[3] A short introduction is therefore in order (further technical details are contained in U4.3 to U4.5).

The purpose of content analysis is to describe the thematic content of a written text by identifying its constituent words (and longer structures) as instances of more general semantic categories, usually referred to as 'tags'. Having chosen a particular set of tags as exemplifying each theme, the investigator can then begin to examine their prevalence and inter relationships by looking at the contexts within which they occur and by counting the frequency of those identified as reflecting the same content. It is a hazardous procedure, partly because of the inherent indexicality of the enterprise (Garfinkel 1967, Ch. 2) but also because of the very much more basic fact that a given written word often has more than one meaning. The problem of such homographs and their disambiguation is more serious than may at first sight appear. Approximately one quarter of words in common use have more than one meaning, and the actual number of distinct senses which a homograph has is by no means fixed.[4]

Take, for instance, the word 'fellow'. The *Concise Oxford English Dictionary* (1976) identifies six distinct uses:
1. Associate or comrade (as in 'fellow-feeling')
2. Counterpart or equal
3. Incorporated senior member of a college (as in 'Fellow of King's')
4. Member of Governing Body of a University (as in 'The Society of Fellows of Harvard University')
5. Colloquial use for 'man', such as 'poor fellow', and
6. In the same relationship, as in 'fellow-traveller'.

The *Shorter OED* (1956) identifies thirteen uses and the *Oxford English Dictionary* distinguishes seventeen. It will therefore be impossible to provide a unique set of word-senses, yet some of the senses distinguished are less different than others; we should find it very difficult to do without the basic distinction between the nominal 'being a member of' sense (cf. 3 and 4) and the adjectival 'being in the same situation' sense (cf. 1, 2, 6), since the role-connotations are rather different from the affiliative connotations of the second. In other words, we should wish to count the former sense as an instance of one set of categories and the latter by another (not necessarily distinct) set. And since each meaning will in general be associated with a different set of categories, a systematic method is needed to determine *from the context* which sense is intended. The development of a workable, effective and reliable disambiguation procedure, which enables the computer 'to discriminate a *useful* set of senses for *some* high frequency words of English, with a reasonable degree of reliability' (Kelly 1970:41) marks the major improvement, and achievement, of Inquirer III.

The task of computer disambiguation was construed in a pragmatic

fashion; no attempt was made to solve the general linguistic problem of
disambiguation, but since the distribution of word-frequency is so skew
(see Fig. 4.1 and U4.2, where the first 10 words account for 27 per cent of
the corpus) a relatively small number of disambiguated high-frequency words
can be expected to cope with a large number of occurrences, especially when
inflected forms of words have been reduced to their root form.[5]

Once inflection and disambiguation have been dealt with, the remaining
and central task of interpretation consists of identifying each resulting
word-sense as an instance of a set of semantic categories. Here again there is
no unique way of proceeding. In principle there could be as many category
systems as social science theories, or indeed as social science theorists. The
purpose of the category system used in the Harvard IV Psycho-Sociological
Dictionary is to distinguish words in terms of their commonly accepted
grammatical properties (word form, sentence structure categories, reference
and person markers, basic semantic markers), and also to cover a wide-ranging
area of content categories in common use among social scientists. The category
system of content tags also reflects the origin of the dictionary within the
Harvard 'theory of action' tradition of analysis, and it is termed 'psycho-
sociological' since this best describes the range of application. Moreover,
since sociology provides categories best suited to roles, objects and cultural
artifacts whilst psychological categories are more oriented to dynamic
processes, most nouns (object names) are given a sociological definition, and
most verbs are given a psychological definition.

Within the Dictionary, each category is extensively defined by the word-
senses which are instances of it, and these in turn are divided into the relevant
part of speech. Take the semantic marker 'male' for instance:

TAG NAME: MALE
Instances:
    (i)   *as a pronoun:*
           he, his, him
    (ii)   *as a modifier:*
           manly, masculine, Mr
    (iii) *as a noun:*
           actor, bachelor, boy, brother, buddy, bully, businessman/men,
           Christ, clergyman, coachman, congressman, dad, daddy,
           emperor, father, fellow, gentleman/men, grandfather . . .

Each word-sense is allocated to one or more such category, of which it serves
as an instance (the theme specifications earlier in this chapter are defined
in this way). Thus, the first sense of 'fellow' is tagged as:
    FELLOW 1: NOUN. HUMAN. MALE.
meaning that it counts as an instance of a noun and of the semantic markers
HUMAN and MALE, whereas the second sense is:
    FELLOW 2: MODIF. AFFIL. PSTV. REL.

i.e. it counts as a Modifier (adjective), as an instance of the Leary's (1957) Affiliative theme, of the Positive evaluation category, and of the Relation category.

In all, Harvard IV–3 (Edinburgh) Dictionary recognises a total of 6822 word entries (of which a quarter are distinguished by two or more senses). As a Dictionary it bears more resemblance to Roget's *Thesaurus* than to a conventional dictionary, since the main organising features are the set of analytic categories, and the word-senses only feature as instances of them.[6]

The categories making up a content analysis dictionary are usually rather disparate, and include such components as:

linguistic categories (verbs, modifiers, pronouns, passive sentences)
semantic markers (animate, male, collectivity, kin)
social science terms (affiliation, affective neutrality, ritual references)
evaluative terms (good, bad, virtue, vice)

and more complex components, such as:

themes ('need for achievement', 'female symbolism', 'class imagery')

These components also feature in Harvard IV–3, whose categories are organised under the following headings: (a fuller specification is given in U4.4 and U4.5)

(i)   *Markers of sentence structure* (nouns, adjectives, verbs etc)

(ii)   *Markers of reference* (pronouns, determiners) *and Person* (1st, 2nd, 3rd)

(iii) *Semantic markers* (used chiefly in disambiguation — animal, human, time, dimension etc)

(iv) *1st order content tags:*
      Behaviour (Communication, Action)
      Concrete objects (Place, Body etc.)
      Psychological States (Need, Think, Feel, Evaluate, Perceive)
      Natural Processes (Nature, Change, Dimension)

(v)   *Second order content tags:* (see U4.5)
      Institutions (Academic, Economic, Political, Religious etc)
      Interpersonal Axes (Affiliation, Hostility, Power, Submission)
      Ascribed Status (Kin, Race, Non-adult)
      Osgood Semantic differential (Evaluation, Potency, Activity)
      Style (Overstate, Understate etc).

Some of the most general categories in the Dictionary such as THINK are further subdivided into more specific tags, such as SOLVE, KNOW and EVALUATE, and this last heading is in turn divided down into MEANS, GOAL, DOCTRINE (a general ideological category), VIRTUE and VICE. Hence the categories form a hierarchical system, and each tag is also distinguished in terms of its constituent part of speech.

4.2 CONTRASTING TEXTS: OCCUPATIONS, COAL AND RELIGION

The most persistent problem facing the content analysts is that of comparison: with what should a particular text be compared? In the absence of any standard reference set of textual material (itself a strange notion), the usual practice adopted by linguists and content analysts is 'contrastive analysis': the selection of relevant contrasting material. Preferably two texts are chosen as contrasts — one deemed similar to the text of interest, and one chosen to display different characteristics.

In this case, the two texts chosen to contrast with the HACONS text are:

(i)   *'COAL'*
       This text consists of official shorthand transcriptions of a number
       of meetings in 1920 of the Joint Standing Disputes Committee of
       the South Wales Coalfield, including both the Coal Owners
       Association and the Miners Federation.[7]

(ii)   *'HTOGOD'*
       A small set of the letters written to the (then) Bishop of Woolwich,
       Dr John Robinson, following the publication of his best-selling
       book, *Honest to God,* and subsequently lodged at Leeds University
       Library.[7]

We may expect the COAL text to be most similar to the HACONS text, due to both its interactive form and economic content, whilst the HTOGOD text, consisting of quite different material and in a contrasting subject area, is likely to be rather different.

We are now going to use Inquirer III to describe the characteristics of, and differences between, these three texts. (In so doing, the punctuation and word-form markers will be ignored.)

Some preliminary decisions need to be made about the form of analysis. First, Inquirer III counts both the number of *words* which are tagged by a particular category and the number of *sentences* in which the category appears. Which should form the basis of analysis? In this case, as in any where sentence length is an unimportant variation in style, the simple word-based count is to be preferred, because the probability of a tag occurring in a sentence will increase with sentence length. Secondly, information will be presented in the form of a percentage of all the words in the document (rather than as a frequency) to facilitate comparison between texts of unequal length. Thirdly, only differences between texts in excess of 1 per cent will be reported in the body of the text.[8]

It will occasion little surprise that, excepting the grossest grammatical categories, the most significant tags differentiating the occupational data are the markers concerned with economic thinking (ECON,ECON* and THINK), that the *Honest to God* letters are distinguished especially by religion and

TABLE 4.1   Distinguishing tags of the three texts

| | | *Texts* | |
Harvard IV-3 (Edin) Dictionary categories	OCCUPATIONAL DATA	COLLIERY DISPUTES	HONEST TO GOD LETTERS
Markers of sentence structure	Nouns, *Adjectives*	Verbs (SUPV)	
Markers of reference and person	Pronominal determiners *Totality* (DEF4)	Pronouns	
	Count/Mass Predeterminer Third person (PRE)	First person	First person, and First person singular
Semantic markers	*Collectivity, Economic* Evaluative, *Dimension* Political	Abstract (General) *Communication Time*	'ism' (Abstract)
Psychological states	*Need* Think Know Evaluate Means *Doctrine* Virtue		
Behaviour		*Work* Communication	
Institutions	*Academic, Economic*		*Religious*
Thinking categories	Generality *Relation* Overstate Understate		
Inter personal		*Hostility*	Affiliation, Power
Osgood semantic differential	*Active*		Passive (= Neg. Active)

Notes to Table 4.1
1. Tags are chosen as 'distinguishing' if there is a difference of $\geqslant 1\%$ between texts in the frequency of tag occurrence.
2. Distinguishing tags are assigned to the text in which the probability of its occurrence is highest.
3. Tags in which the ratio between minimum and maximum percentage is three or more are underlined.
(See U4.6 for numerical details.)

references to the first person (RELIG,FRSTP), and that the Colliery disputes are especially characterised by abstract nouns, communication and hostility (ABS, COMN and HOSTILE).

But other, less obvious, distinguishing characteristics reveal more subtle features of our material.

First, the occupational data show a more extreme profile: it differs in a very wide variety of ways from the other two sources. To some extent this is a consequence of the formal characteristics of the hierarchies task − the prevalence of Totality ('Anyone and everyone'), Count and Mass nouns (all, more, some, most, no . . .), and to a lesser extent, the Third person marker and the Relation category all illustrate this point.

More important, and reassuring, is the prevalence of the 'Psychological States' and 'Thinking Categories' among the occupational text, since these two categories reflect most closely the explicitly cognitive operations that are supposed to be the central focus of the task:

Psychological States:
    NEED (indicating need or desire)
    (e.g.) We *need* more teachers
            They *need* more knowledge and certificates, ken, to get in
            They meet a *need* when people are in trouble
            Before we buy a house we *have to* consult these chaps
            Both *have to* know about management structures
            They always *want to* be moving on to something new
    THINK (a very general category with very wide coverage)
            I would *think* that the life styles are very similar
            Well, I *think* the executive grade is the bottom grade
            All *think* of themselves as unskilled
            I *believe* he is a skilled man
    KNOW (somewhat broader than merely cognition; indicates awareness of knowledge)
    Their minds must be *alike* − one could fit into the other's job
    We must *assume* that people can read and write
    He *knew* how to cook, he *knew* how to dig holes in the ground
    I don't *know* where to put the Teacher
    He might have to *know* various metals

EVALUATE (an extremely broad category)

More *respectable* than a Labourer, yet they're really no better

There's no such thing as a *bad* Commercial Traveller

They were socially *desirable* jobs

(MEANS) (covers assets, needs, capabilities, and includes such occupational means as income, salaries, job)

Both are *necessary* in what I regard as a civilised society

Concerned with upholding law and *order*

It *requires* a fair amount of devotion

(DOCTRINE) (disciplines and orientations)

All on the highest *academic* level

... involve *technical* skills and some limited *theoretical* knowledge

(VIRTUE) (positive evaluation)

The *virtues* of behaving in an orderly and *honest* way of life

As people they were reasonably *dynamic*

Semi-skilled chaps who are *good* with their hands

The *good* of mankind is behind his motive

THINKING CATEGORIES

GENERALITY (covers abstract and general uses)

Have a *general* accountibility in the community

A professional person in the same *general* career-structure

They do it out of *some kind* of British instinct

Their *type* of work is very similar

They're in a *general class* of the same *type* of people by virtue of having the same *type* of occupation

He deals with a *wide* variety of people

All want to constrain society in some way

Almost *all* males

All were now administrative

RELATION (includes a range of relations and relatives)

Similar in the context of their work

In terms of status probably *similar*

Under- *versus* over-paid

The *basic* skills are not dissimilar

They all had the *same* political views, and follow the *same* sport

The prominence of the Understate and Overstate categories, which indicate strong over- and under-emphasis respectively, are usually taken to connote a defensive style (Stone *et al.* 1966:176, 185), but here probably represent exaggeration due to the fact that the subject is repeatedly required to make detailed comparative judgements between the occupations.

More unexpectedly, the occupational material is more similar to the *Honest to God* letters than it is to the Colliery disputes minutes, except in the most pertinent substantive areas.

4.3 LEVEL, GENERALITY AND CONTENT

We now turn to the internal analysis of the HACONS text, first to see what meaning can be attributed to the different levels of the hierarchies task, and then in the next section we shall examine how far a subject's social identity affects his linguistic and semantic descriptions.

The subject's construction of his occupational hierarchy was intended to represent a process in which the generality of his judgement would systematically increase, level by level. As we saw above, this expectation was not in fact borne out. Instead, the significant variable characteristic seems to be whether the subject is *pairing* an initial 'core' of a branch, *chaining* new instances or *joining* already existing branches. Since these stages typically succeed each other, and can reasonably be interpreted as representing stages of increasing abstraction (or 'concept formation'), and it seems better to use these three states as the meaningful levels of judgements. Inspection of Figure 3.4 will confirm that a reasonable approximation to this tripartite division (in terms of the predominance of stage concerned) is:

Stage	Description	Levels of hierarchy	Number of	
			Words	*Sentences*
A	Low levels: predominantly pairing	1–5	10,160	843
B	Middle levels: predominantly chaining	6–10	10,963	886
C	Top levels: predominantly joining	11–15	8,425	636

(The summary data for the transcripts of the verbal material, by levels and stage, are given in U4.6.)

It can be said immediately that although the Generality category increases systematically by stage (2.5 per cent Pairing, 2.9 per cent Chaining, 3.4 per cent Joining) and fairly clearly by level, most of the other tags that one would expect to increase in a similar fashion do not do so. We shall return to this point.

Table 4.2 presents in summary form the tags which distinguish the three stages.

At the Pairing stage, the predication process is most clearly at work, with Nouns and Adjectives predominating, and reference being chiefly to Totality, Counting and possessives. In this stage, too, the economic categories (ECON, ECON* and WORK) are most frequent, as are the cognitive and evaluative states. The picture conveyed, then, is overwhelmingly one consisting of the basic description of the content of jobs, people and their properties.

Chaining is predominantly concentrated upon verbal action, and now the pronoun usage has shifted primarily to the third person – and in particular to

TABLE 4.2 Tags that distinguish the three stages of hierarchy construction

General type of category		Stage:	
	A: Pairing	B: Chaining	C: Joining
Harvard IV-3	(Levels 1-5)	(Levels 6-10)	(Levels 7-10)
1. Markers of sentence structure	Nouns Adjectives (modif)	Verbs (esp. Auxiliary, Having, Doing, Modal and Infinitive)	Prepositions Conjunctions
2. Markers of reference and of person	All, Each (DEF4) Count Possessives They (Nominative)	Pronouns First person (I, Nom.) Third person (They, Their/ his)	Det Pron Count/Mass
3. Semantic markers	Econ Communication (Noun)	Male Dimension	Collective
4. Psychological	Think, Know, Evaluate (Means)		Virtue, Vice
5. Behaviour	Work		
Second Order			
6. Institutional	Econ*		
7. Thought forms	Relate	Neg	Overstate, Generality

Based upon: i) Differences ⟩ 2% between each stage
      ii) Stage at which maximum proportion/word occurs.
See U4.7 for numerical details

'they' (nominative) and 'their' (genitive) — with the job(s) and the person(s) as the main intended reference. Correlatively, the heightened use of the male marker indicates the largely male occupations, whilst the dimensional marker picks up the comparative and quantitative estimates of length of training, amount of skill etc. In the chaining stage, then, it is the active aspects of jobs and people which comes into prominence.

The final joining stage is one of linguistic elaboration and semantic complexity. Propositions increase, as do the conjunctions which link properties:

It all really depends on how you are brought up	*and*	one's education
Similar in responsibility	*and*	status
A skilled group	*and*	perform necessary functions
They don't have qualifications	*but*	they are non-manual
All necessary to society	*but*	not to man's life

Collective nouns, including 'Group', 'Profession' and 'Class', are also at their maximum in this stage, and adjectives such as 'public' and 'social' are used to describe these social entities and groups. More surprising is the fact that over-emphatic style (OVRST) occurs with highest relative frequency in the joining phase, as do the evaluative categories of VIRTUE and VICE (which denote the characteristics of persons and objects generally regarded as virtuous or vicious by conventional middle class morality — beneficial, competitive, important, rich, polite, respectable, responsible . . . as opposed to arrogant, careless, disorganised, ignorant, poor, unqualified and unsuccessful . . .)

It is as if the strongest approbation and disapprobation is being reserved for the final differentiation into the large social collectivities. Examples of such usage are contained in U4.13.

To summarise, the joining phase has a readily understandable character typified both by greater syntactic complexity and by semantic generality. It is collective nouns (and especially social collectivities) which dominate and these are differentiated largely on moral grounds. The joining phase is, above all, the phase of generalisation where judgement concentrates on the relationships between groups, and upon their more persistent and distin-guishing properties. It is here that we may expect social classes to be delineated and the relations between them discussed, as opposed to the use of class as simply a superset ('these occupations are instances of class x'), as in the earlier stages. We shall see.

Having described the three stages, we now return to the question of whether these syntactic and semantic properties increase systematically through the three stages, as we originally hypothesised. As can be seen from Table 4.3, the answer, broadly, is no. Of the 84 tags which differentiate between levels and stages, less than half show even a weak monotone relation (that is, either increase or decrease with the three stages). The tags which do show a consistent trend have by and large been commented on above. But this lack of relationship makes it necessary to reassess the significance of the levels and of the hierarchies task itself. Although there is some evidence of a

TABLE 4.3 Trend patterns in tags across stages

% Difference (*)				
P − C	C − J	MARKERS AND TAGS (HARVARD IV)	N	Trend (*)
U	U	PRE2, OVRST, GENRLTY,	3	SMI
U	U	TO; FRSTP; EGOP; PLACE; EVAL; NEG	6	WMI
U	D	SUPV; VERB; MOD; PRON; DEF1; THRDP; MALE	7	(NM)
S	U	PREP; CONJ; CONJ1; DETPRON; COLL; VIRTU; VICE; QUAL	8	WMI
S	S		32	(NT)
S	D	ART; HU; PERCV; KNOW; MAKE; LABOUR; ACAD; COMV; POLIT; POWER; ACTIV	11	WMD
D	U	NOUN; DEF4; PSV (OSGOOD)	4	(NM)
D	S	BE; PASSIVE; NEG; GEN; ECON; THINK; MEANS; WORK; ECON*; REL	10	WMD
D	D	MODIF; PRE1; DOCTR	3	SMD

| Pairing-Chaining | Chaining-Joining | | | N = 84 (subjects) |

(*) *Percentage Difference* (Words)

U: (up)   increasing percentage (⟩ 0.2%)
S: (same) no difference (⟩ 0.2%)
D: (down) decreasing percentage (⟩ 0.2%)

(**) *Trend* (Ordinal)

			48.8	(% of tags)
SMI	:	Strongly monotone increasing	3.6	
WMI	:	Weakly monotone increasing	16.7	
WMD	:	Weakly monotone decreasing	25.0	
SMD	:	Strongly monotone decreasing	3.6	
		(Non-monotone)	51.2	
NM	:	Increasing-Decreasing (or v/v)	13.1	
NT	:	No trend	38.1	
		Total	100.0%	

systematic increase in generality, as the levels and stages increase, it does not seem to be the most important factor. The key to the problem seems to be that the chaining phase is not generically different from the pairing phase; the real and substantial differences occur when shifting to the joining phase. Such an explanation also makes eminent sense in terms of the task itself.

In the free sorting task, for instance, pairing and chaining are the primary options open to the subject when forming his groups and relatively few subjects in fact go on to merge the groups which they have initially made. So pairing and chaining may well correspond to the category formation stage, whereas the joining phase makes the subject become more explicit about the *relations* between the groups.[9] In any event, the subjects' verbalisations in the joining phase provide plenty of evidence that the more abstract general social differentiation goes on at this stage, and it is here that effects of the peculiarities of a particular set of occupational titles is likely to be least important.

4.4 CLASS LANGUAGE? . . .

The proposition that distinct forms of social language are associated with different social groups is by now a truism in sociolinguistics. Much of the supporting empirical work has been associated with the name of Basil Bernstein, who has consistently argued that major differences exist in language communities with respect to the type of coding which is employed in various situations, contexts and roles. The most famous distinction he makes is between varieties of the so-called 'restricted' and the 'elaborated' codes of communication. (By 'code' Bernstein means a regulative principle which guides the selection and organisation of speech acts, and a code is defined in terms of how easy it is to predict 'the syntactic alternatives which speakers take up to organise meanings', Bernstein 1972:466 *et seq.*) In his earlier papers, these two codes are specified largely in lexical and syntactic terms. The restricted code, in pure form, is one where 'all the words, and hence the organizing structure, irrespective of its degree of complexity, are wholly predictable for speakers and listeners' and where individual difference must therefore be signalled through extraverbal signals, whereas the elaborated code is characterised by low syntactic predictability, and involves greater verbal explicitness (Bernstein 1964).

In his later work, Bernstein is at pains to stress that his earlier formulations gave the distinction too great a syntactic flavour, whereas his intention was to include the semantic component, to ground the distinction sociolinguistically and stress how the manifestations of either code (and in particular the choice of one code rather than another) are limited and constrained by the social situation. Especially in restricted coding, the social actors have to make use of their shared background knowledge to interpret and flesh out the context-dependent speech, and the meaning supplied is carried not in the actual words, but is available only to those who have the necessary background knowledge, as Edwards (1976:92) puts it.

The difficulty of specifying precisely the ways in which the codes can be identified has been one of the main shortcomings of Bernstein's research effort. Yet a good deal of the criticism from linguists—and especially their objection that the syntactic and other items used are a heterogeneous and unprincipled mix — is ill-conceived: what Bernstein is (or was) doing is to try to make what Edwards rightly calls 'a *sociologically* consistent attempt to describe what context-dependent speech might be like' and this is an entirely laudable, and more complex, ideal.

Yet it is not unfair to say that most sociological interest in Bernstein's work was initially roused and is maintained because of its early linkage to social class differences. Bernstein has said regularly and repeatedly that there is not, nor was there ever intended to be, any suggestion of a one-to-one link between codes and class: both codes are available to all social classes; the problem is rather to investigate the contexts within which the codes are used, planned and elicited.

The research evidence now fairly well confirms that the dominance of one code over another does not transfer systematically across all situations and contexts. (A nice example is provided by Hawkins (1973:240 *et seq.*) who set children the task of telling a bed-time story, and found that in this case working-class *girls* were most fluent and working-class *boys* were most hesitant, since the task was well within the social competence of the girls and outside that of the boys.) But *within* given restricted social contexts, the predominant tendency to select one code still seems to be a persistent finding, and as a phenomenon it is demonstrably class-linked (cf. Hawkins 1977).

Probably the most stark statement of the relationship between social class and code selection is made by Bernstein himself (1972:472) in support of his claim that 'the genes of social class may well be carried not through a genetic code but through a communication code that social class itself promotes.' The reasons he adduces are more relevant to our concerns than his conclusion, and justify extended quotation:

> If a social group, by virtue of its class relation, i.e. as a result of its common occupational function and social status, has developed strong communal bonds; if the work relations of this group offers little variety; little exercise in decision-making; if assertion, if it is to be successful must be a collective rather than an individual act; if the work task requires physical manipulation and control; if the diminished authority of the man at work is transformed into an authority of power at home; if the home is over-crowded and limits the variety of situations it can offer; if the children socialise each other in an environment offering little intellectual stimuli; if all these attributes are found in one setting, then it is plausible to assume that such a social setting will generate a particular form of communication which will shape the intellectual, social and affective orientation of the children.

Without entering the debate as to whether occupational groups are to be accounted classes, it is obvious that Bernstein's argument applied *pari passu* to the types of occupational groups we have designated 'quadrants'. The same arguments might equally well be made to justify the likelihood that people-oriented occupations will also generate differences in communication compared to the others. In any event, the constraints of social structure are such that not many 'working class' occupations are primarily people-oriented, as we have already commented in accounting for the small number of subjects in Quadrant C.

Before proceeding to investigate such differences, a word of caution is in order. The interview is not a common or natural social context, and the interviewer/interviewee role is quite likely to reproduce in miniature the 'cultural discontinuity' between community and school which the working-class child may experience. For these reasons, we may expect that the interview itself will tend to elicit elaborated coding, and this tendency is likely to be accentuated by the selection and editing process to which the protocols have been subjected (but see U4.8). But all these considerations would work *against* evidence of the survival of the restricted code, hence any evidence that remains of differences in coding among occupational groups will be that much more surprising.

GRAMMATICAL ELEMENTS

Although subject to the criticism that they are context-dependent, the syntactic characteristics of the elaborated and restricted codes which were elaborated in Bernstein's (1962) early work have proved to be surprisingly useful and methodologically resilient. The starting point is the description of the elaborated code which 'facilitates the verbal elaboration of subjective intent whilst a restricted code limits the verbal elaboration of such intent' (ibid.: 108).

Most of Bernstein's 15 grammatical instances of such structural selection and lexical choice can be investigated simply and straightforwardly using the Harvard IV-3 Sentence Structure and Reference Markers (see U4.9).

The groups to be used in the comparative analysis are the fairly heterogeneous quadrants, and selected occupations. (The third quadrant will be excluded as the number of subjects is too small for stable estimation, leaving the basic 'class' contrast of the higher-status quadrants A and B *versus* the lower-status, non-people-oriented, quadrant D.) The only single occupation groups with enough numbers to justify direct comparison are also drawn from these three quadrants—namely Doctors ($n=11$), and Engineers/Fitters ($n=15$).

The first group of grammatical elements (denoted A in Table 4.4) are those which indicate non-individuated speech and signal the fact that intent is not explicated verbally. These include indices of restricted use (or selection) of modifiers; infrequent use of uncommon forms, and simple verbal structure. Bernstein finds such instances of restricted coding to be significantly associated with working-class, as opposed to middle-class, subjects. In our case, this leads to the prediction that such indices will be

Groups (Quadrants)

	A and B		D		Ratio	x^2
	f_1	p_1	f_2	p_2	p_1/p_2	
A: Selection of Modifiers etc						
1. Use of adjectives (chance expectation)	1334^+ (1276.5)	.0854	636^- (693.5)	.0737	1.16	7.36, p < .001
2. Uncommon conjunctions	591^+ (575.5)	.0378	309^- (324.5)	.0358	1.06	1.16, NS
3. Passive verbs	106^+	.0068	49^-	.0057	1.19	1.42, NS
B: Pronominal use						
4. Use of 'I'	254^+ (201.3)	.0163	68^- (120.7)	.0079	2.07	36.81, < .001
5. Ratio: 'I' as fraction of total no. of personal pronouns (pp)		.3175		.1687	1.88	
6. Ratio: 'I' as fraction of all words		.0163		.0079	2.06	
7. Use of 'you'	46^- (66.3)	.0030	49^+ (28.7)	.0057	$1.90\ (p_2/p_1)$	20.58, < .001
8. Use of 'they'	474^- (498.5)	.0304	286^+ (275.6)	.0331	$1.08\ (p_2/p_1)$	1.58, NS
9. Ratio: 'You' and 'they' as fraction of pp		.6500		.8313	$1.28\ (p_2/p_1)$	
10. Ratio: 'You' and 'they' as fraction of all words		.0333		.0388	$1.16\ (p_2/p_1)$	
C: Miscellaneous						
1. Ratio: 'Of' as fraction of 'of', 'in', 'into'		.5312		.6105	0.87 (contrary direction)	
2. 'I think' (egocentric)	40^+ (25.5)	.0026	3^- (17.5)	.0003	$8.67\ (p_2/p_1)$	18.89, < 001
3. 'Sympathetic circularity' sequences: see U4.8						

higher for Quadrant A and B ('middle-class') occupations. But although the relative preponderance of use is in the direction which Bernstein predicts, only in adjectival usage does the difference differ markedly from chance fluctuation.

The second group of indicators (Section B in Table 4.4) is concerned with the use of pronouns, and especially with the markers of reference. (We have already had occasion to comment on the general preponderance of third person usage, but now we concentrate only on nominative case usage (DEF1), and exclude objective and genitive forms.) In Bernstein's interpretation, use of the first person singular is primarily regarded an egocentric signal, although it is not entirely clear why middle-class social relationships should lead to its greater frequency, unless it is used to articulate individualised ideas, or because it simply reflects greater self-confidence and assertiveness. None the less, in these data too, the class differential is clearly evident, both in actual frequency and as a proportion of all personal pronouns.

By contrast, the use of 'you' and 'they' (which signal the 'concretizing of experience' and non-specificity respectively) reflects restricted coding, and is associated with our working-class subjects. The same holds for our data, although the differential usage of 'they' is scarcely worth commenting on, being comprised almost entirely of repeated indirect reference to the occupational groupings which are under discussion in the hierarchies task.[10]

Finally, Bernstein draws particular attention to two indicators of what he terms 'semantic uncertainty'. (See Section C in Table 4.4.) In the sociocentric restricted code it takes the form of 'sympathetic circularity' sequences, which require expansion in terms of the common understandings which the listener is assumed to share — 'y'know', 'isn't it?' are good examples of such sequences. In elaborated coding, by contrast, they take the form of egocentric 'I think' sequences (which signal differentiation) and 'translate in palpable form the sociological relationship constraining the participators' (ibid.: 113). Unfortunately it was not possible to make an acceptable estimate of sympathetic circularity sequences (see U4.8), but the use of 'I think' — even in such edited texts — is overwhelmingly associated with our 'middle-class' subjects.

There is, of course, no question of restricted coding being *equated* with working-class usage, nor elaborated coding being simply identified as middle-class. None the less it is noteworthy that the whole range of differential structure and lexical selection should be evident, even in these selective accounts of an interview situation which naturally calls upon elaborated coding skills.

If Bernstein's suppositions are correct, then membership of occupational communities and the effect of work experience should have a more marked influence upon coding than these somewhat gross 'class' categories. But, at least as regards linguistic selection and restriction, this supposition is not borne out for our data. The occupational groups which have sufficient numbers to allow a fair assessment — doctors, social workers and fitters —

TABLE 4.5 Indicators of coding, by occupational group

| | Occupational Groups | | | | | |
	Doctors	Social Workers	Fitters, Engineers	(The Rest)	Total	x^2
A: Selection of modifiers						
1. Use of adjectives	490⁺	401⁻	378	886	2155	1.29 NS
(chance expectation)	(472.2)	(418.8)	(380.5)	(885.5)		
2. Uncommon conjunctions	208⁻	207⁺	160⁻	396	971	2.85 NS
	(212.8)	(187.8)	(171.4)	(398.9)		
3. Passive verbs	36	33	25	73	167	0.99 NS
	(36.6)	(32.3)	(29.5)	(68.6)		
B: Pronominal use						
4. Use of 'I'	72	124⁺	24⁻	120⁻	340	75.94 $p < .001$
	(74.5)	(65.8)	(60.0)	(130.7)		
5. Use of 'you'	22⁻	14⁻	19	57⁺	112	5.65 NS
	(24.5)	(21.7)	(19.8)	(46.0)		
6. Use of 'they'	187⁺	114⁻	131⁻	410⁺	842	28.7 $p < .001$
	(184.5)	(162.9)	(148.7)	(345.9)		

do not differ significantly from chance expectation in their employment of modifiers, conjunctions or of passive verbs (see Table 4.5), although there are considerable and significant differences in their employment of 'I' and 'they' (though not of 'you'). In making their hierarchic occupational judgements, fitters rarely rely upon the authority of their own word for their opinions, and restrict themselves either to commenting on 'what everybody knows', or at least limit themselves to the safety of straight assertion. By contrast, the two professional groups — and above all the social workers — give much more extensive expression to their own opinions, and frequently differentiate their opinions from what others may think. Indeed, the use of 'I' by social workers exceeds by a comfortable margin their reference to 'they', whilst the fitters' use of 'I' is only one-fifth that of their third-person reference.

Whilst differences in restrictive selection do not seem to distinguish our occupational groupings, differences in pronominal references do so to a marked degree. But a degree of caution is in order: it would be much more dramatic if the differences in third-person usage were exophoric, for we should then have very clear indication of the shared identifications and common expectations which Bernstein predicates of occupational groups. In the context of this task, however, most subjects use 'they' anaphorically (referring back in this case to the occupations which have just been joined). Nor should the predominance of 'I' among the professional groups be misconstrued. Given the constraints of the hierarchies task, most first-person reference is *not* straightforwardly descriptive, it is rather a way of expressing caution, qualification, possibility — in a word, modality.[11] The context of 'I' usage then, turns out to be highly significant. Descriptive contexts (such as 'I have worked with ambulance drivers', 'I once shared a flat with one', 'I avoid contacting that sort of chap') are not very common. But on the other hand modal contexts are much more predominant ('I should think', 'I would have thought that', 'I would feel that', 'I could argue that') and this is the form typically chosen by the middle class to describe their cognitions and evaluations (see Table 4.6). The significant contrast, then, lies not so much in simple differences in the relative frequency of these contexts, but in the fact that the professional occupations make very much more frequent and obvious use of qualification, caution, hesitancy and guardedness in expressing their judgements. Does this reflect greater subtlety in their cognitive judgements? Or greater verbal articulateness? Or is it simply a class-linked habit of style? These questions are moot, and need some discussion. There are three components of the Harvard IV-3 Dictionary which may assist us. First, the THINK structure among the psychological states; secondly, the categories of thought; and thirdly, the stylistic tags. If the differences are largely those of class or educational *style,* then the occupational differences should be evident only in the third component. But if the differences are also evident in the cognitive components, then we may conclude that the differences are not merely stylistic artefacts, but reflect genuine differences

TABLE 4.6   Contexts of 'I' usage

---

1. POSSIBILITY/MODAL
    CONTEXTS

    e.g.   I can imagine . . ., I suppose you could say . . ., I would think that . . . ,
            I would say that . . . , I don't know that I would . . . , I could
            probably . . . , I tend to . . . , I would feel that . . . , I imagine there
            is . . . , . . . I would guess, I would assume . . . ,

            I wouldn't be very happy to . . . , I shouldn't have thought . . . ,
            I feel very diffident about . . . , I get the impression that . . . , if I
            have it right . . . , I would argue that . . . , I don't know that . . .

2. FACTUAL/DESCRIPTIVE
    CONTEXTS

    e.g.   I have worked . . . , I am biased . . . , when I retire . . . , I shared a flat
            with . . . , I am a tradesman . . . , I avoid contacting . . . , I used to be
            an X myself . . . , I'm intimately acquainted with . . .

3. GROUPING (Method-specific)
    CONTEXTS

    e.g.   I would put them together . . . , I classify . . . , I am tempted to
            put . . . , I would put . . . , I bracketed them . . . , I put them in . . . ,
            the only thing I can do with him . . . , I don't think I can put him
            elsewhere . . .

---

of usage. The relevant data are presented in Table 4.7.

Both stylistic tags (see Table 4.7c) differ significantly between the groups. The professional groups tend to use qualified *understatement* (considerable, some, relatively, suppose, tendency . . .) in their verbal judgements, whereas the fitters and engineers are accustomed to more sweeping *overstatement* (all, always, certainly, entire, essential) in their statements.

The THINK structure is hierarchically organised, and the differences must therefore be traced from the general to the particular. In the grosser aspects of this very general category, there are indeed important differences in usage (see Table 4.7a). In general, fitters and engineers use Thinking categories much less than the Professions, but within the Professions it is the social workers who rely most strikingly on this mode of expression. (Since Evaluation is not used in significantly different ways, it is analysed no further.) But when we turn to the finer details of the categories and to the relationships of thinking, the contrast between occupations disappears, and we are left simply with 'Generality' as a distinguishing tag. But unfortunately the GENERALITY tag is not well specified, and its instances overlap to a considerable degree with those of OVERSTATE. As a result, we cannot

TABLE 4.7   Differences in Thinking and Stylistic categories

(a) THINK structure

TAGS	Doctors	Social Workers	Fitters, Engineers	(The rest)	Total	x^2
			Occupational Group			
THINK	824$^-$	809$^+$	610$^-$	1630$^+$	3891	13.60 (p⟨.001)
(expected)	*(852.7)*	*(752.6)*	*(687.0)*	*(1598.8)*		
Solve	–	–	–	–	89	(frequencies too small
Know	232$^-$	256$^+$	175$^-$	440$^-$	1103	11.34, p⟨.001
	(241.8)	*(213.3)*	*(194.8)*	*(453.2)*		
Evaluate	548	483	420	1020	2471	0.76 NS
Means				(797)		
Goal				(57)		
Doctrine				(606)		
Virtue				(732)		
Vice				(157)		

(b) Categories of Thinking

TAGS	Doctors	Social Workers	Fitters, Engineers	(The rest)	Total	
QUALI-FICATION	149	122	155	274	660	0.44
GENERAL-ITY	136$^-$	105$^-$	170$^+$	355$^+$	766	32.71 p ⟨.00
(expected)	*(167.9)*	*(148.2)*	*(135.3)*	*(314.7)*		
CAUSAL DIMENSION	36	38	25	70	169	1.66 NS
(REL.)	178	142	122	323	765	2.40 NS
IMPLIED NEGATION	32	26	58	66	182	6.09 NS
NEGATION	84	74	61	146	365	0.66 NS

(c) Stylistic categories

TAGS	Doctors	Social Workers	Fitters, Engineers	(The rest)	Total	
i) OVER-STATE	238$^+$	135$^-$	225$^+$	416	1014	31.98 p ⟨.00
(expected)	*(222.2)*	*(196.1)*	*(179.0)*	*(416.6)*		
ii) UNDER-STATE	133$^+$	105$^+$	63$^-$	212	513	12.53 p ⟨.01
	(112.4)	*(99.2)*	*(90.6)*	*(210.8)*		
Ratio i/ii	1.79	1.29	3.57	1.96	1.97	

be sure that it is measuring much else of significance here. So no sure conclusion can be reached: the obvious differences between the occupational groups are certainly due to more than stylistic (and educationally-linked) factors, and they continue to show in the grosser characteristics of the categories of thought. But they do not persist into the more detailed aspects of cognitive relations.

Yet there is now enough evidence to conclude with some assurance that important, systematic and socially-patterned differences *do* exist in the language by means of which our subjects make their occupational judgements. These differences would be even more marked, and might well persist into finer levels of detail, if a full set of verbal protocols were available for analysis. In any event, differences in syntactic and semantic usage pervade these data, despite the fact that the interview situation, the topic of discourse and the nature of the task predispose towards the eliciting of elaborated coding. We do not argue that the same differences would be evident in naturally-occurring, task-oriented social settings, but this does not detract from the most salient point — that differences which are undoubtedly rooted in occupational cultures and communities are still discernible in the edited protocols of the subjects' hierarchical judgements.

4.5 . . . AND LANGUAGE OF CLASS

Sociologists remain fascinated by 'models of class' — those conceptions of social stratification which are brought to bear upon everyday matters of power, prestige and wealth. With the exception of an occasional foray, we have been decidedly reticent — some have said coy — about this important area. Our self-denying ordinance arose neither out of indifference nor contempt. Rather, our whole strategy has been to get behind the issues which normally pervade 'class analysis' in sociology. Because of this none of our subjects have been asked directly about class. One reason for making such a rule is historical. There have been periods when any Briton would discourse freely and without embarrassment on the subject of 'social class' and when detailed and probing questions about their (perceived) arrangement would have been entirely natural. But with income usurping sex as the taboo area in social enquiry, this is no longer the case. Class conceptions, so to say, have gone underground. This is not to say that such imagery does not exist — of course it does, and often in a well-articulated form. The issue, rather, is how these conceptions may be elicited naturally, and indeed whether they are of any sociological import when they have been obtained.

'IMAGES OF CLASS STRUCTURE'

We have argued in *The Images of Occupational Prestige* (section 1.3) that although the tradition of research into 'images of class' has been interesting, it suffers from a number of important defects. Chief among these is the often unspoken assumption that a person can be characterised as having a single dominant 'image'. For all their justified insistence on the diversity of images of social class, the *Affluent worker* authors (Goldthorpe *et al.* 1969:116 *et seq.*) slip easily from a description of ideal types of class imagery into talking about their subjects as having some (one) 'communicable image', and in their later work the question of the reliability of subjects' conceptions of the occupational order looms large. But to imply that a subject only operates with *one* such model, and independently of the social situation, is, we believe, both ill-conceived and misleading. By contrast, our assumption has been that people have a range of such 'images', 'perspectives', 'models' or 'codes', which they deploy to differing extents, and which will vary according to the situation. Even the most committed marxist militant is usually perfectly *capable* of describing the finer details of a prestige distinction, and will do so in the right circumstances. Equally, despite his professional concern with issues of status, the Garter King of Arms is perfectly *aware* of other bases of stratification and capable of articulating them:

> Social classes and economic classes are not the same thing and, though at times they coincide, often they do not.
> The concern with social niceties is, I take it, largely a consequence of long-standing social mobility producing finely graded groups and classes in close enough juxtaposition to cause anxiety about identity. This is perhaps a specially English phenomenon. The differences between rich and poor on the other hand are world-wide, and the kind of mobility which England has known more of and for longer than many countries has sometimes been seen as a cure or palliative.
> However that may be, it seems important to distinguish the two complaints.
> (*The Times*, 24 Dec 1976)

The parallel with sociolinguistic codes is deliberate. Bernstein has been at pains to avoid identifying single codes with individuals in a given class, and to insist that a given individual has a repertoire of codes which he will deploy in differing social circumstances. In the same way, we wish to avoid the notion that subjects possess a single 'model of class', and direct attention rather at how distinguishable *aspects* (such as 'money', 'power' and 'prestige') are found useful, relate to each other, and are articulated. The sociological puzzle is then to see what social patterning there is to such multiform codes, how far their meanings are socially shared, and how different social situations 'select' different codes. In any event, there is abundant evidence that our subjects generate accounts of social stratification to any desired level of specificity. Most people in fact 'tune' their responses to the level expected in the particular situation, which of course includes the interview.

Our strategy has been to take a 'permissive' approach to class terminology and class images, in the sense that we have employed no direct questions or probes on 'conceptions of class'. If these matters arise in the focused context of a particular task, then they do so according to the reasoning, and by the choice, of the subject concerned. Naturally, the subjects bring expectations about the kind of answer that is appropriate to bear on their answers and may well make informed guesses as to 'what it is we are driving at', as this comment by a psychiatrist makes clear: 'The Porter and the Building Site Labourer — they're both in Social Class Five — *but you don't want me to say that* . . .' (emphasis added)

Secondly, the literature on 'models of class' notwithstanding, the supposedly distinct 'dominant conceptions' in fact occur as themes in almost all subjects' protocols, as we have seen in Chapter 3. Moreover, there are some very salient themes which feature in most subjects' verbalisations, but do not appear to do so to any extent in sociological accounts of subjective social stratification. (In part this is because of the actual occupations chosen for judgement — but it *is* only in part.)

CLASS TERMINOLOGY

The term 'class' is used about one hundred times in the HACONS material (exactly one hundred times if usage such as 'professional class' and 'the same class of people' is excluded). The contexts of use are presented in Table 4.8.

Let us start by examining the grosser properties of such usage. First, class terminology is not in fact used very extensively. One third of the subjects talk in terms of class, and those who do so are drawn over-representatively from Quadrant D, the lower educated, non-people-oriented occupations (see U4.11).

We have said several times that class terminology is most likely to occur in the generalising phase of occupational judgement, and so it is. Using the crudest form of assessment, references to 'class' are slightly more common at the higher levels (especially when the amount of verbal material at each level is taken into account). Rather more significantly, class references occur considerably more frequently in the subjects' joining phase than at any other (see U4.11c). This is precisely what one would expect if the sort of two-step process postulated by Nosanchuk (1972:109) in fact obtained — that in social interaction, the first step in locating a new acquaintance socially is to 'screen' him to see whether he is eligible for more extended interaction. The process, Nosanchuk suggests, consists of a search from high to low generality, beginning with the most general (often stereotypical) predicates such as social class, and then switching in the second phase to much more specific bases, which 'are probably *not* the objective variables used by most sociologists', as he nicely puts it. On this basis it is worth reminding ourselves again of Moore and Tumin's (1949:793) assertion:

It is only where the specific attributes of individuals and the specific contexts of action are unknown, ignored or irrelevant that the category of class is likely to have any significance.

But this is not the whole story, by any means. Class citations are certainly concentrated in the generalising phase, but a very respectable number occur

TABLE 4.8   Contexts of class terminology

Key variants

i)		*WORKING CLASS* (33 occurrences)
	(pre)	unskilled–, semi-skilled– better–, common–, average–, lower–,
	(post)	–occupations, –job, –people, –group –qualifications, –background
ii)		*MIDDLE CLASS* (18)
	(pre)	upper–, middle–, intelligent–, so-called–
	(post)	–jobs, –people, –origins, –look, –background
iii)		*UPPER CLASS* (17)
	(pre)	middle–, not quite–
	(post)	–type of job, –people
iv)		*SOCIAL CLASS* (10)
	(pre)	higher–
	(post)	(–V) (–Groups) –background, –division
v)		*CLASS* (20)
	(pre)	same–, general–, one–, own– wealthy–, status–, professional– 'no such thing as–, but there is'
	(post)	–of people, –group, –of professions, –of parents –society, –consciousness, –distinction –terms, –reasons
vi)		*CLASSES* (2)
		professional–, lower–

---

even at the earliest stages of hierarchy construction. Before going on to assess the significance of this fact, let us pause briefly and raise a number of particular questions about the validity and acceptability of the data we are relying on. Is there not a danger that we are doing just what we accuse others of — counting frequencies of occurrence as a substitute for assessing the significance of the usage? Moreover, is there any evidence that anything more than chance is involved in deciding who actually happens to come out with class words?

On this latter point, it appears that the conditions under which class terms are triggered are more subtle than is usually recognised. But our evidence is rather indirect. In the earlier stages of the Research Project (and especially in the similarities task (*Images,* Ch. 3) we were struck by the very low frequency of any spontaneous mention of class, and one of our interviewers commented:[12]

> It has been my firm impression (for which one must obviously amass evidence) that 'class' is taboo. Those foolhardy enough to use the word follow that use with an apology, and have to be comforted with soothing words like 'We use it every day in the Social Science Faculty'. Many pauses seem to be caused by a stifled desire to express a class difference between two occupations. The manual/non-manual distinction, and the skilled/unskilled, are more acceptable, apparently.

Bernstein too, in his discussion of the role of public language (1958:170) has commented that the terms used to denote social status within the class environment are often judged unacceptable for use outside it, and our subjects certainly gave verbal expression to a similar view, often in a characteristically Scottish, to-the-point, manner: 'There's no' supposed to be such a thing as class, but there is, and these are working class.' (telephone engineer)

Further evidence of caution before starting to talk in class terms comes from the taped record, in the form of hesitation phenomena. A lecturer in Town Planning is discussing his pairing of the Barman and the Commercial Traveller:

Subject I suppose the Barman and the Commercial Traveller in a sense don't need any . . . well . . . Commercial Traveller might need to be trained but the Barman might . . . but on the other hand they are the people who . . . involved in . . . face to face (laughs) relationships and therefore might need . . . to have perhaps more social skills and er . . . sorry, as unskilled, or rather untrained people . . . mm. I suppose I am to a certain extent, um, conditioned by, or . . . slight familiarity with social classes, y'know, er categories . . . um . . . but that doesn't matter (laughs) . . .

Interviewer Well, we're very interested in all your personal values.
Subject   Yes, well you know, I mean having . . .
Interviewer That's what we want to find out . . .
Subject   . . . having, having to do in planning, having something to do
              with data of that sort, I'm sort of, I'm *aware* of it, so y'know . .
              I think it's probably fitting into my, into the way of my
              decisions . . . um. I think Carpenters and Machine Tool
              operators seem to me to be similar in that they are both skilled
              manual workers . . . um . . .

In this case, the subject is trying to exclude his professional knowledge about
the Registrar-General's Social Classes as irrelevant to the task in hand, but the
argument remains: he, too, recognises strong normative expectations against
expressing class terminology. Not only he, but several other subjects
indicated — verbally, paralinguistically or even simply by the knowing glance
or smile — that they were not sure whether the sociological interview is a
permissible forum for such talk. (But equally, those who entirely disavow
the relevance of class terms — 'it's a one-class society' — still feel it necessary
to affirm their view in the face of what they think of as a mistaken, but
none the less widespread, belief.)

In order to delve further into understanding how class terminology is
used in this context, we now have to abandon any pretence of
representativeness, and concentrate attention upon those subjects for whom
class is clearly a salient and important (but by no means the exclusive) way
of looking at occupational structures.

The main points can be illustrated by reference to the hierarchies of the
six subjects presented in Figure 4.2.

(i) *SW08* is a social worker with some sociological training and professional
knowledge of the Registrar General's classification. In the hierarchies task, as
well as in his subsequent free-grouping task, he said he was 'doing it on the
status ascribed to the job'. He mentions 'common status' as a basis in levels
5, 6, 7, 10 and 12, and clearly uses 'status' as equivalent to 'social class' in
several contexts.

He produces a two-class structure, as he recognises: 'I've probably made a
social class division with the Commercial Traveller rather uncomfortably sitting
in the middle' (level 15).

He uses class terms to do three things:
(*a*) *to name membership of the working class:*
Level 2: BSL and RP are 'both unskilled working class'.
Level 9: BM, though not a manual labourer, is 'most likely in bars with
working-class people'.

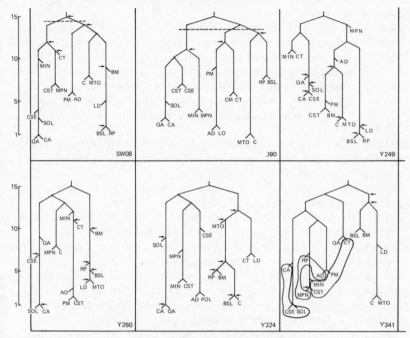

Figure 4.2 Class in hierarchies

(*b*) *to explain the anomalous position of the Commercial Traveller*
Level 11: 'He's one of these classless characters difficult to characterise.
Not working class, not doing a service . . .'
(*c*) *to explain the general basis of his hierarchy*
Level 12 (Join): 'On the basis of status or class qualification . . .'
Level 14 (Join): 'They have more in common − social class background −
to them' (pointing to the working class group).
Level 15 (Join): 'I've probably made a social class division . . .'

Notice that his judgements that particular occupations *belong to* a specified
social class occur in the lower (pairing, chaining) phases, whereas the 'structural'
information occurs at the most general (joining) phase.
    (ii) *Y090* is an aircraft fitter who left school at 15 and subsequently
served his apprenticeship in Fife. As in the previous case, status references
(here 'social standing') occur at the earlier stages (levels 1, 2 and 8), but class
terminology only appears at the joining phase to describe his three main
class groupings: 'upper class' (level 11), 'middle class' (level 12) and 'working
class' (level 13).
    (iii) *Y249* is a jobbing heating engineer. He makes extensive use of class

terminology, and he launches into a genuine occupational grading exercise entirely of his own accord:

Level 1: He begins by joining Building Site Labourer and Railway Porter, describing them as 'unskilled working class' and saying that 'anyone could flip between them'. These are joined at

Level 2: by the Lorry Driver, and are all called 'less paid labour'.

Level 3: Now the Carpenter and Machine Tool Operator are described as 'better working class, unskilled', and 'better trades'. They are, he says 'not quite so far down the scale' as the previous group. Next, at

Level 6: The Chartered Accountant and the Civil Servant are joined, and described as upper class: 'You're in the upper class type of job when you get to these people'; they are 'highly qualified'.

Level 7: The Country Solicitor is added, with the comment 'Again, you're going up the scale of job grading', and at

Level 8: the group is completed with the addition of the Qualified Actuary. These are all 'upper class people'. 'How?' enquired the interviewer. 'Well, they've got easy conditions, posh accent, they sit at a desk and dictate matters, and they can take time off at any time . . .'

Level 9: This stage is most important, because it shows the process of revision and gradation clearly at work, and it illustrates the fact that the Joining phase often involves reassessment. The Comprehensive School Teacher, the Barman and the Policeman — 'the trustworthy' — are now merged with the 'better working class, skilled trades' into a single group and called 'middle-class people . . . (a pause) . . . well, O.K., average working class'. (This brief flirtation with the 'middle class' category is strongly reminiscent of the Cleansing Department Worker in Macaulay's (1976:173) study of social class and language in Glasgow, who confided to him: 'I don't really believe in that middle class, you know, myself, to be honest.')

As a consequence of introducing the new distinction 'average working class', he goes on to reassign the initial 'unskilled working class' group (levels 1 and 2) to a new category, the 'lower working class'.

At the end, then, his main contrast is between the upper class and the working class, with the latter graded into 'average' (the trades) and 'lower' (the unskilled

(iv) *Y260* is a public-school educated shop-salesman. When he was giving an order to his groups in the free grouping task he insisted that the sequence reflected 'not social structure — I don't like class terms [sic] — but wealth', but he went on nevertheless to name them as 'upper class', 'skilled classes', 'the devoted' and 'working class'!

In producing his hierarchy, he also forms two main classes: 'the upper class, the more wealthy class' (Accountant and Solicitor at level 1) — diluted by the addition of the Civil Servant (Executive) at level 7 to 'upper middle class' — and the working class occupations (levels 4, 5, 6). As in the case of

SW07, the Commercial Traveller occupies a marginal, ambiguous, position: 'working class qualifications with a middle class look'. None of his class terminology occurs at the joining phase, and once again the class information is primarily concentrated in specifying what occupation belongs in which class.

(v) *Y324* is a heating engineer, aged 53. His class references simply refer to the fact that the given occupations belong to the same (unspecified) class, and he uses 'class' almost synonymously with 'type of home'. To a very large extent, his references specify a 'working-class' branch.

(vi) *Y341* is a maintenance engineer. His hierarchy is included more by way of a contrary example to warn against too ready an identification of class groups with branches of a person's hierarchy. He refers primarily to the 'working class' (levels 13 and 14) in the course of constructing the hierarchy. (But *after finishing the task,* he began talking about his groupings — saying that the Accountant, Solicitor and Civil Servant 'are upper class' (a term not hitherto used by him), that the Policeman, Commercial Traveller, School Teacher and Minister 'have the same status, moneywise', and that the Ambulance Driver, Railway Porter and Male Nurse 'are in the same class' (unspecified). These last two class identifications obviously cross-cut his earlier descriptions, and underline the fact that the use of class terminology should not be thought of as a straightforwardly descriptive predicate on a par with the other bases we have isolated.

4.6 SUMMARY

However hazardous it may be to generalise on the basis of these few cases, a number of regularities are evident which are of sociological significance.

(i) Reference to class terminology in the more specific judgements is virtually entirely restricted to stating that a given occupation *belongs in* a given social class. At the generalising (joining) levels, by contrast, information occurs about structural aspects, and especially about the interrelationships between classes. In this sense, class terminology is more an operation upon occupational structure than a description of it.

(ii) Class naming seems to be more akin to adaptive discrimination than a matter of simple static identification. When further occupations are added to an existing set (or indeed when any further information is provided), the earlier, lower-level simple classifications are often further discriminated, and even entirely re-specified. The question 'how many social classes are there?', without further specification of occupational content, social context or purpose of the research project is akin to the man walking into a greengrocer's shop and asking 'How many are there?'[13]

(iii) When an indirect method such as the hierarchical task is used to elicit class terminology, some occupations are more often located in a class than others are. It is as if some occupations are more 'class-worthy' than others.

The third point needs elaborating. The two social classes referred to most
frequently (with greater or lesser specification) are 'middle class' and
'working class' (see Table 4.8), and they serve as excellent examples. For
our set of occupational titles, the term 'upper class' is used entirely by
subjects in lower educational/status occupations (Quadrants C and D), often
as a synonym for 'professionals' in the mouths of subjects from Quadrants
A and B. (For our 'middle-class' subjects no 'upper-class' occupations are
represented in our list; indeed, 'conspicuous non-occupation' could be an
important factor in describing an upper-class person.)

In all, 31 subjects naturally refer to the fact that one or more occupations
belong to either the middle or working class. The allocations they make are
depicted in Figure 4.3.

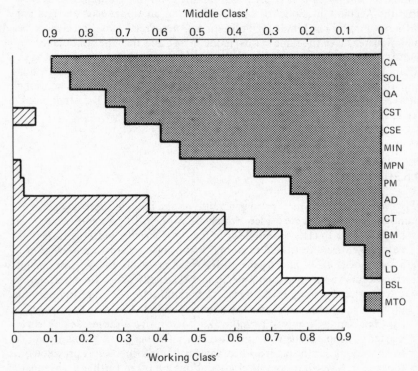

Figure 4.3 Class assignment of occupations

Some care should be taken in reading the diagram, since the two horizontal
scales of proportions refer to different (but overlapping) groups of subjects,
namely (i) those (20) who make middle-class identifications and (ii) those
(19) who make working-class identifications (10 subjects make both middle-
class *and* working-class identifications). Hence the upper and lower sections

of the diagram should be interpreted separately: e.g. 20 per cent of those who make middle-class identifications assign 'Ambulance Driver' to that class, whereas 37 per cent of those who make working-class identifications assign it to the working class. The most striking feature is the closeness of fit between the two sets of identifications — for the 'top' and 'bottom' occupations. There is little consensus, however, about the intermediate occupations — Ambulance Driver, Commercial Traveller and Policeman — and a further group of occupations is in effect defined negatively — thus, the Civil Servant and the Minister are never identified as working-class by this group of subjects, but neither are they overwhelmingly identified as middle-class either.

(iv) Finally, the references to 'class' as such do not, of course, exhaust the language and imagery of class. *'Status'* has a modicum of mentions, as do *positional terms* and their cognates (top, high, upper, middle, low, bottom); *relative positionings* (upper, lower) and *spatial or ordering terms* (order, level, scale, grade, ladder). It would be intriguing to pursue such imagery further, but the restricted number of subjects, the relative infrequency of mention and the involuntary (but none the less real) selection involved in the editing process would all make it a difficult decision to justify, at least with reference to the hierarchies data. But the analysis has now been carried to the point where the central question now becomes: how are these conceptions and beliefs about the occupational world actually interrelated and socially structured? To that question we turn in the next chapter.

5 Belief Systems about Occupations

INTRODUCTION

One way to characterise a belief system about occupations is to make a 'credal' abstract of what seem to be its major premises. Caplow (1954) used this approach in his examination of the principles underlying the 'socioeconom scale of occupations' published by A.M. Edwards in 1943. On Caplow's account, the Edwards scale embodies five evaluative assumptions, which may be seen as the core of its designer's occupational belief system. The five premises were:

1. White-collar work is superior to manual work.
2. Self-employment is superior to employment by others.
3. Clean occupations are superior to dirty ones.
4. The importance of business occupations depends upon the size of the business, but this is not true of agricultural occupations.
5. Personal service is degrading, and it is better to be employed by an enterprise than to be employed in the same work by a person. (from Caplow, 1954:42-3)

These five premises are hardly well-specified. One would wish to know whether they are to be interpreted strongly, (e.g. 'any white-collar job is superior to any blue-collar job'), or in a much weaker sense as 'other things being equal'. One would also want to have some specification of rules for ordering *combinations* of the occupational characteristics involved in those five premises.

A similar attempt to outline the basic assumptions of a belief system about occupations was made by W. Lloyd Warner and his colleagues in *Democracy in Jonesville*. Their final chapter discusses the 'social logics' of Jonesville — those assumptions of social life which, though contradictory, are each affirmed as basic values in one situation or another (p. 293). Selecting out those assumptions to do with occupations and earnings, Warner's 'social logics' are as follows:

1. All occupations are to be respected, for all are necessary for the common life; but they have varying degrees of prestige and power and are ranked accordingly.
2. The values inherent within occupational ranking place the skilled jobs above those with less skill, and reward them accordingly.

3. Those same occupational values rank jobs demanding more schooling above those requiring less.

4. Clean jobs outrank dirty ones; white-collar men those who labour.

5. Jobs may be organized into interconnected hierarchies (factories etc.) where the success or failure of a man may be measured by his movement up or down the hierarchy.

As regards the sources of income, Warner's 'social logics' are:

1. Unearned income is better than earned, and unearned income derived from inherited wealth is better than income from any other source.

2. Profits and fees as forms of income are better than salaries, but salaries *as forms* of getting money are better than wages (the emphasis is Warner's).

3. Wages, while low, are earned money and as such are better than public or private aid.

4. Recipients of 'public welfare aid', the lowest form of income, are ranked accordingly, and are penalised by social sanction.

Neither Caplow nor Warner considered that the average belief systems they were describing were correct (indeed Caplow devotes a chapter to listing many counter-examples). Furthermore, the reader will notice that these 'belief systems' consist of ground rules for the *evaluation* of occupations, and take for granted the existence of a socially shared structure of cognition about the meaning (in a dictionary sense) of occupational titles and of the phrases normally used to relate them.

DEFINING BELIEF SYSTEMS

In the past, belief-systems have been considered either as relatively monolithic and undifferentiated systems (think of how we use 'capitalism', or 'communism' or 'christianity' as categories of description in everyday use) that are basically definable in terms of credal statements, or else the attempt to describe such systems empirically was given up, and attention was concentrated instead on certain 'structural' aspects of belief-systems (their rigidity, for instance). Even when attempts were made to refer directly to identifiable beliefs — such as radicalism, fascism, ethnocentrism — this was part of a narrowly-conceived attempt to represent them as numerical 'dimensions', and summarise a quality of an individual's beliefs as a single number. Belief systems existed to be measured in the narrow sense; that is, only *aspects* and properties of belief systems were of scientific relevance, and if belief systems could be treated as 'structurally identical' by evacuating the content of those beliefs, then this also was a scientific advance. So very often the *meaning* of the beliefs a person held was lost sight of — science was basically interested in what degree of a particular property you had, and how this related to other properties and behaviour. The semantic dimension of beliefs faded from view.

Recent developments have radically changed this orientation. Psychologists in particular have come to conceive measurement generally not so much as a prerequisite for the establishment of quantitative laws, nor yet as parsimonious summaries of complex data, but rather as *models* of the *internal representations* of a person's environment. This has meant that memory, cognitive structure (including the cognitive structure of social structures) and the self have become organising, central concepts. Work in simulation of mental processes, and of problem-solving in particular, has had a profound effect, and because of what we know of the sheer complexity of problem-solving, straightforward numerical measurements — perhaps totally justified — help very little in understanding and explaining even very basic examples of 'understanding', searching, problem-solving and adaptive changes in cognitive systems. The representational problem, in a rather extended sense, then becomes centred round a justification of the faithfulness and adequacy of representation for even stating the cognitive processes of theoretical interest.

In order to represent belief systems, we need to explore in detail not only what beliefs are held, but exactly how they are organised; more than this, we shall want to know how such systems are formed, how they change, how new information is processed, and what processes operate upon them. Conventional scaling procedures almost by definition exclude learning, and are concerned with *stable* attitudes and beliefs. Moreover, whilst selection and abstraction is obviously necessary for any model-building, the purely technical constraints which scaling models often impose (e.g. upon what items can enter the set to feature in the measurement) should be avoided.

To summarise the criteria advanced so far: the representation of a belief system should model in as faithful a way as possible the 'internal representation of the environment', and especially the structural features that characterise such systems. In addition, it should allow the 'meaning' of beliefs to be stored in such a way that, in principle, input can be broken down (selected and stored) and can be generated for output in linguistically acceptable form.

Fortunately, a whole body of research in other areas is available to help in meeting these criteria, since basically similar problems have been faced in the areas of simulation of cognitive tasks on the one hand, and the analysis of semantic and syntactic structures on the other. The relevance is perhaps best seen in the related areas of memory and cognition, since similar problems of internal representation arise there. The classic view is that cognitive structure is organised associatively; here the words are the elements and the relation is that of (differential) association.

For meaning interpreted in associative terms, empirical research has shown that 'associations exist in well-organized, and in some cases tightly organized networks' (Deese 1962:163), and that the principles of organization include a strong clustering and hierarchical element (not only with respect to the semantic lexicon, but also in the way in which the concepts themselves are organised).[1] It is also known that, allowing for the exclusion of so-called 'interstitial' words (such as 'a', 'the', 'and' which occur very rarely as associates but very frequently in natural discourse), the 'average probability that a given word will be emitted as a response in the word-association experiment is the same as its probability in general discourse' (Howes 1957:84).

Another tradition in the study of semantic cognition is characterised by representing meaning not, as in the association instance, by a locus in a complex relational net of associational links, but rather by describing the concept in terms of its co-ordinates or values in a (not necessarily common) set of *attributes*. Thus, Osgood's Semantic Differential analyses in *The Measurement of Meaning* of connotative, affective meaning locate a concept in terms of its (numerical) co-ordinates in basically 3 factor space (labelled Evaluation, Potency and Activity), whilst Kelly's Personal Construct theory technique (Kelly 1955) attempts to elicit from the subject the attributes (in this case dichotomies) he uses by presenting him with triads of 'objects' (e.g. jobs) and asking him to say how two of them are similar and differ from the third, thus locating the concepts in an attribute space (of the subject's choosing). Scott (1969) has carried the dimensional, 'semantic space' model for belief systems further, by suggesting that the dimensions (attributes) be thought of as varying in coarseness or fineness of discrimination. Quite apart from other reasons, attributes are essential for encoding affective orientation to belief-components, and it is this that basically distinguishes a belief or attitudinal system from a purely cognitive system such as memory.[2]

Directed graphs have been extremely useful in representing complex structures, with several relations involved. For our purpose the most relevant example is the representation of semantic structures where the connotative meaning of a concept (a node in the structure) is thought of as the complex of associative links spreading out from one concept to others. Perhaps the most extensive and influential example of this approach is found in the work of Ross Quillian (1968, 1969), who asks the basic question: 'What sort of representational format can permit the 'meanings'' of words to be stored, so that humanlike use of these meanings is possible?' (1968:227). Whilst he is mainly interested in the structure of long-term memory, his concerns are clearly linked to those of this book, especially since belief systems must have a substantial semantic component.

In Quillian's representation, memory consists essentially of one large complex set of nodes (each usually labelled by a word, or concept, or property) and associative links between them. A node is related to the meaning of the word it names in two quite distinct ways. Each word has a unique node (termed its Type node) and a 'plane' or sub-graph. In this plane is an interrelated structure of other nodes (Token nodes) specifying the meaning of the type node. Each token node has an associational link back to its 'parent' type-node at the head of some other plane. Within each plane, meaning is thus represented as being built up from a collection of token nodes (each associatively pointing back to its parent), but is built up in a very structured way. To specify a word's meaning fully always involves entering the relevant type-node plane and beginning to trace through the interrelated tokens, and at each token branching off to the associated type node:

A word's full concept is defined in the memory to be all the nodes that can be reached by an exhaustive tracing process, originating at its initial . . . node, together with the total sum of relationships among the nodes specified by within-plane, token-to-token links. (Quillian 1968:238)

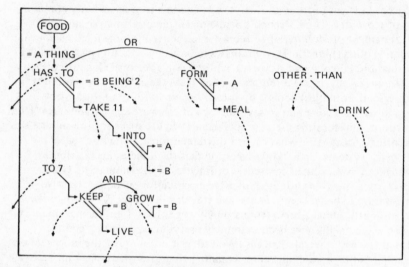

Figure 5.1   Quillian's representation of the meaning of 'Food' as 'That which living being has to take in to keep it living, and for growth. Things forming meals, especially other than drink', (Simplified version of Quillian, 1968: 237.)

Figure 5.1 is taken from Quillian (1968) and illustrates *one* of these planes. This plane represents the meaning of the type node FOOD as 'That which living being has to take in to keep it living and for growth. Things forming meals, especially other than drink'. Within a plane, the token nodes are organised in a basically associative manner, but six *different types* of association are used. In part this is to allow natural language forms to be input, represented and output, but it is also quite deliberate in that the undifferentiated associations of many theories of verbal learning are not sufficiently flexible or subtle for a reasonable semantic representation to be made.

The six basic associative links are:

1. A SUBCLASS TO SUPERCLASS POINTER: used to specify the superclass of which a type-node is a subclass, e.g. Food is a subclass of 'thing'.
2. A MODIFIER LINK: to indicate that a node modifies (usually adjectivally or adverbially) another, e.g. 'has-to' modifies 'thing', i.e. 'food is thing which being has-to take . . .'.
3/4. CONJUNCTIVE AND DISJUNCTIVE SET ASSOCIATIONS: to express

the 'and'-ing of modifiers in the case of conjunction, and the 'or'-ing
of modifiers in the case of disjunction. The latter is normally used to
distinguish distinct meanings of a word. Examples of each are 'keep'-AND-'grow'
and in distinguishing the 'being'-'has-to'-'take' OR 'thing'-'form'-'meal'
meanings of food.

5/6. GENERAL RELATIONAL LINK: of an open-ended and somewhat
residual sort, since 'in natural text almost anything can be considered as a
relationship so that there is no way to specify in advance what relationships
are needed' (ibid., 241). An example is 'being'-'has-to'-'take'.

These relational links apply *within* planes, and a tracing proceeds through
these structures within the plane, but also follows token-to-type node links
across planes. The major differences between this process and a branching
trace through a conventional dictionary are that information about structure
is necessarily preserved and that repeated occurrences of the same word (token)
within a plane are in essence referred back to the first occurrence in Quillian's
model.

Quillian sees this representation not only as a 'reasonable description of
the general organization of human memory for semantic material' (p. 235),
but also as a theory of how natural language text is understood, hence
'understanding' in this account can be viewed as being essentially the creation
of a symbolic representation.

This account has been oversimplified, and the programme which might
operate upon the semantic structure has hardly been mentioned. Perhaps
more importantly the major and controversial linguistic implications have
been neglected. None the less, the implications for belief-systems are clear:

1. The nodes of elements of the nets are probably best thought of as
   properties rather than words as such (a point long made by concept-learning
   theorists), and a concept is then thought of as a collection of properties,
   together with the relations linking them — which is natural in this
   representation. Since a property can be thought of as an attribute with an
   associated state or value, this also provides a reasonable way to encode
   the valuation attached to concepts in belief-systems, and this is readily
   implemented in list-processing languages. It also allows grammatical
   inflexions and gradations (such as 'much', 'not', 'probably') to be represented
   (but only as restrictions on the stored root-form of the word).
2. In order to represent anything at all of the complexity of semantic
   linguistic structures, a range of quasi-logical relations or associations is
   necessary, enabling at least set-inclusion, con- and dis-junction and
   modification.

Whilst Quillian uses dictionary definitions as input data, there is no reason
why the model should not be made more directly relevant to social science
concerns (e.g. the modelling of actual or ideal-typical semantic or cognitive
systems) by inputting either individual (idiosyncratic) or cultural definitions.

We do not propose to embark on any computer simulation approaches in this chapter, or indeed in this book. In fact, our purpose is straightforwardly empirical. We shall be further exploring the types of relationship that would have to be represented in *any* belief system about occupations. We shall also be searching for clues about the bases for differences between individual belief systems. As we have indicated, scaling methods are unlikely to be useful for studying the dynamic aspects of belief systems. Nevertheless, we shall still use such techniques as heuristic devices for data reduction and the detection of individual differences.

5.1 OCCUPATIONAL DESCRIPTIONS AND THE CONTRAST RELATION

As a preliminary step in our analysis of occupational belief systems, we constructed a series of 50 statements about occupations. This was accomplished by reading through transcripts of interviews already performed, as well as through newspapers and the Department of Employment's *Classification of Occupations and Dictionary of Occupational Titles* (CODOT). By way of auto-criticism, we might remark that we found this task of sampling occupational predicates (statements about occupations) to be both novel and rather difficult. We (and perhaps other sociologists) find it much easier to frame the problem of sampling occupational titles than to consider how occupational predicates should be selected.[3]

The list of 50 statements about occupations that we decided upon has been shown earlier in this book (as Table 2.2). The statements were constructed with the general form 'They (have a certain property), for example, 'They are often self-employed', or 'Society could not continue to exist without them', or 'No special training is required to be one'.

Several investigations were carried out with this set of 50 descriptions as stimuli. One of them serves to illustrate a basic element of occupational belief systems — the contrast relation. Students attending a first-year sociology class were asked to carry out a free sorting of the 50 occupational descriptions. As in other free-sorting tasks we have reported, the respondents were asked to sort the descriptions into piles (non-overlapping clusters) on the basis of overall similarity. Sorting data of this kind can be analysed in numerous ways, but here we restrict ourselves to simple visual inspection of the aggregated data. We look for those pairs of occupational descriptions that *none* of the students sorted into the same pile, on the basis of overall similarity. Putting it the other way round, we look for those pairs of occupational descriptions that were sorted into different piles by each and every one of the respondents. The clear meaning of a pair like this is that *no respondent* has been able (in the absence of prompting) to envision an occupational category for which both statements apply. This can be interpreted as a cultural or subcultural assumption that there are no occupations for which both statements — (we might call them statement (i) and statement (j) — are true. Such an assumption provides the basis for a syllogism of *contrast* having the form:

(a) there are no occupations for which both statements (i) and (j) are true;
(b) for a particular occupation, statement (i) is true;
(c) therefore statement (j) is false (for that occupation).

We had sociology students make free sortings of the 50 occupational descriptions, and we examined their aggregated data for pairs of descriptions that were in contrast in the sense defined. We found 60 contrasting pairs (just under 5 per cent of the 1225 possible pairs of the 50 occupational descriptions). Some of the contrast relationships are strictly definitional. For example, 'They are paid by the month' contrasts with 'They are paid by the week' and with 'They are paid by the hour' (the contrast here is what survey analysts would describe as 'dummy variable dependency'. Other contrast relationships are not at all definitional, but indicate more or less 'obvious' aspects of the social organisation of work. For example, 'They are paid by the month' contrasts with 'They earn a lot when young, but their incomes don't rise much after that'. Similarly, 'They have to clock in and out of work with a time card' contrasts with 'They have to have a high standard of academic education'; further, 'They are required to have high educational qualifications' contrasts with 'They have a strong trade union'. The vast majority of the contrast relationships which are not simply definitional are of this 'working-class' versus 'professional, managerial or white-collar' type.

A small number of the 50 occupational descriptions were evaluative rather than purely descriptive in content. 'Society could not continue to exist without them' is one of these, and contrasts (so far as these students were concerned) with 'They are paid by the month', and also with 'They are involved in managing people as part of their work'. These students (of sociology) appear to be taking a 'status dissent' perspective. Clearly we should expect other social groups to make contrasts between some quite different occupational descriptions and 'Society could not continue to exist . . .'.

This simple example shows how data from a free-grouping task can be used to uncover what may be a basic element of occupational belief systems — the *contrast* relation such that one description immediately excludes several others. Unfortunately this is as far as the free-grouping method will take us in the analysis of occupational descriptions. It is of course possible to use multidimensional scaling methods in an attempt to uncover a spatial representation of occupational descriptions. We constructed overall indices of similarity between the 50 occupational descriptions, from the free-sorting data and used smallest space analysis (Roskam's MINISSA algorithm) to scale them in two and three dimensions. This gave a useful, though static snapshot of our 50 descriptions in the occupational belief system. We do not show the scaling solution for students' sortings of the 50 occupational descriptions, since it was broadly similar to the results discussed on pages 45 to 53 above and in U2.12 of the third volume.

There was a strong tendency for the scaling solution to fall out into two large and opposing clusters — one cluster containing descriptions relevant to professional and managerial jobs, while the other contained descriptions concerned with aspects of shop floor work.

Where the scaling of similarity measures (derived from aggregated free sortings of the 50 occupational descriptions) seemed to fail was, first, in that the technique appeared ill-suited to any search for systematic individual differences; and, second, in that it lumps together a number of distinct relations among occupational beliefs into a single numerical index of 'similarity'. D'Andrade (1976) puts the argument well:

> Multidimensional scaling techniques place objects in a space on the basis of overall similarity. The objects may be alike in that one may be a sub-set of the other, or one may be a member of the class named by the other, or one may be part of the other, or both may be members of some third class, or one may be the antonym of the other . . . [etc.] All of these relations lead to objects being assessed as similar . . . Once the information about the difference kinds of relations has been reduced to one overall similarity measure, there is no way to retrieve the information about how objects are really related to each other. (1976:160-1)

With these considerations in mind, it was decided to abandon the free-grouping method of investigating occupational descriptions, and to turn instead to the use of an approach known as 'sentence frame analysis'. The objective here was to adopt a procedure that would be sensitive to individual differences in the perceived interrelationships between occupational descriptions and would also be interpretable in terms of cognitive operations.

SENTENCE FRAME DATA

The purpose of collecting sentence frame data is to find out the acceptable usage of 'properties', or 'predicates' which respondents believe to be more or less applicable in a given semantic domain (in our case, the domain of occupations). The basic method is that respondents are presented with 'linguistic frames' (belief sentences), which each have one component or 'slot' removed.[4] In our investigation, this 'slot' is for an occupational title. As the task is used in linguistics and anthropology, the respondent either *provides* an acceptable (to him) range of 'fillers' for the 'slot', or *judges* the acceptability of a systematically chosen (by the investigator) range of alternative 'fillers'. Buchler and Selby (1968) have summarised the method as follows:

> First, one learns the linguistic shape of questions in the local language. Second, one seeks the appropriate questions that can be asked in the culture. One asks an informant, for example, 'What kind of question

could I ask about 'X'?' Third, one forms 'substitution frames' on the basis of information gained in steps one and two . . . The fourth step is to turn all the questions into assertions, and check the body of information with other informants, with whom the elicitation had not taken place. The fifth step is a summary of the data by domains and contrast sets, within contrast levels (or taxonomic levels). (p. 22)

We carried out two investigations using the sentence frame method. The first was a pilot study using students in a first-year sociology class as respondents in a classroom situation. Here we used 50 sentence frames (closely similar to the 50 statements about type of work-related activity whose analysis as grouping data is described earlier). We selected 20 occupational titles for use with the sentence frames, 16 of them being the same set that we had used in research on similarity judgements and on invidious comparisons between occupations, (see *The Images of Occupational Prestige*) and the remaining four being taken from the set used in the British investigation by Hall and Jones (1950).

We administered the task in such a way that each of a large number of students used a different subset of 15 from the total 50 sentence frames. A respondent would be asked to judge each combination of sentence frame

TABLE 5.1 List of 20 occupational titles used in a pilot investigation of sentence frames with students

1.	MIN	Church of Scotland Minister
2.	BM	Barman
3.	BMG	Business Manager (10 to 99 Hands)
4.	C	Carpenter
5.	CSE	Civil Servant (Executive Grade)
6.	CT	Commercial Traveller
7.	SOL	Solicitor (Country Practice)
8.	MPN	Male Psychiatric Nurse
9.	JMB	Jobbing Master Builder
10.	LD	Lorry Driver
11.	PM	Policeman
12.	RP	Railway Porter
13.	WMG	Works Manager (Industrial)
14.	CST	Comprehensive School Teacher
15.	QA	Qualified Actuary
16.	AD	Ambulance Driver
17.	BSL	Building Site Labourer
18.	MTO	Machine Tool Operator
19.	NT	Newsagent and Tobacconist (One man shop)
20.	CA	Chartered Accountant

Note: The 20 occupational titles are composed of the same 16 as were used in a paired similarities task, supplemented by 4 from the Hall-Jones list.

and occupational title into one of three categories, 'Always', 'Sometimes', or 'Never'. As an example, a 19-year-old psychology major, daughter of a railway worker and describing her political sympathies as 'conservative', used the sentence frame: '(. . .) have high social standing in the community'.

She judged eight occupational titles as follows:

Church of Scotland Minister	'Always'
Barman	'Never'
Carpenter	'Never'
Male Psychiatric Nurse	'Sometimes'
Policeman	'Always'
Chartered Accountant	'Sometimes'
Qualified Actuary	'Sometimes'
Lorry Driver	'Never'

We shall try to make inferences about cognitive structure from data such as these.

AGGREGATE ANALYSIS OF 20 FRAMES AND 50 OCCUPATIONS

It is conventional, in studies of occupational images, to try to present an answer to the question, 'What does the average person think about certain occupations?' This enterprise usually yields a list of the attributes which characterise each occupation. Table 5.2 is useful here, for it shows the percentages of respondents considering each of the 50 sentence frames 'Always' appropriate for each of the 20 occupational titles.

For example, 100 per cent of respondents say that Church of Scotland Ministers 'often work at weekends', and that they 'have a secure job'. Similarly, 100 per cent of respondents say that Male Psychiatric Nurses, 'are involved in helping other people', 'have to be physically fit to do their job', and (not surprisingly) 'are almost always men'. *No* respondents say that Chartered Accountants 'spend a lot of time at work clock-watching', or that 'they are often self-employed', or that 'they have mainly physical skills', or that 'they have irregular hours', and so forth. The large number of zero percentages is an interesting characteristic of this table, since it suggests the role of contrast relationships in occupational thinking.

We used a method called parametric mapping analysis, directly on these data. This is a metric scaling technique, which allows the distances between the data points to be *any* smooth (not necessarily monotonic) function of the distances between corresponding points in the solution space[5] (see Shepard and Carroll, 1966). It yields a cognitive map of the occupational titles only (and not of the sentence frames), though the distances between occupations in this map reflect their different profiles over the 50 sentence frames. The two-dimensional configuration is shown as Figure 5.2. It is very striking how the 16 occupations which were the same as those used in pairwise scaling

TABLE 5.2 Percentages of respondents considering sentence frames 'always' appropriate for occupational titles (50 sentence frames and 20 occupational titles; respondents were 47 sociology students)

		MIN	BM	BMG	C	CSE	CT	SOL	MPN	JMB	LD	PM	RP	WMG	CST	QA	AD	BSL	MTO	NT	CA
STRIKE	1	59	46	66	39	33	66	73	19	33	39	39	33	59	13	66	19	26	39	66	79
HOURS	2	13	33	33	0	0	6	6	19	13	59	33	7	13	13	6	13	13	6	46	6
MANAGE	3	28	14	92	0	50	50	35	64	21	26	42	19	85	92	21	21	0	7	7	7
CLOCK-W	4	0	33	0	0	0	0	0	6	0	26	6	19	0	19	0	0	39	53	0	0
S-EMP	5	0	6	0	6	0	0	18	0	18	0	0	0	0	0	0	18	0	0	50	0
PHYS	6	0	18	0	75	0	0	0	18	75	62	12	68	6	0	0	0	100	68	6	0
SERVE	7	76	58	11	52	29	11	35	88	35	35	82	47	17	76	29	100	41	29	58	29
CLOSED	8	36	10	21	15	36	5	42	26	36	21	42	36	21	26	31	31	21	36	10	31
APPR	9	52	43	12	88	23	43	47	29	70	11	41	5	17	47	41	17	5	29	0	41
IRREG	10	75	0	17	0	41	0	76	56	6	68	62	25	12	0	0	50	6	6	18	0
ACAD	11	64	0	0	0	0	0	0	11	0	0	0	0	70	70	88	50	0	0	0	70
SWITCH	12	0	39	0	0	39	39	0	6	6	39	0	19	0	6	0	13	59	13	0	0
OTIME1	13	0	17	0	41	0	41	0	0	41	64	23	41	5	6	13	23	70	58	5	0
SONS	14	19	0	46	19	19	39	26	0	19	0	13	0	0	6	19	0	0	0	6	13
PERKS	15	59	19	53	0	46	39	53	0	6	6	19	19	6	6	39	8	0	0	19	26
MOST	16	0	8	0	0	8	8	16	0	6	25	41	0	33	50	0	8	0	8	0	0
OTIME2	17	0	53	26	53	19	19	6	26	53	79	33	86	19	6	19	59	100	93	0	19
CASUAL	18	0	50	7	50	0	14	7	7	28	78	23	0	14	50	14	0	42	50	85	7
TU	19	0	0	7	15	30	0	7	15	46	53	23	84	38	69	15	76	61	76	0	7
DAY OFF	20	13	19	19	0	19	19	13	6	6	6	6	13	0	0	0	6	19	13	6	7
ANY	21	14	92	7	28	14	42	0	14	28	85	71	92	28	14	0	64	92	78	85	0
WKENDS	22	100	93	6	6	12	12	0	62	6	31	56	37	0	0	0	37	12	6	81	0
MEN	23	85	28	71	92	14	85	57	100	100	92	42	100	71	0	50	100	100	42	0	57
PAYWK	24	0	92	0	100	0	38	0	46	76	92	46	84	0	0	0	76	92	84	30	0
CLOCKIN	25	0	0	0	7	7	0	0	0	15	15	7	46	15	0	26	30	46	92	7	0
30	26	19	0	46	13	39	6	46	0	53	6	0	13	59	0	0	6	0	6	59	39
PROF	27	66	0	50	25	66	0	100	41	25	0	41	0	16	66	91	0	0	0	0	91

TABLE 5.2 continued

		MIN	BN	BMG	C	CSE	CT	SOL	MPN	JMB	LD	PM	RP	WMG	CST	QA	AD	BSL	MTO	NT	CA
TRAIN	28	91	0	16	50	16	0	75	50	25	8	25	0	0	75	75	0	0	0	0	75
HELP	29	83	8	8	16	8	0	58	100	8	0	66	41	8	83	16	91	0	0	8	16
BORING	30	7	28	0	0	21	21	0	0	0	21	7	64	0	0	7	14	57	78	14	14
MONTH	31	71	0	85	0	78	21	57	42	21	7	28	0	64	85	57	7	0	0	0	71
MONEY	32	0	0	33	0	41	0	58	6	8	25	0	0	25	0	25	0	25	16	0	50
STATUS	33	79	0	46	0	59	6	93	0	23	0	26	0	19	39	53	0	0	0	15	59
FEES	34	0	7	0	0	0	30	61	0	0	15	0	7	0	0	0	0	23	15	15	23
MOVE	35	0	0	0	8	0	14	0	0	8	14	0	7	0	0	0	0	28	14	0	0
VARIOUS	36	8	41	0	0	0	25	0	0	0	41	23	0	8	0	0	16	41	8	8	0
CTY	37	84	15	7	0	7	0	38	0	0	0	7	25	0	15	0	7	0	0	30	0
YOUNG	38	7	30	0	15	0	38	7	15	15	46	41	23	0	7	7	15	38	30	15	15
HOUR	39	0	66	0	58	25	0	0	25	50	58	54	75	0	16	0	58	91	75	8	8
PEOPLE	40	90	63	63	18	18	63	81	90	41	0	0	0	36	100	9	27	0	0	81	18
SPEC	41	75	8	16	41	16	0	66	66	0	0	25	0	8	41	66	8	0	8	0	66
EDUC	42	58	0	8	0	33	33	91	0	0	0	0	0	91	0	83	8	63	0	0	83
ESSE	43	36	36	27	45	36	18	45	36	36	36	63	18	36	54	36	54	75	54	27	45
N-TRAIN	44	0	91	0	8	0	0	0	0	0	50	0	91	0	0	0	33	0	41	75	0
LATER	45	16	0	50	0	66	33	50	0	16	0	33	0	50	0	33	0	16	0	16	50
YOUNGER	46	0	16	0	0	0	0	0	16	0	16	0	0	0	0	0	0	0	0	0	0
FIT	47	22	55	22	77	22	88	22	100	88	77	88	55	33	33	22	88	100	22	22	11
SECURE	48	100	0	16	50	100	0	100	33	16	0	66	0	16	100	100	16	0	0	16	66
EXAM	49	66	0	0	0	50	0	100	16	16	0	0	0	0	100	100	0	0	0	0	100
SOLIDY	50	50	0	16	16	16	0	50	16	16	33	66	33	16	50	33	50	33	66	0	33

analyses occupy much the same relative positions in this cognitive map as they did in the map derived from a different scaling method applied to a different kind of data, collected over different respondents (see *The Images of Occupational Prestige*).

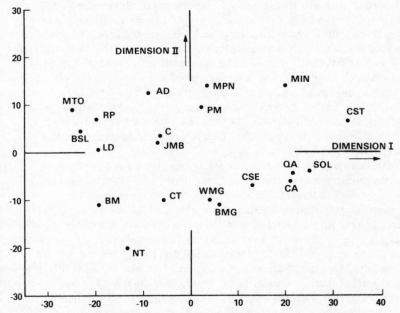

Figure 5.2   PARAMAP representation of cognitive map for 20 occupations

The four extra occupations fit in roughly as one might have expected, with Jobbing Master Builder close to Carpenter, Newsagent/Tobacconist close to Commercial Traveller and the two Managers near to Civil Servant.

THE MAIN INVESTIGATION WITH SENTENCE FRAMES

The sentence frame data we collected from students were used in other analyses which we describe later in this chapter. We profited by our experience with this pilot investigation by modifying the sentence frame task slightly, so as to make it easier to administer in full-scale interviews with adult men sampled from the Edinburgh area. The modifications were:

(i)   to *reduce* the number of sentence frames from 50 to 15;
(ii)   to *increase* the number of occupational titles from 20 to 25;
(iii)   to use an entirely new set of occupational titles wich much more detail in the wording of each;
(iv)   to ask respondents to use four response categories rather than three.

The wording of the new categories was 'Always', 'Usually', 'Seldom', and 'Never'.

These modifications were made with a view to focusing attention on implicative relationships between the *social class* characteristics of occupations expressed in sentence frames. Only 15 sentence frames were used because it was thought that any more (each being judged in combination with 25 occupations) would cause the interviews to drag on too long. It turned out that very few respondents took longer than an hour over this task, and one man took as little as 21 minutes. The number of occupational titles to be judged was increased to 25 because we wished to compute indices of association between each pair of sentence frames, *for each respondent*, and a 'sample size' of 25 occupations seemed to be the bare minimum necessary for such an enterprise. We had the usual problems of making a rational selection of occupational titles, and of deciding how generalised or specific they were to be.

With this version of the sentence frame task, we made a novel approach to these problems of selection. Reasoning that, so far as social interaction is concerned, an occupational title is what a person says in response to the question 'What is your occupation?', we went through the 371 completed questionnaires for enumeration district 160 in Edinburgh, and examined what the interviewer wrote down as the man's occupation. For example, if a railway engine driver finds it relevant to say that he is a 'second man on diesels', then that specification becomes part of his occupational title; if a school-teacher finds it relevant to say that he is a 'teacher in a boys' boarding school', then that is the occupational title he uses; if a refrigeration engineer points out that he is self-employed then we include that as part of his occupational designation.

Since we required 25 occupational titles for the sentence frame task, the most natural way to obtain them was to draw a random sample from those 'naturally occurring' on the 371 questionnaires completed for households in Edinburgh enumeration district 160. By using this method of selection, we could be sure that the occupational titles we used were of the form currently known to our subjects. We could also be sure that the dispersion of our stimulus set of occupational titles (on dimensions such as salary level, educational requirements, degree of contact with people, and so forth) was of the same order of magnitude as the people in Edinburgh at that time saw in their daily lives. So far as we are aware, little or no attention has been paid to this last point in previous studies in the field (see Coxon and Jones, 1974b).

INTERPRETATION OF THE TASK

A small but significant minority of the respondents who carried out the sentence frames task found difficulty with the 'social standing' sentence frame

TABLE 5.3 List of 15 sentence-frames used in the main investigation with adult men.

1.	TRA	A _____	would have served a trade apprenticeship to get into the job.
2.	EDQ	A _____	would have high educational qualifications
3.	OVT	A _____	would have the opportunity of working at overtime rates.
4.	STU	A _____	would be a member of a strong trade union.
5.	STA	A _____	would have high social standing in the community
6.	PBW	A _____	would be paid by the week.
7.	CLK	A _____	would have to clock in and out of work with a time card.
8.	PRO	A _____	would regard himself as a member of a profession.
9.	PUB	A _____	would be involved in meeting the public in his job.
10.	BOR	A _____	would have a boring repetitive job.
11.	LAB	A _____	would vote labour.
12.	OWN	A _____	would own the house or flat he lived in.
13.	SEC	A _____	would have financial security in his job.
14.	FEE	A _____	would send his children to a fee-paying school.
15.	CLA	A _____	would regard himself as working class.

Notes: These 15 sentence frames have only a tenuous connection with the 50 use used in the pilot investigation. Nos. 5, 9, 11, 12, 13, 14 and 15 are essentially new while 1, 3 and 8 involve terminological changes.

The abbreviations used in data anlysis are shown to the left

('A — would have high social standing in the community'). The wording here is quite similar to that of the classical NORC 'prestige' question,' ... your own personal opinion of the general standing that such a job has' (Reiss 1961:19).

One respondent (Y319, a publisher's representative) flatly refused to judge occupations on this criterion. Another (S029, an architect) refused on the 'voting' sentence frame ('A — would vote labour'). Two other respondents conformed to the pressures of the interviewing situation, but only to the extent of making precisely the same judgement for each occupation on the 'social standing' sentence frame. (These were S165, a civil servant with the Forestry Commission, and Y035, a retail adviser.) Many respondents made remarks indicating their dislike of the task, or their decision to reinterpret it according to their own view of the world. We report some of these now.

1. An anaesthetist. The interviewer recorded that he didn't believe social standing is job-related. He said, 'My answers depend upon what I think of the job; ... whether it is demanding, responsible, difficult ...'. (S004)

2. A chief agricultural officer worked silently, and only argued about the interpretation of 'social standing', which he would have preferred to grade with reference to smaller groups than the same 'community' in all cases. Of 'social standing' he remarked, 'This is very politically sensitive, as we say in the civil service.' (S005)

3. A chartered accountant found 'social standing' the most difficult. 'It's so subjective!' At 'vote labour' he asked if he should put 'Always' all down the line and laughed. He refused to give an answer for the Civil Servant on the grounds that a Civil Servant — at that level — would *never* vote. (S006)

4. A professor of computer engineering said his answers did not and could not represent his views. He described how much social standing people have *because of their job only* but stressed that this is not the only source of social standing. (S042)

5. A partner in a firm of quantity surveyors argued that social standing is dependent on the community and on the individual. Age is also relevant, he said; ' — the trainees have to be considered as low.' (S061)

6. A man with multiple interests as an insurance broker, a property owner

TABLE 5.4   List of 25 occupational titles used in the main investigation with sentence frame data

1.	AR	Architect
2.	ADM	Mini Ambulance Driver
3.	CSA	Civil Servant Assistant Secretary
4.	WCK	Wages Clerk for Engineering Firm
5.	ICR	Industrial Compositor (Typesetter)
6.	DBF	Director of Brass Foundry (Self-Employed)
7.	ED	Engine Driver (Second Man on Diesel Engine)
8.	RE	Refrigeration Engineer (Self-Employed)
9.	EI	Engineering Inspector (Steel Plant)
10.	HGR	Head Groundsman
11.	IT	Inspector of Taxes
12.	MJ	Master Jeweller
13.	CJR	Carpenter/Joiner (Self-Employed)
14.	LLD	Long Distance Lorry Driver
15.	TMG	Trainee Manager in Burton's Tailors
16.	MMG	Motor Mechanic in Garage
17.	NM	Nursery Man (Self Employed with Two employees)
18.	PS	Police Sergeant
19.	TBS	Teacher in Boys' Boarding School
20.	LTT	Laboratory Technician Trainee (Brewery)
21.	TR	Tyre Repairer
22.	WH	Warehouseman (Groceries)
23.	SF	Shop Floor Superintendent (Engineering Factory)
24.	TF	Turner and Fitter
25.	ADM	Assistant Officer Manager (Stockbroker's Office)

and an antique dealer found the social standing frame difficult. He thought it was 'unfair' to 'lump together' members of a trade into one category of social standing. (S121)

7. A civil servant with the Forestry Commission claimed, 'Social standing is not related to occupation. It has to do with individual qualities. The only honest answer is to put "Usually" all the way down.' And he did! (S165)

8. Another anaesthetist (a consultant) seemed according to the interviewer to enjoy the sentence frame task. At 'social standing', he claimed to be a 'middle-of-the-road' man, and wished there was a 'possibly' response category. (S166)

9. A retail adviser started with the 'social standing' frame by giving a 'Usually' and a 'Seldom'. Then he stopped and announced smugly (according to the interviewer) that social standing was not dependent on occupation, and that everyone would get a 'Usually'. (Y035)

10. A salesman for a firm supplying industrial protective clothing also commented on the difficulty of drawing firm inferences from an occupational title to knowledge about social standing. He said, ' "Never" and "Always" are impossible; too strong. You wouldn't know, would you?' (Y060)

11. The owner of a sub-post office/newsagent's shop (also the absentee landlord of a public house) argued of the 'social standing' frame, 'This is a group thing; how people fit into a community in different ways, and it's all wrong. This is not my ideas: it's all the same to me whether a man's a Lord Provost or a scaffie.' (Y070)

12. The sales manager of a large garage was uncertain about the meaning of 'social standing'. He asked, 'What social standing? Are you talking mainly of possessions?' The interviewer noted his strong reaction to the title Inspector of Taxes, at which he exclaimed 'Never! Never!' (of social standing). (Y139)

13. The assistant pensions secretary in a life insurance company considered that the social standing of a Police Sergeant might be variable. 'It all depends on the community – contrast Muirhouse (an area of the Edinburgh conurbation) and a tiny Highland village.' Eventually he decided to base his answer on the Edinburgh area. (Y300)

14. A publisher's representative took 55 minutes to finish the sentence frames task, even though he left two frames unanswered ('social standing' and 'vote labour'). His reasons were, 'A man's occupation doesn't give him social standing', and 'this (question) is unfair'. Of 'vote labour' he remarked 'This is hypothetical – going by the rules, I could tell you which vote labour, but it doesn't always follow. This is nonsense! You can't tell people's political views by their occupations – it's like social standing.' (Y139)

15. A foreman in an engineering works asked of the list of 25 occupational titles, 'Why do they put "self-employed"? Does that give higher standing or something?' (Y332)

16. A plant fitter was asked by the interviewer why all his answers on the 'social standing' frame were either "Always' or 'Usually' and none were 'Seldom' or 'Never'. His explanation was, 'Well, these are all people like me, more or less – they are in the same category; there are no weirdos there . . .' (Y364)

17. An auctioneer of motor cars objected to the 'social standing' frame. He said he would rather not answer, since 'You're trying to find out how big snobs people are.' The interviewer asked him if he could answer the question on the opinions of people in society at large. He replied, 'There are more snobs in this country than anywhere else. Yes, I suppose I could.' On 'vote labour', he said, 'That's a bloody snobbish question that. There's only one way you can answer that – answer "Usually" right down the list; assuming labour is the popular party.' But he did not do as he said he would. Instead of a blanket 'Usually' response, he differentiated quite markedly, giving a total of 16 'Seldom' and 9 'Usually' responses. (S180) as we shall see later, this respondent was very poorly fit by the INDSCAL model.

18. A part-time salesman was extremely reluctant to answer the STA sentence frame at all. He argued that occupation should not, and need not correlate with status since 'Regardless of occupation, one merits a place in social standing relative to activities outwith work.' He was finally persuaded to answer on the basis of what the general opinion might be (the classic sociological method of framing the concept); though he gave his opinion that this would be largely determined by income rather than by occupation itself. (Y006) This man turned out to have a well organised belief system.

The 18 respondents whose problems with the 'social standing' sentence frame have been quoted comprised about one-third of the total number who were interviewed with the sentence frame task. This seems hardly an insignificant minority, especially in view of the fact that other respondents reacted with paralinguistic and other signs of tension when using class related concepts in free and constrained grouping tasks (see Chapter 4).

These observations that some people deny the reality of social classes, or argue that status is not dependent upon occupation should not be misunderstood. Depending upon one's theory, they might be counted as evidence for, against or irrelevant to the proposition that occupation determines social status in modern societies. Our concern is to understand why people *think* that occupations do or do not determine social position.

A number of respondents adopted a very wide definition of 'apprenticeship', in the sentence frame TRA ('. . . would have served a trade apprenticeship to get into the job'). Our intention has been that *trade* apprenticeship should be interpreted narrowly, but we seem to have been only occasionally successful.

1. An architect told us that 'Architects were in the past apprenticed, but now they never serve their time.' (S029) This is a 'correct' interpretation.

TABLE 5.5 Expository tabulation of two sentence frames over 25 occupational titles

	Never (8)	Sometimes (6) Usually (6)	Always (5)
Always (7)		Refrigeration Engineer (S/E) Engineering Inspector Teacher in Boys' Boarding School	Architect Civil Servant Director of Brass Foundry (S/E) Inspector of taxes
Usually (5)	Trainee Manager Police Sergeant	Carpenter/ Joiner (S/E) Nurseryman (S/E) Assistant Office Manager	
(1) Sometimes		Shop Floor Superinten- dent	
(12) Never	Engine Driver Motor Mechanic Trainee Lab. Technician Tyre Repairer Warehouseman Turner & Fitter	Ambulance Driver Wages Clerk Compositor Head Groundsman Long Dist. Lorry Driver	Master Jeweller

Note: A number of the occupational titles have been contracted in this presentation

2. The interviewer had to insist when interviewing an anaesthetist that an apprenticeship could hardly be equated to 'some training', but he paid little attention, and still assigned 16 out of the 25 occupations to the 'Always' category. (S004)

3. A precision sheet metal worker commented that 'apprenticeship' is rather 'loose'. He pointed out that 'An Inspector of Taxes will have training', and throughout the task he interpreted apprenticeship as 'training of some sort for the job'. (Y284)

These individual differences in the interpretation of 'trade apprenticeship' might be counted annoying. Nevertheless, they show how one occupational category (trades with formal apprenticeships) seems to be blurring over time, though with some people hanging on to the obsolescent interpretation.

Our list of 25 occupational titles was unusual (as such lists go) in that four of them had the additional specification, 'self-employed'. One of our interviewers noticed that the mention of this qualifier seemed to be of prime importance to those subjects who were themselves self-employed, (though not to other subjects). The retail adviser, (though not himself self-employed) seemed to use the concept quite frequently for making inferences.
He commented, 'self-employeds don't pay themselves overtime' and 'self-employeds don't vote labour' and 'self-employeds don't necessarily have financial security', and 'self-employeds aren't in unions'. (S035) These are all relationships of contrast or exclusion.

PRESENTATION AND ANALYSIS OF SENTENCE FRAME DATA

The essential element in presenting these data is the two-way table of sentence frame (i) against sentence frame (j). An example for one person judging 25 occupational titles is given as Table 5.5.

The two sentence frames in the table are:
I. (rows)   A — would be paid by the month.
J. (columns)   A — would own the house or flat he lived in.

One can read from the table that this subject sees an Architect as being 'Always' paid by the month, and 'Always' owning the house or flat he dwells in. Ranging more broadly over the figure, it is evident that this subject sees the two attributes of monthly payment and home ownership as being strongly inter-related (though not completely so). He might well be equipped to use the reciprocal implication rule that payment by the month implies home ownership, and vice versa. However, there are exceptions to this rule. An advantage of this mode of presentation (where the titles of the elements in the cells of the cross-tabulation are written out rather than being left as homogeneous replications) is that one can immediately see the occupational titles where the rule does not work. These are

(*a*) Trainee Manager in Burton's Tailors
(*b*) Police Sergeant
(*c*) Master Jeweller

The first and second of this trio (Trainee Manager and Police Sergeant), were judged as 'Usually' being paid by the month, though 'Never' owning their own home. When questioned on these exceptions, the subject recalled that he had considered a Trainee Manager in a multiple tailors as being likely to be very young and therefore almost certain to be renting accommodation or living with his parents. The position of the Police Sergeant was explained quite simply on the grounds that such a person would have a police house provided for him. Finally the Master Jeweller had been seen as 'Always' owning his home, but 'Never' being paid on a monthly basis. The subject recalled that he had been thinking of a Master Jeweller as being very well off financially, but as not being any kind of employee. He admitted that this was somewhat unsatisfactory, since he had been prepared to consider four other 'self-employed' occupations as being 'Always' or 'Usually' paid by the month. He supposed that the specification of *Master* jeweller may have set off medieval guild-related associations in his mind.

To present this sort of table and this sort of analysis for each pair of 15 sentence frames (105 pairs) for each individual subject would be out of the question. Simplifications are therefore desirable. One possibility is to compute coefficients which express the strength and direction of association between sentence frames (i) and (j). Some candidate coefficients are the Goodman and Kruskal *gamma* index of weak (non-decreasing) monotonicity, Kendall's *tau-b* index of strict monotonic association, and asymmetric coefficients such as Somers' *d* and Guttman's *lambda*. Such coefficients are sometimes useful, but must of course be regarded merely as a supplement to detailed examination of the tabulations, and in particular, examination of which occupational title goes where in the tabulations. If this approach is followed, each respondent can have his data summarised by 105 coefficients of association (which can be cast in the form of the lower triangle of a 15 by 15 matrix).

Sentence frame data can also be used to generate information about similarities between occupational titles. Once such similarities data are available, multidimensional scaling and clustering techniques can be used to explore the principles underlying belief systems about the occupations. A primitive similarity coefficient between each pair of occupations can be produced by treating the sentence frame data as a series of 'context-bound' sortings of the occupational titles. If a respondent 'treats' two occupations in the same way on a particular sentence frame (both occupations rated 'Always' for example, on the same sentence frame), then that can be treated as a 'vote' for the similarity between those two occupations, (for that respondent, in that context, or sentence frame). For any pair of occupations, these 'votes' of similarity can be added up:

(*a*) for each respondent, over all the sentence frames in which he judged occupations (yielding one similarities matrix for each respondent);
(*b*) for each sentence frame, over all respondents (yielding one similarities matrix for each frame);
(*c*) over all frames and over all people (yielding one overall similarities matrix).

Once generated, the similarities matrices which summarise the relationships between occupational titles can be visually inspected, (for example to see which occupations are *never* judged similar to one another, and which are *always* judged as being alike. One might also wish to try out a *dimensional* representation of the underlying 'model of society', by some multidimensiona scaling technique. A final possibility is to seek a non-dimensionsl (dimension-free) classificatory representation of those aspects of the underlying belief system captured in matrices of similarities between occupations. It could be argued that similarities derived from such context-bound sortings data as these are easier to interpret than similarities data obtained from a respondent' direct judgement of 'overall similarity'. Our own feeling is that both approach are useful.

We have already reported the cognitive map which resulted from 'parametric mapping' the profiles of 20 occupational titles over the 50 sentence frames. (These were data collected from students attending a sociology course.) It was shown as Figure 5.2 and may be compared with Figure 5.3, the cognitive map resulting from INDSCAL analysis of the similarities matrix derived from 'context-bound sortings' aggregated over all subjects and all 50 sentence frames.[6] An eyeball comparison shows that the two representations are broadly similar. This convergence between the results of two different scaling methods is encouraging.[7]

5.2 DIFFERENCES IN OCCUPATIONAL BELIEFS

THE ASSOCIATIONS BETWEEN SENTENCE FRAMES

We computed measures of the strength of association between all possible pairs of 15 sentence frames, and we did this for each of our 52 respondents. We tried using both the Goodman and Kruskal gamma coefficient (measuring the extent of weak monotonic association), and Kendall's tau-b (measuring the extent of strict monotonic association). Our results were much the same in both cases, and so we shall confine ourselves to presenting only the results which make use of gamma coefficients.

It is of some interest to know which pairs of sentence frames are strongly associated with one another (and whether strong associations are positive or negative in sign). Naturally enough, there was a certain amount of variation among the 52 respondents, we found 12 out of the 105 mean gamma coefficients to have an absolute size larger than 0.80 (a strong correlation). Six of the 12 were positive in sign, and were as follows:

Pair of Frames	Mean Gamma
FEE with EDQ	0.83
FEE with EDQ	0.86
FEE with OWN	0.88
CLK with OVT	0.82
CLK with PBW	0.81
PBW with CLA	0.86

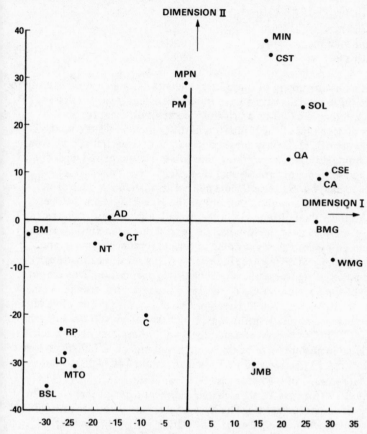

Figure 5.3 INDSCAL Representation of cognitive map for 20 occupations (dimensions I and II of a three-dimensional solution)

FEE (= '. . . would send his children to a fee-paying school') is strongly positively related to EDQ (= '. . . would have high educational qualifications'), to STA (= '. . . would have high social standing in the community'), and to OWN (= '. . . would own the house or flat he lived in'). Similarly, CLK (= '. . . would have to clock in and out of work with a time card') is strongly positively related to OVT (= '. . . would have the opportunity of working at overtime rates'), and to PBW (= '. . . would be paid by the week'). In turn, PBW is strongly positively related to CLA (= '. . . would regard himself as working class').

  Similarly, the six strong *negative relationships* were:

Pair of Frames	`Mean Gamma
CLA with EDQ	−0.83
CLA with STA	−0.81

CLA with FEE	−0.92
CLA with OWN	−0.82
OWN with PBW	−0.81
PBW with FEE	−0.87

It seems clear that for many of our 52 respondents (though not necessarily for all of them) these six pairs of sentence frames were 'contrast pairs', useful for making inferences based on a principle of *exclusion* (that for an occupation to have one of the properties in the pair excludes the possibility of its having the other). Clearly these contrast pairs are each made up from a sentence frame describing a working-class job-attribute, paired with one describing a managerial or professional characteristic.

Needless to say, our 52 respondents had rather different values of the gamma coefficient for any given pair out of the 105. This seemed to be partly due to individual differences in the overall 'tightness of cognitive organisation' exhibited by the respondents, partly due to intrinsic variability (possible caused by ambiguous wording in certain sentence frames), and partly reflective of real differences in belief systems about occupations. As a rough index of tightness in overall cognitive organisation, we computed the average of the absolute values of the 105 gamma coefficients for each respondent. The idea here is that large positive or negative values of gamma hint at the presence of relationships which the respondent can use in chains of reasoning. If this is valid then respondents with many gamma coefficients which are large in absolute size ought to have well-organised belief systems. There is certainly a fair degree of individual variation. The highest value is a mean absolute gamma of 0.82 (for case S013, an insurance broker) closely followed by 0.77 (for case Y248, a chargehand heating engineer) and 0.76 (for case Y145, a photographer). The lowest values are 0.48 (for case Y326, a master jeweller) and 0.54 (for cases Y349 and Y364, a sales manager (ex-miner and ex-mechanic) and a plant fitter respectively).

We thought it possible that there might be a difference in terms of this variable between High Education and Low Education respondents (as coded in terms of our quadrant system). The previous literature does in fact suggest that the experience of higher levels of formal education makes people organise their thoughts better. However analysis of variance showed no significant effect of our Educational Requirements classification upon any index of tightness of cognitive organisation.

Another possible cause of variation between respondents in the sizes of gamma coefficients is that the wording of some sentence frames may be ambiguous. Given such an ambiguous stimulus, some respondents may interpret it one way, and some another. Unless the direction of interpretation is influenced by the individual's belief system, the role of 'pure' ambiguity in the sentence frames should be simply to add variability to the data, such variability being unsystematic between respondents. Where the between-respondent variation is patterned, even after allowances have been made for differences in overall tightness of cognitive organisation, then we have *prima facie* evidence of differences in belief systems.

The between-respondent variation in sizes of gamma coefficients can be expressed by calculating the standard deviation of the gammas (over the 52 respondents) for each of the 105 pairs of sentence frames. There is wide variation between a standard deviation of 0.10, for the highly agreed upon negative relationship between FEE ('. . . send his children to a fee-paying school'), and CLA ('. . . would regard himself as working class'), to one as high as 0.52, for the 'multiple-viewed' relationship between TRA ('. . . would have served a trade apprenticeship to get into the job') and PRO ('. . . would regard himself as a member of a profession'). Other pairs of sentence frames which have relatively large standard deviations are as follows:

Pair of Frames	Standard Deviation of Gammas
TRA with EDQ	0.46
TRA with SEC	0.41
SEC with LAB	0.41
TRA with PBW	0.39

Together with the TRA with PRO pair, these make up the five most variable pairs of frames. Putting it another way, these are the five pairs about whose correlations there is most disagreement. It is noticeable that the frame TRA ('. . . would have served a trade apprenticeship to get into the job') crops up several times, a point which shows the extent of disagreement about what it is to 'have a trade to one's name'. A comparison of the gamma coefficient between TRA and EDQ as generated in four individual respondents may illustrate the range of variation. Gamma between this pair of sentence frames is −0.91 for case S013 (an insurance broker); it is −0.38 for S039 (a manager's personal assistant); it becomes positive, though small, at +0.18 for Y349 (the service manager, ex-miner); and finally it becomes large and positive with the value 0.78 for case S220 (an insurance manager). These same four cases show considerable agreement if we shift attention to a more stable pair of frames. The gamma coefficients for the relationship between CLA ('. . . would regard himself as working class'), and OWN ('. . . would own the house or flat he lived in') are −0.97, −0.75, −0.75 and −0.88 for the four cases.

INDIVIDUAL DIFFERENCES SCALING OF ASSOCIATIONS BETWEEN SENTENCE FRAMES

As one method of searching for systematically patterned differences between respondents, we used Carroll's Individual Differences Scaling, (INDSCAL) procedure to analyse the 52 sets of gamma coefficients.[8] Each of the respondents had his data summarised in a lower triangle matrix containing the 105 gamma coefficients (one coefficient for each pair of the 15 sentence frames). In the present application of the method, the gammas are regarded as similarity coefficients. The gammas range in size from −1.0 (which denotes extreme dissimilarity between the two sentence frames concerned) to +1.0, (which indicates very close similarity). The INDSCAL model seeks to find a parsimonious description of the 52 matrices of gamma coefficients such that each of the 52 is a systematically distorted version of the similarities between the 15 sentence frames in a constructed 'group space' (also called a

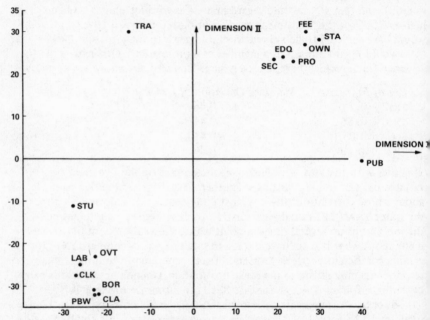

Figure 5.4 INDSCAL representation of 15 sentence frames (group space)

'compromise space', or a 'cultural space'). Depending upon the number of dimensions of the group space, each of the respondents is characterised by a certain number of *weights* which are such as to differentially stretch or shrink the similarities in the group space (which is the same for all respondents) into the closest possible conformity with his own similarities data.

An INDSCAL representation of the data yields four types of information. The pattern of relationship between stimuli in the group space suggests the culturally available 'cognitive map'. Examination of the relative sizes of the weights for individual cases indicates the extent to which systematic individual differences exist. The goodness of fit between the data for each case and the 'fitted values' predicted by the model tells how successful the INDSCAL representation has been in summarising the raw data. Finally, the indiivdual weights for each respondent can be used in conventional data analysis as variables which summarise the cognitive styles of the respondents.

INDSCAL analysis in two dimensions yielded the group space which is shown as Figure 5.4. The pattern is a very simple one, since two tight clusters of points (each point representing one sentence frame) dominate the solution. Three other sentence frames (TRA, STU, and PUB) float between the two main clusters. Not surprisingly, one tight cluster is composed of the six attributes of professional and managerial jobs, (EDQ, STA, PRO, OWN, SEC and FEE). The other cluster contains OVT, PBW, CLK, BOR, LAB and CLA – all of which are attributes of shop floor work. It seems highly plausible that the INDSCAL solution is dominated by these two clusters because whatever the disagreements between our respondents about inferences and implications between job characteristics *within* each cluster (and with respect to the three 'floating' sentence frames), there was massive agreement about the existence of strong *contrast* relationships (36 in all) between job-attributes in the 'upper-class' cluster and those in the 'lower-class' cluster.

At one point in the project, we concluded (rather prematurely as it turned out) that this INDSCAL analysis was degenerate or otherwise uninformative because of the two-cluster solution. The fit between the data and the values predicted from the solution was very close (the correlation here was 0.91), but one normally expects such high correlations when there is a two-cluster solution. Furthermore, the two dimensions of the solution were highly correlated (the value was 0.78), which suggested that a one-dimensional solution might be equally satisfactory. However, we persisted with the two-dimensional analysis because it turned up interesting individual differences. Picking out extreme cases, S013 (an insurance broker) and S039 (a manager's personal assistant) had comparatively large weights for the first (left-right) dimension, and small ones for the second (up-down) dimension. The pattern was reversed for Y349 (the service manager, ex-miner and ex-mechanic) and for S166 (a consultant anaesthetist), who had a much larger weight for the second dimension than for the first one. Two cases whose data are exceptionally well fit by the model were S220 (an insurance manager in a bank) and Y116 (machine engineer in Ferranti). Finally, there was only one case (S180, a car auctioneer) whose data were very badly fit by the INDSCAL model. Figure 5.5 shows these seven respondents, plotted as points in the coordinates of their weights on the two dimensions of the INDSCAL solution. (The remaining 45 respondents are not shown. However the seven extreme cases serve as 'boundary markers', so that other cases fall between them.)

Although we prefer the two-dimensional INDSCAL solution, we computed a one-dimensional solution as well. The subject-weights are the same numerical value as the goodness of fit correlations when one analyses data with the INDSCAL model in only one dimension, so that this extra effort in data reduction yielded only one extra variable. It was noticeable that some cases were fitted almost as well by the one dimensional model as by two dimensions, but that other cases were dramatically affected by the loss of the second dimension. For case Y349 for example, the correlation between his data (gamma coefficients) and the values fitted from the INDSCAL solution dropped from 0.92 with two dimensions to a value of 0.68 with one dimension.

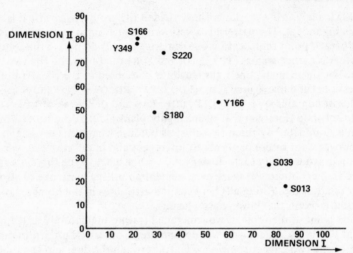

Figure 5.7 Seven extreme subjects in INDSCAL subject space

ANALYSIS OF INDIVIDUAL DIFFERENCES

Taking those characteristics of individual respondents that were derived
from INDSCAL analysis, and also taking other information into account, we
were able to embark on a conventional variable-centred analysis of the sentence
frame data (see Table 5.6). The variables were:

(a)   the individual's weight on the first dimension of the INDSCAL
      solution;
(b)   the individual's weight on the second dimension of the INDSCAL
      solution;
(c)   the goodness of fit correlation between the individual's data (gamma
      coefficients) and the values predicted from the INDSCAL solution
      in one dimension (also interpretable as the subject-weight for the
      one-dimensional solution);
(d)   the goodness of fit correlation between the individual's data
      (gamma coefficients) and the values predicted from the INDSCAL
      solution in two dimension;
(e)   the total number of minutes taken for the sentence frame task
      (we reasoned that respondents who worked very quickly might
      adopt a stereotyped belief system);
(f)   the arithmetic mean of the absolute values of the individual's
      105 gamma coefficients (this was used as a rough index of the
      'tightness' of cognitive organisation).
(g)   the standard deviation of the individual's 105 gamma coefficients
      (introduced as a slightly different operational index of 'tightness' of
      cognitive organisation).

We also used the usual background information, such as age and level of formal education received. (Sex was held constant, since all our respondents were men.) We routinely used our fourfold classification of respondents on the basis of their current and past occupations. This classification divides up individuals according to whether their jobs require high or low levels of formal education, and also according to whether their jobs require more contact with other people, as opposed to more contact with data or machines. Finally, we noted which of our four interviewers conducted the interview.

Correlation analysis showed a strong negative association between weights on the two dimensions of the INDSCAL solution ($r = -0.91$). Cases who placed heavy weight on one of the dimensions would weigh the other dimensions comparatively light. These dimension-weights are not significantly correlated with variable (d), the goodness of fit correlation between data and fitted values for the two-dimensional INDSCAL solution. However, they are quite strongly related (but with opposite signs) to variable (c), the goodness of fit between data and fitted values for the one-dimensional solution – the correlations are $+0.90$ and -0.64 respectively. This pattern of relationships seems to argue that the second dimension of the two-dimensional solution is required for an adequate account of the data.

As one might expect, the better the fit between data and fitted values for each case in the one dimensional solution, the better the fit in the two-dimensional solution ($r = 0.67$). The number of minutes taken for the sentenc frame task was not related to any of the response variables. However, there was a significant tendency for older men to take longer ($r = 0.34$). Variables (f) and (g), the two rough indices of tightness in cognitive organization (or perhaps of strength in the relationships of implication and contrast) were almost perfectly correlated with one another. They were each correlated with age (older respondents being more tightly organised); and they were also correlated with variables (c) and (d), the two case-by-case measures of goodness of fit between data and solution. They were also positively correlated with the sizes of the individual weights on dimension I of the INDSCAL space. This seems to indicate that performing the sentence frame task in a way that can be easily fitted by the INDSCAL model has something to do with having large values of the gamma coefficient (be these positive or negative in sign) between sentence frames. One strategy for attaining this goal with the 15 frames we used in this study would be for a respondent to adopt a rather simple two-class model.

The number of years of formal education experienced by respondents was not significantly correlated with any other variable. Age was positively correlated with INDSCAL weights on dimension I, and negatively correlated with INDSCAL weights on dimension II. As we have mentioned, age was significantly correlated with the length of time required to do the sentence frames task. Age was also intriguingly but non-significantly associated with the tightness of cognitive organisation measures, (c) and (d), and with goodness of fit in the one-dimensional INDSCAL solution. These results suggest that

TABLE 5.6 Pearson correlation coefficients between characteristics of 52 adult male respondents.

	(a)	(b)	(c)	(d)	(e)	(f)	(g)	(h)
(a) INDSCAL Solution: weights on dimension I	1.00							
(b) INDSCAL Solution: weights on dimension II	−0.91	1.00						
(c) INDSCAL Solution in one dimension: correlations	0.90	−0.64	1.00					
(d) INDSCAL Solution in two dimensions: correlations	0.29	0.11	0.67	1.00				
(e) Minutes taken for the Interview	0.10	−0.07	0.10	0.06	1.00			
(f) Mean of Absolute Gamma Coefficients	0.25	−0.05	0.41	0.51	−0.17	1.00		
(g) Spread (s.d.) of the Gamma Coefficients	0.31	−0.10	0.47	0.55	−0.15	0.99	1.00	
(h) Age in years	0.28	−0.27	0.23	0.05	0.34	0.21	0.20	1.00
(i) Number of years of formal education	0.18	−0.19	0.14	0.01	−0.10	0.04	0.04	0.15

Note: Those smaller then 0.28 are not significant at the 5 per cent level.

age has some relationship with the structure of occupational belief systems. However, it is not clear whether age effects should be interpreted as indicating that older men have experienced *more* of the occupational world, or as indicating that they have experienced a *different* occupational world from younger men.

The effects of our quadrant classification were investigated by using two-way analysis of variance, with each of the characteristics of our 52 respondents taking a turn at being the dependent variable.[9] No statistical interaction was found between the 'educational requirements' and the 'people orientation' components of the quadrant classification. The 'people orientation' predictor has a significant effect only upon variable (*b*), the INDSCAL weight on dimension two (which stretches or shrinks the vertical axis of the group space). The 'educational requirements' predictor is significantly related to three rather highly inter-related variables — the INDSCAL weights on both dimensions of the two-dimensional solution, and the individual goodness of fit correlations for the one-dimensional solution. For a short time we thought that these results indicated that people whose jobs demand high levels of formal education are simply able to respond more systematically and fluently to a paper-and-pencil task. However, this interpretation will not stand up, since there is no relationship between the 'educational requirements' predictor and the mean value of the absolute gamma coefficients. In fact not one of variables (*d*) through (*g*) is related to either of the predictors in the quadrant classification.

SHORTCOMINGS OF THE INDSCAL ANALYSIS

The scaling analyses we have reported above are rather unsatisfactory for a number of reasons. First, the INDSCAL solution divided the 15 sentence frames into two opposed clusters, and this hardly seems to be an adequate representation of any belief system. Second, none of the scaling solutions give any information about the extent to which belief elements might serve as concepts applicable at particular and different levels of generality. Third, none of the scaling models has any generative capability.

In view of these problems, we decided to use the individual differences scaling methods and variable centred analysis in order to find subjects who were likely to have occupational belief systems of differing types. The INDSCAL analyses were to be conceived not so much for *representing* belief systems, as for the heuristic purpose of finding deviant cases. Individual analyses of implicative and contrasting logical relationships between sentence frames were then carried out for these subjects.

5.3 IMPLICATIVE RELATIONS AND SOCIAL CLASS

Implication and Exclusion

In order to model a belief system using the building blocks of propositional (classical) logic, we have followed the example of D'Andrade (1976). D'Andrade's concern was to analyse cultural belief systems about diseases, while we are interested in occupations. Nevertheless his methodology seems to be highly appropriate for our purpose.

The basic technique is again the cross-tabulation of one sentence frame against another. If each sentence frame is a dichotomy, this generates the familiar two by two table, with the 25 occupational titles distributed in some way over the four cells. If there are two sentence frames A and B, then each of the occupations either (i) has property A and also has property B; (ii) it has property A, but not property B; (iii) it has property B but not property A; or (iv) it has neither property A nor property B.

A completed two by two table can reveal the presence of an element in a belief system. If simple inspection of the table shows that one or more of the four cells is empty this indicates that we may identify one of the building blocks of classical (propositional) logic there. As an example, if requiring high educational qualifications is a necessary condition for an occupation to have high social standing in the community, then there will be no examples of occupations which have high social standing, but which do *not* require high educational qualifications of their incumbents.[10] Putting the relationship in terms of subsets and supersets, the set of occupations which have high social standing will be a subset of the occupations requiring high educational qualifications. One may or may not wish to interpret an empirical relationship like this as indicating the presence of causal imagery in the belief system being investigated. Such an inference would require additional evidence from the subject's unstructured comments or from some other such source. Nevertheless, the method would seem to have considerable potential for investigating the properties of occupations that lead them to be placed in various social class categories, or under other kinds of generalizing concept.

A 'necessary' condition is not the same as a 'necessary and sufficient' condition. If requiring high educational qualifications is regarded as being both necessary and sufficient for an occupation to have high social standing, then there will be no examples of occupations having high social standing, but not requiring high educational qualifications, and *nor* will there be any examples of occupations having low social standing, but requiring high educational qualifications. This 'necessary and sufficient' relation predicts the existence of two diagonally opposite zero cells in the two by two tabulation of the pair of sentence frames — a pattern that shows the row and column classifications of the table to be identical.

Each of our 52 subjects made 375 judgements, rating each of 25 occupations on 15 sentence frame properties. For each subject, we examined all 105 possible pairs of sentence frame properties. The same computer program which had constructed a four by four table and computed the gamma coefficient between each sentence frame pair was slightly modified–so that it would collapse the four by four table into a two by two table (combining

'Always' with 'Usually', and 'Seldom' with 'Never') and then scan this for evidence of zero cells.

Six tables are given below, each of which corresponds to one of the logical types of relationship between sentence frame properties. Each table has one or more zero cells, and it is the positions of these zero cells that show which type of logical relation is present.

		Property B	
		no	*yes*
	yes	0	9
1. Property A			
	no	8	8

If any occupation has property A then it also has property B. Occupations with A are a subset of occupations with B.

		Property B	
		no	*yes*
	yes	9	8
2. Property A			
	no	8	0

If any occupation has property B, then it also has property A. Occupations with B are a subset of occupations with A.

		Property B	
		no	*yes*
	yes	9	0
3. Property A			
	no	8	8

If any occupation has property A, then it does *not* have property B. Contrariwise, if any occupation has property B, then it does *not* have property A. The presence of property A excludes the presence of property B, and vice versa. (In D'Andrade's term, the property A *contrasts* with the property B. To distinguish this relation from the one below, we call it the *positive contrast* relation.)

		Property B	
		no	*yes*
	yes	8	9
4. Property A			
	no	0	8

If any occupation does *not* have property B, then it has property A. All occupations have either property A or property B, but no occupation has neither A nor B. This is called the *negative contrast* relation.

| | Property B | |
	no	yes
yes	0	12
5. Property A		
no	13	0

If any occupation has property A then it has property B, and if any occupation has property B then it has property A. Properties A and B are identical (or perfectly correlated positively).

| | Property B | |
	no	yes
yes	12	0
6. Property A		
no	0	13

If any occupation has property A, then it does not have property B, and if any occupation has property B, then it does not have property A. The properties are perfectly correlated negatively.

As a concrete example, Table 5.7 shows the two by two by two table for the two sentence frames, 'A——— would have to clock in and out of work with a time card' (abbreviated as CLK), and 'A——— would be paid by the week' (abbreviated as PBW). The 25 occupations are distributed over the four cells of the table according to the judgements of SO13 (a 63-year-old insurance broker) and it can be seen that there is no case of an occupation which is said to have the CLK property but not the PBW property. So far as SO13 is concerned, all of the nine occupations which have the CLK property also have the PBW property. PBW implies CLK.

Tables 5.8 and 5.9 show similar tabulations, also from the data of SO13. Table 5.8 shows the relationship of positive contrast (exclusion) between EDQ ('. . . high educational qualifications'). Table 5.9 shows the relationship of negative contrast between SEC ('. . . financial security in his job') and CLA ('. . . would regard himself as working class').

PUTTING BELIEF ELEMENTS TOGETHER

One way to describe a belief system is to show the relationships, (implicative or contrasting as the case may be) between all possible pairs of elements in the system. So far as the present study is concerned, we need to depict the relationships between 210 pairs from the 15 sentence frames. This turns out to be useful, and by way of illustration, the complete belief system for SO13 is shown in Table 5.10. Such a table can readily be translated into a picture, of the kind that will be shown as Figure 5.6.

TABLE 5.7 Expository tabulation showing subsumption in the data of case SO13

	no	PBW	*yes*
yes			Laboratory Technician Trainee
			Tyre Repairer
			Shop Floor Superintendent
			Industrial compositor
			Motor Mechanic
			Turner and Fitter
			Wages Clerk
			Engine Driver
			Long Distance Lorry Driver

CLK

	no		*yes*
no	Engineering Inspector		Mini Ambulance Driver
	Trainee Manager		Police Sergeant
	Architect		Warehouseman
	Civil Servant Assistant Secretary		Head Groundsman
	Director of Brass Foundry		
	Refrigeration Engineer		
	Inspector of Taxes		
	Master Jeweller		
	Carpenter/Joiner		
	Nurseryman		
	Teacher in Boys' School		
	Assistant Office Manager		

This is an example of the relation of *implication*.
If any occupation has the CLK property, (have to clock in and out of work), then it also has the PBW property, (paid by the week). Occupations with the CLK property are a subset of occupations with the PBW property. Row classification implies column classification.
Note: Occupational titles have been contracted slightly.

.t is convenient to have a short abbreviation for each of the six elementary relationships between frames.
1. If A implies B, we say A 'IMPL' B.
2. If B is implied by A, we say B 'SUPR' A. (Since B is a superset of A.)
3. If A excludes B, we say A 'EXCL' B. (This is also called the relation of positive contrast and is a symmetrical relationship.)
4. If not—A implies B, we say A 'NEG' B. (This is the relation of negative contrast and is also symmetrical.)
5. If A and B are identical, we say A 'IDENT' B. (Symmetrical of course.)
6. If A and B are perfectly correlated negatively, we say A 'OPP' B. (Since they are opposites of one another, the relationship is symmetrical.)

These six abbreviations are used in Table 5.10 whose aim is to show the complete belief system for SO13.

For example, EDQ excludes OVT and this is indicated by EXCL in the cell of the table where the row belonging to EDQ intersects the column belonging to OVT. Since the relationship of exclusion (positive contrast) is symmetrical, EXCL also occurs in the cell of the table where the OVT row intersects with the EDQ column. In the same way, OVT implies PBW, and this is indicated by IMPL at the intersection of the OVT row and the PBW column, and by SUPR at the intersection of the PBW row and the OVT column.

We have chosen to represent belief systems in diagrammatic form by using sentence frames (belief elements) as points and indicating their degree of generality by writing the number of occupations which were linked to them as a suffix in brackets. Thus PRO (6) indicates the 'professionals' sentence frame, and that six occupations were linked to it. One-directional arrows are used to indicate the logical relationship of implication, and broken lines are used to show positive contrast. The identity relationship is indicated by a

TABLE 5.8   Expository tabulation showing positive contrast in case SO13

		EDQ	
	no		*yes*
yes	Industrial Compositor		
	Engine Driver		
	Head Groundsman		
	Long Distance Lorry Driver		
	Motor Mechanic		
	Turner and Fitter		
OVT			
no	Mini Ambulance Driver		Director of Brass Foundry
	Wages Clerk		Refrigeration Engineer
	Trainee Manager		Engineering Inspector
	Tyre Repairer		Laboratory Technician Trainee
	Warehouseman		Civil Servant Assistant Secretary
	Shop Floor Superintendent		Master Jeweller
	Carpenter/Joiner		Police Sergeant
	Nurseryman		Assistant Office Manager
			Architect
			Inspector of Taxes
			Teacher in Boys' School

This is an example of the relation of *exclusion,* or *positive contrast.*
If any occupation has the OVT property, (have opportunity of working at overtime rates), then it does not have the EDQ property, (would have high educational qualifications). No occupation has both the OVT property and the EDQ property.
Note: Occupational titles have been contracted slightly.

TABLE 5.9   Expository tabulation showing negative contrast in case SO13

	no	SEC	*yes*
yes	Motor Mechanic Tyre Repairer Warehouseman Turner and Fitter Engine Driver		Wages Clerk Industrial Compositor Head Groundsman Long Distance Lorry Driver Trainee Manager Laboratory Technician Trainee Shop Floor Superintendent
CLA			
no			Mini Ambulance Driver Police Sergeant Civil Servant Assistant Secretary Engineering Inspector Nurseryman Architect Teacher in Boys' School Director of Brass Foundry Assistant Office Manager Refrigeration Engineer Inspector of Taxes Master Jeweller Carpenter/Joiner

This is an example of the relation of *negative contrast*. If any
occupation does not have the CLA property, (regard self as working class),
then it has the SEC property, (financial security). Contrariwise, if any
occupation does not have the SEC property, then it has the CLA
property. All occupations have either the SEC property or the CLA
property (or both).
Note: Occupational titles have been contracted slightly.

mathematical equivalence sign. We have found that the negative contrast
relationship often clutters the diagrams without adding anything by way of
understanding, and so this relationship is not represented.

A number of types of 'reasoning chain' are possible when the six varieties
of zero-cell relationship are put together in one pattern or another. We may
illustrate by using the belief system of subject SO13, as shown in Table 5.10
and Figure 5.6.

(a)   *Inference from subset to superset, by a transitivity relationship*
For SO13, the property STA implies the property FEE, and the property
FEE implies the property SEC. Therefore (by transitivity) the property
STA implies the property SEC. Social standing implies financial security.
Positive instances are carried *up* the chain of arrows.

TABLE 5.10   Tabular presentation of the belief system of SO13

Subject SO13

		1 TRA	2 EDQ	3 OVT	4 STU	5 STA	6 PBW	7 CLK	8 PRO	9 PUB	10 BOR	11 LAB	12 OWN	13 SEC	14 FEE	15 CLA
TRA	1															
EDQ	2			EXCL												
OVT	3					EXCL	IMPL		SUPR	EXCL	EXCL	IMPL	EXCL	IMPL	EXCL	IMPL
STU	4					EXCL		EXCL	EXCL	EXCL	EXCL					EXCL
STA	5						EXCL	EXCL	EXCL	EXCL	EXCL	EXCL		IMPL	EXCL	IMPL
PBW	6							SUPR	SUPR	SUPR	SUPR	SUPR	EXCL	NEG	IMPL	
CLK	7								EXCL	EXCL	EXCL	EXCL			EXCL	IMPL
PRO	8									EXCL	EXCL	EXCL	IMPL	IMPL	IMPL	EXCL
PUB	9										EXCL	EXCL	IMPL	IMPL		
BOR	10											IMPL	EXCL	EXCL	EXCL	IMPL
LAB	11												EXCL	EXCL	EXCL	
OWN	12													IMPL		
SEC	13												NEG		SUPR	NEG
FEE	14															
CLA	15															

(b)   *Inference from superset to subset*

For SO13, the *absence* of the property SEC implies the absence of the property FEE (since all occupations positive on FEE are also positive on SEC). The absence of property FEE in turn implies the absence of property STA, and therefore (again by transitivity) the absence of SEC implies the absence of STA. As a general rule, then, negative instances are carried *down* the chain of arrows. This means that so long as we can begin with a negative instance at the top of a chain of arrows, we can generate a set of implications about the absence of properties. Such a negative instance is provided if an exclusion (positive contrast) relationship is attached to the top of the chain.

(c)   *Attaching of an exclusion relationship to a superset-subset chain*

For SO13, the presence of property PRO implies the absence of property CLA (by exclusion, or contrast). The absence of CLA implies the absence of CLK, and so the presence of PRO implies the absence of CLK. Since CLA is also a superset of OVT and BOR, the presence of PRO also implies the absence of OVT and BOR. All this can take place because of the strategically useful exclusion relationship which links PRO to the top of a hierarchy of arrows by positive contrast.

(d)   *Attaching of a negative contrast relationship to a positive contrast relationship (or to a superset-subset chain).*

For SO13, the presence of property PRO implies the absence of property PBW (by exclusion, or positive contrast). The absence of PBW implies the presence of SEC (by the negative contrast relationship). It follows that the presence of PRO implies the presence of SEC through this intervening relationship with PBW. (Negative contrast relations are shown in tables, but not in figures.)

GENERATIVE ASPECTS OF THE LOGICAL IMPLICATIONS REPRESENTATION

Since the logical relationships of implication and contrast obey transitivity rules, it is possible to describe this sort of belief system in a way that leaves many relationships unstated. The nature of the system allows them to be generated as, and when required.

A further examination of SO13's belief system shows how the four types of reasoning chain can be put together. Suppose that SO13 can identify that a particular occupation has the property PRO. Further properties can be generated as follows:—

(a)   It must also have the properties FEE, OWN, EDQ and SEC (through subset-superset relationships).

(b)   It must *lack* the properties STU, LAB, PWB and CLA (through subset-superset and exclusion relationships).

(c)   It must also *lack* the properties OVT, BOR and CLK (through subset-superset, exclusion and superset-subset relationships).

S013 decided that six occupations had the property PRO ('. . . would regard himself as a member of a profession'). These were:

Architect
Teacher in Boys' Boarding School
Civil Servant Assistant Secretary
Master Jeweller
Inspector of Taxes
Refrigeration Engineer

The part of his belief system we have just described allows S013 to make inferences about eleven other properties of these occupations. As soon as he knows that they have the property PRO, his belief system can generate the prediction that they also have FEE, OWN, EDQ and SEC; and that they all *lack* STU, LAB, PBW, CLA, OVT, BOR and CLK.

Our representation of S013's occupational belief system is shown as Figure 5.6. As with all of the diagrams of belief systems in this chapter, we show only the relationships of implication/subsumption (indicated by a directed arrow), those of exclusion (or positive contrast, as this relationship indicated by a dashed line is also called), and in the small number of cases where it occurs, the relationship of identity. The total number of occupational titles linked to each sentence frame is placed in brackets as a suffix to its abbreviation on the diagram. Finally, we have shown the abbreviations for the linked occupational titles under each of the 'root elements' of the belief system (at the bottom of the figure).

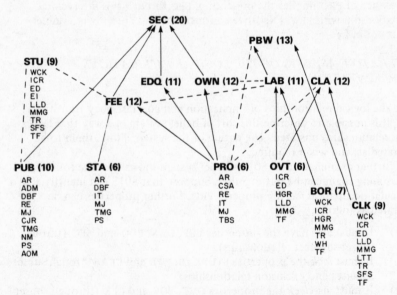

Figure 5.6 Belief system of SO13

One of the things that we seek in representations of belief systems is evidence of superordinate (or 'generalising') concepts. Such concepts may or may not correspond to sentence frames that we have thought to include in the empirical investigation. Where they can be thus identified, we try to find belief elements which subsume many other elements. But subsumption is not enough. What is also required is that a generalising concept should be in contrast with other belief elements. It is also desirable though not essential that a generalising concept should be in contrast not merely with other belief elements, but with other generalising concepts. When this pattern occurs, the belief system will have considerable power to generate further predictions about an occupation, once given a small amount of 'priming' with some initial data.

It further seems desirable that we should be able to infer the existence of a generalising concept, even when this concept had no direct expression in the sentence frames devised for the interviewing task. It is in the nature of things that a generalising concept should be applicable to more instances than is any more specific concept which it subsumes. However, an investigator might very well select a list of sentence frames of which a subset imply the same generalising concept but are all at about the same level of specificity. If such a state of affairs were to occur, the belief elements which were subsumed by the absent generalising concept ought all to have the same contrast relationships to any other (opposed) generalising concept. They would also have the same contrast relationships to all of the belief elements subsumed by such opposed generalising concepts. Finally, there is the possibility that an investigator may select a list of sentence frames that are all at the same level of specificity. In that unhappy event, his only option would be to form clusters of belief elements which had the same pattern of contrast relationships. The generalising concepts would have to be inferred from the contents of the clusters.

The SEC belief element in Figure 5.6 is a good example of a belief element which subsumes many others, but does not seem to be a generalising concept, since an occupation's possessing it does not exclude that occupation's posessing any other property. On the other hand, LAB and PBW appear quite plausible candidates to be generalising concepts (again in Figure 5.6), since they subsume other belief elements, and also have many contrast relationships. We mention LAB and PBW in the same breath here, since they appear very closely related in this belief system. FEE and OWN, on the left-hand side of the figure, are each in contrast with LAB, and we might feel tempted to suggest the existence of a 'left out' (of our list) belief element which is superordinate to both of them, and in contrast with LAB.

INDIVIDUAL VARIATION IN BELIEF SYSTEMS

The logical implications approach seemed an appropriate way to represent the belief systems of those subjects who had been identified as deviant or

extreme cases either by the interviewer's comments on their way of carrying
out the sentence frame task, or by INDSCAL analysis. Eight cases were chosen
for individual examination.

S013: insurance broker (Figure 5.6)
As the figure shows, the logical implications representation of S013's belief
system can be drawn as two hierarchies of implications, linked by
strategically placed relationships of positive contrast, (exclusion). One
important contrast relationship occurs between OWN, ('. . . own one's
home'), and LAB ('. . . vote labour'), with OWN being implied by PRO, and
LAB being implied by BOR and OVT. The contrast relationship between
OWN and LAB is 'strategic' because each of them is implied by (or is a superset of) other belief elements. The positive contrast between OWN and LAB
implies positive contrast between PRO and LAB, OVT and BOR. The positive
contrast relationship between OWN and LAB also came out in S013's
comments during the interview. On the OWN sentence frame, he remarked,
'This is important. If a man owns his house or flat, hs is almost sure to be an
independent type who doesn't want to live off the country. It almost
determines his political allegiance.'

   A similarly strategic contrast relationship occurs between FEE, ('. . . send
children to a fee-paying school') and LAB. In fact, the FEE belief element has
more logical linkages than does the OWN element, and because of this it seems
more plausible as a generalising concept for the left-hand side of the diagram.
It is opposed, of course, to LAB, which (possibly with PBW) serves as the
overall concept for the right hand side.

S220: an insurance manager in a bank (Figure 5.7
The belief system of S220 may be compared with that of S013. In both
systems, OVT, BOR and CLK are 'root elements' for CLA, LAB and PBW
in the right-hand side hierarchy of working-class belief elements. A further
similarity is that FEE, STA and PRO are in contrast with all six working-class
elements for S220, and with five of them for S013. The two subjects are in a
certain amount of disagreement over which occupations have the STA
property ('. . . social standing'), and this contributes to the overall difference
of pattern between the left-hand side hierarchies of 'professional/
managerial' belief elements.

   The belief system of S220 is organised with redundancies in the sense that
inferences can flow between left and right-hand side hierarchies via two
'bridging' relationships of contrast. There are also alternative routes within
each hierarchy. A simple count (using the complete data in the appendix
table)[11] shows that S220 has 31 positive contrast relationships generated by
his belief system. This is a relatively high proportion of the total 105 possible
links (between all pairs of sentence frames) and was the highest count for any
of our subjects. When S220's data (in the form of gamma coefficients) were
multidimensionally scaled (using Roskam's MINISSA—not shown) the

presence of so many contrast relationships served to push the final scaling
solution into the form of two tight and mutually opposed clusters, with only
PUB being a 'floater' (located near to the 'professional/managerial' cluster).
The belief system for S220 seems to be a good example of *la vision
dichotomique*, since it is eminently suitable for generating a two-class
structure.

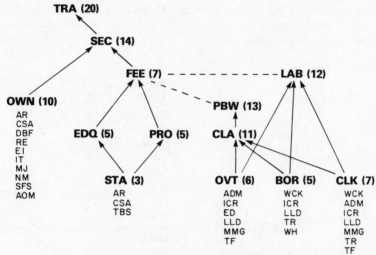

Figure 5.7 Belief system of S220

S220 contrasts with S013 in that he weighted the second dimension of
the INDSCAL solution rather than the first, and his data were much better fit
by the solution in two dimensions than by the solution in one dimension.
However the 'logical implications' representations of the two belief systems
seem quite similar, especially in terms of their organising concepts. Like
S013, S220 appears to use FEE as an umbrella for the left-hand side, and
PBW and/or LAB for the right-hand side.

Y006: a part-time salesman (Figure 5.8)
The belief system of Y006 is rather different from that of S013. Five of the
belief elements form a perfect cumulative scale with the most 'difficult'
element being PRO ('. . . professionals'). Only three out of the 25 occupations
were judged 'Always' or 'Usually' to have the property PRO. However, by a
series of direct subset relationships, this trio of Architect, Teacher and
Assistant Office Manager possess the properties EDQ ('. . . qualifications'),
STA ('. . . social standing'), FEE ('. . . fee-paying school'), and OWN ('. . . own
their houses')—and all this by virtue of their having the property PRO. There
are also some useful contrast relationships which branch off from this chain
of nested implications. For example, FEE is in contrast with (i.e. excludes)

PBW ('. . . paid weekly'), and since PBW is at the top of an 'implication tree'
involving BOR ('. . . boring job'), and CLA ('. . . working-class'), it follows
that all four belief elements in the chain from FEE down to PRO are in
contrast with all three belief elements in the other chain from PBW down to
CLA. In all, 12 contrast relationships are generated between these two chains
of implication. If the three belief elements PBW, BOR and CLA are treated as
being 'reversed' items, they can be combined with PRO, EDQ, STA and FEE
to form a seven-item cumulative scale which divides occupations into eight
groups which are ordered in the mind of Y006 (the basis of the ordering
presumably being social class).

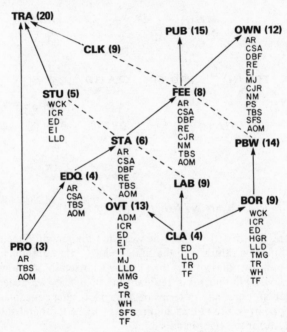

Figure 5.8 Belief system of YOO6

We have mentioned previously that Y006 had been very reluctant to
answer the STA ('. . . social standing') sentence frame at all, and that he had
argued that occupation should not and need not correlate with status. The
interviewer had finally persuaded him to answer on the basis of what the
general opinion might be, which Y006 had said would be largely determined
by income, rather than by occupation itself. It is all the more interesting
then, that the STA belief element fits so snugly into the logical implications
representation of Y006's belief system. It shows how people may behave
according to one set of beliefs, while claiming to behave according to another.
Y006's belief system is perhaps the most tidily hierarchical that we have

found with the sentence frame method. As with many other cases, FEE and PBW seem to be generalising concepts.

Y006 weighted the dimensions of the INDSCAL solution approximately equally (weights being 0.54 and 0.51), but this seems to bear no obvious relationship to the 'logical implications' representation of his belief system. His total count of contrast relationships was 30, which made him second only to S220 in the degree to which his belief system was polarised.

S166: consultant anaesthetist (Figure 5.9)

The belief system of S166 is 'flat' and loosely organised by comparison with those of S013, S220 and Y006. (The system of Y006 is particularly 'mountainous'.) This metaphor of the height of belief systems refers to their appearance when drawn out in diagrams. Tall belief-hierarchies with only two or three 'root elements' typically permit long chains of inference involving many belief elements. Respondent Y006 (see above) provides an excellent example. Flat systems on the other hand seem to have many 'root elements', and their chains of inference involve only a few elements. Another way of putting it is to say that flat systems have little generative capacity. One interesting characteristic of flat belief systems is that they have comparatively few positive contrast (exclusion) relationships. S166 had a total of only nine (compared with 31 for S220 and 30 for Y006). This is related to the 'short implication chain' pattern, and the overall result seems to be a rather poorly developed belief system. It is relevant that the interviewer found S166 to be one of the most reasily biased people she had met, since he seemed to pick up many of the terms that she used. This may be a hint that S166 either did not have any well-developed belief system about occupations, or if he did, was uninterested in revealing it.

The next two cases we shall discuss had similarly flat belief systems.

Y349: a garage service manager, though recently a miner, then a garage mechanic (Figure 5.10)

Y349, S166 and S220 were the three cases with high weights on the second dimension of the INDSCAL solution. From this, one might have expected that their belief systems would show chains of inference which were different from the normal. So far as Y349 is concerned this is not so. His only distinguishing characteristic is the paucity of strict implication and contrast relationships in his data. His total count of exclusion relationships was only four, and eight of the 15 belief elements were unrelated to any of the others. This belief system is not well represented by the logical implications model. There may or may not be any model which will provide an adequate representation for this case.

S180: auctioneer of cars (Figure 5.11)

S180 was the respondent whose data (in the form of gamma coefficients) were worst fit by the INDSCAL model in one, two and also in three dimensions. When examined for evidence of logical relationships between belief elements, the belief system is notable for having only three relationships of positive contrast (exclusion). None of these relationships were strategic and so they are not shown in the figure. In addition to its poverty in

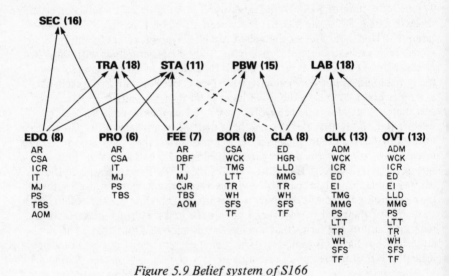

Figure 5.9 Belief system of S166

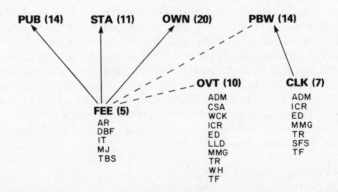

Figure 5.10 Belief system of Y349

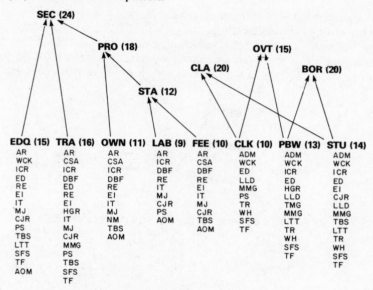

Figure 5.11 Belief system of S180

contrast relationships, the S180 belief system is comparatively 'flat', in the sense that long chains of implications are absent. Furthermore, S180 places the TRA and LAB belief elements in the left-hand side 'professional/ managerial' hierarchy, while most other respondents place them along with 'shop-floor' belief elements. We mentioned earlier that this man threatened to refuse to answer some questions which he connected with 'snobbery', and among these was the 'vote labour' (LAB) sentence frame. S180 mentioned that he would answer, '. . . assuming labour is the popular party', which makes it rather interesting that the nine occupations he identified as having the LAB property also had STA, PRO and SEC. He may possibly have been being deliberately contrary, but it is not clear why he should do so in such a systematic manner with one particular sentence frame.

Y139: sales manager in a car firm and garage (Figure 5.12)

Y139 is an interesting case, for the 'logical implications' representation indicates a larger hierarchy for 'professional/managerial' than for 'shop-floor' belief elements. In the left-hand side of the figure, EDQ implies FEE which in turn implies OWN, which finally implies SEC. Both STU and TRA would usually be attached to the 'shop-floor' hierarchy of beliefs; but for Y139 the only element that each of them implies is SEC. Notice however that STU is in positive contrast with PRO, EDQ and STA. The total count of positive contrast relationships for Y139 is only seven. There is a certain amount of doubt as to which are the organising concepts in Y139's belief system. One might argue for FEE or OWN in the left-hand hierarchy, and for LAB (or possibly CLA) on the right.

The figures do not show relationships of negative contrast. For Y139, this is a rather unfortunate convention, since such relationships exist for the pairs, SEC-CLA, SEC-LAB, OWN-CLA and OWN-LAB. However, negative contrast

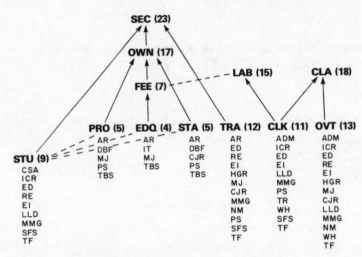

Figure 5.12 Belief system of Y139

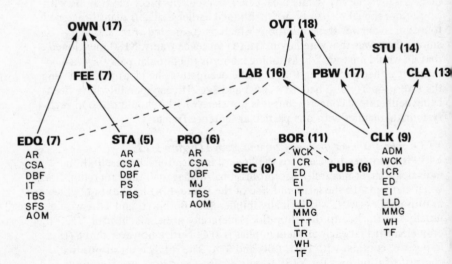

Figure 5.13 Belief system of Y116

relationships are rather difficult to chain together with implication or contrast relationships, and so it is difficult to see how they are useful for explaining the belief system of Y139, or anyone else.

Y116: machine engineer in Ferranti (Figure 5.13)
Like Y006 and Y139, subject Y116 weighted both dimensions of the INDSCAL group cognitive map approximately equally. However, by comparison with Y006's hierarchy of belief elements (which was 'tall' and possessed strategically-placed positive contrast relationships, useful for performing a 'bridging function') the belief system for Y116 was of only moderate hight, and had no positive contrast relationships of any strategic importance (the total count of all positive contrast relationships was 12). TRA was not linked to any other belief element (most likely because Y116 adopted an extremely wide definition of 'trade apprenticeship'). His organising concepts seemed to be FEE (or possibly OWN) on the left, and LAB (or possibly OVT), for 'shop-floor' occupations.

THEMES FROM CONSIDERATIONS OF VARIATION IN INDIVIDUAL BELIEF SYSTEMS

(*a*) The sentence frame data appear to be compatible with a hierarchical type of representation in which some belief elements serve as more general organising concepts.

(*b*) There are individual variations, but the belief elements most commonly used as superordinate concepts were FEE ('. . . send children to a fee-paying school'), and PBW ('. . . paid by the week').

(*c*) Some belief systems are highly organised when examined with the logical implications method, while others are hardly organised at all.

(*d*) Individual differences which were identified by INDSCAL analysis had no obvious counterparts in the logical implications representation of belief systems.

REPRESENTING AVERAGED BELIEF-SYSTEMS

The logical implications method can be applied to aggregated data as well as to the judgements of a single case. In order to do this, we took the data in Table 5.2, which shows for each combination of the 50 sentence frames and 20 occupational titles the percentage of respondents who made an 'Always' judgement. For example, 100 per cent of the sociology students considered that Building Site Labourers, 'get paid overtime for the work they do out of normal hours', and none considered that Building Site Labourers 'are involved in managing people as part of their work'. Where the percentages were in between 0 per cent and 100 per cent we dichotomised them, with 40 per cent and over being considered the presence of a link between occupational title and sentence frame. This choice of cutting-point is to some degree arbitrary, but the logical implications method requires that each sentence frame either is or is not to be considered attached (as a property) to each occupational tiile.

As in the analyses we have shown for individual belief systems, the sentence frames are interpreted as belief elements, and they differ in the degree to which they were seen as applying to occupations. For example ANYONE ('Anyone with average intelligence could do the job . .') was a property of nine out of 20 occupations, while MONEY ('. . earn a great deal of money') was a property of only three of them.

Figure 5.1 gives diagrammatic representation to the logical relationships of implication, contrast and equivalence between 29 of the 50 belief elements. (The remaining 21 belief elements are excluded because they were properties for two or fewer occupations of the 20 used.) The general pattern of Figure 5.14 is similar to that shown for individual subjects (in Figures 5.6 to 5.13). The left-hand side of this average belief system is made up of elements which refer to the characteristics of professional and managerial work, while on the right we have belief elements concerned with unskilled and shop-floor occupations. It is noteworthy that the triplet of belief-elements which relate to the 'helping' occupations (SERVICE, PEOPLE and WKENDS) fall naturally *between* the middle-class and working-class sides of the diagram. (Sentence frames of this kind were not represented in the set of 15 frames used for individual analyses.)

The important higher level concepts that emerge are ANYONE ('. . . could do the job') and PAYWK ('. . . paid by the week') on the right-hand side of the diagram, and MONTH ('. . . paid by the month') on the left. (Perhaps

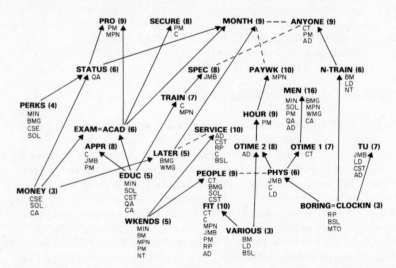

Figure 5.14 An averaged belief system with 29 elements

SERVICE should be included as the superordinate concept for the 'helping' group of belief-elements.) Broadly speaking, working-class types of occupation are attached to belief elements on the right-hand side of the diagram while professional and managerial jobs are found on the left. Male Psychiatric Nurse, Policeman and Carpenter are exceptions to this rule, being attached to various belief elements on both sides of Figures 5.14.

Our purpose in showing Figure 5.14 is heuristic and illustrative. The average belief system we have portrayed might have come out differently if we had used different cutting-points or a different sampling of subjects to generate the data. This particular belief system uses relationships of implication and contrast to show the relationships between concepts. A computer simulation approach to studying occupational belief systems might very well begin here, and proceed by adding other relationships and modifiers, perhaps by using list processing languages and the methods adopted by Quillian. However, that would be a different kind of analysis.

5.4 SUMMARY AND CONCLUSIONS

(i) This chapter has been devoted to considering the 'occupational belief system' in the sense of the implication and contrast rules which link the properties of occupations. Three empirical investigations have been discussed. In the first, respondents simply sorted 50 descriptive phrases about occupations into piles, on the basis of 'those that naturally go together'. Analysis of the data from a large number of respondents suggested that respondents acted as if most descriptive phrases were 'semantically marked' with either an 'upper class' or a 'lower-class' designation. There are strong contrast relationships between upper and lower-class properties of occupations.

(ii) A second investigation used student respondents in a 'sentence frame substitution' task. Each student judged 20 occupational titles as to their applicability in 15 sentence frames. A total of 50 sentence frames were used, the respondents each being assigned a different subset of 15. It was shown how such data can be viewed as 'context-bound' sortings of occupational titles, and therefore as a simple model of the way in which overall similarities between occupations can be generated from lists of the properties of occupations.

(iii) The third empirical investigation was carried out in order to examine implicative as well as contrast relationships, and to test the possibility that the previous treatment of data in aggregated form might conceal important individual differences. To this end, 52 adult respondents were asked to carry out another 'sentence frame substitution' task. This was arranged so that each respondent made judgements of the suitability of 25 occupational titles in each of 15 sentence frames. The occupational belief system of each respondent was then summarised by a set of 105 Goodman-Kruskal gamma coefficients—one to indicate the strength of the reciprocal implication between each pair of the 15 sentence frames. An individual differences scaling analysis of these data showed that except for some 'oddball' cases, the data provided by every respondent could be accounted for in terms of their making use of a very simple 'two-cluster configuration' in two dimensions, the two clusters being interpretable as 'upper-class' and 'lower-class'.

(iv) There were individual differences which were statistically related to the age of the respondents. The data of some subjects could very easily be accounted for in one dimension, while the data of other subjects required two dimensions if they were to fit the overall group configuration without distortion. It was concluded that the major individual difference in this sample of subjects lay in the simplicity and consistency of .the decision rule they used in deciding whether the sentence frames were or were not applicable to the various occupational titles. Some respondents appeared to use a very simple social class-based decision rule, and to do so with great consistency. A respondent of this kind would have his belief system summarised as a set of 105 gamma coefficients, each of which tended towards either— 1.00 (strong inverse implication; if A then not B); or +1.00 (strong implication; if A then B). Such a respondent's data would be scaled as two tight clusters in one dimension.

Other respondents were characterised by sets of gamma coefficients whose values were fairly evenly spread between the logically possible extreme values of plus or minus one. The scaling solutions for respondents of this kind are much less likely to be one-dimensional, but it is not immediately clear what inferences can be made from such data to the characteristics of the belief system which produced it. Two candidate explanations are as follows:

(a)   A simple decision rule being used inconsistently due to the belief system's being complex enough to have superordinate rules concerning exceptions, ranges of convenience and so forth (i.e. rules about other rules and when those other rules can be applied).

(b)   A simple or complex decision rule being used inconsistently due to the respondent's being tired, or ignorant of what was required in the sentence frame task, or simply contrary. Since the data were in fact collected by carefully trained interviewers, and respondents' comments as they carried out the sorting and sentence frame substitution tasks were recorded, we have evidence to support the first explanation rather than the second.

(v) The belief systems for selected subjects were drawn out as hierarchical schemes by a technique which shows the relationships of implication and contrast between belief elements, in such a way as to represent a structured memory. Analysis of individual differences showed that respondents generally shared the same basic pattern in which middle and working class jobs are opposed to one another. The main differences were to do with some belief systems having more contrast relations than others, and with the lengths of implication-chains (nested subsettings) being greater in some belief systems than in others.

One weakness of our work on belief systems in this chapter is that we have confined ourselves to *logical* implication and *logical* exclusion (contrast) relationships. In future work, we should wish to explore other and less formalisable kinds of implication, such as associative or sequential (linkages). We should also want to use operators which modify the actions of other relationships. Empirical analysis would be difficult or impossible with models of the required complexity, and we are led to propose computer simulation approaches to the modelling of occupational belief systems.

6 Subjective Aspects of Occupational Structure

The researches we have been reporting upon were started in 1971. Our first working paper outlined our basic concerns with the subjective or 'mental' aspects of occupations. We were concerned:

1.   that sociologists often appeared to view the occupational structure as having objective, 'given', quality – an easily measurable, countable and palpable manifestation of social constraint.
2.   that the only 'subjective' aspect of occupations that sociologists appeared to be interested in was a variously defined phenomenon called 'occupational prestige'.
3.   that sociologists had a grossly over-simple model of the processes by which people make prestige judgements. The sociological notion of a 'grading operation' left out what we felt to be an important distinction between cognitive and evaluative processes.
4.   that the evidence cited in support of theoretically important propositions concerning between-society agreements about occupation prestige hierarchies was methodologically suspect, in that it depended upon insufficiently sensitive techniques for measurement and for aggregation.
5.   Finally, that sociologists seemed to treat the subjective aspects of occupations as derivative, citing public opinion surveys of occupation prestige in order to give credence to their scales of 'socioeconomic status', but refusing to take seriously any notion that 'subjective' factors could be anything other than dependent upon the 'objective' structure of occupations. We ourselves have been accused of psychologism and worse.

As it turned out, our work fell naturally into two parts, so much so that each half was funded by a different research grant, took place over a different time-period, and ended up as a separate book. In the discussion which follows, we shall refer to the first book (*The Images of Occupational Prestige*) as *Image* and we shall refer to the present one simply as 'this book'. There is a distinct shift of emphasis, as one moves from the material presented in *Images* to that covered in the present book. In *Images,* we reported upon data collected as paired and triadic judgements of similarity, and upon invidious comparisons between occupations made by ranking and rating methods. In this book, we discuss unconstrained and also hierarchical sortings data, and we use a sentence frame substitution task as well. There are contrasts in the style of analysis as well, for we used techniques of multidimensional scaling a great deal in *Images*, but much less so in the present book. It may be fair to say that *Images* represents our being seduced into a rather conventional sociological application of new techniques to a long-standing problem area (the study of prestige judgements), and that the second book is a more accurate reflection of our basic interests in the subjective aspects of occupations.

In *Images*, our attention was focused upon matters which have concerned sociologists for many years – the measurement of occupational images, and the collection and analysis of data on occupational rank orderings. Our treatment of these topics was novel from the methodological point of view, but our substantive questions were much the same as those of other sociologists. We wanted to find a valid scheme for representing images (both cognitive and evaluative), and we wanted to look for systematic differences between social groups. Since *Images* went to the printers, we have received valuable criticisms and suggestions from colleagues and students. Furthermore, a number of important books and papers have been published over this period, and as happens in academic life, we have become aware of work which had been available for many years but which had escaped our attention. We shall use the opportunity which this review offers, in order to correct some ambiguities of presentation and to insert references to relevant further work.

One of the objections most strongly made against our research (both in *Images*, and in the present book) has been aimed at our procedures for sampling subjects. One anonymous reviewer captured this feeling when he wrote;

The data base here is not in keeping with the scale of the problem addressed. A few males in Edinburgh are asked to evaluate a few occupations in terms of prestige, earnings, societal usefulness and deserved rewards. Who cares ?

It is not difficult to crush this objection. Had we wished to make statistical generalisations to some (say national) population, it would have been essential that we allow every member of the population to have a known (and non-zero) probability of being included in the sample. However, as even a cursory reading of our work will show, our aims have been partly to produce empirically based counter-examples to very general propositions made by other sociologists (our position is similar here to that of the *Affluent Worker* group), and partly also to use our data in heuristic, illustrative and exploratory style. Neither of these research objectives required us to draw a properly random sample. The procedures that we did use were more along the lines of what Arnold (1974) has called 'dimensional sampling'.

Another charge, that of psychologism, may perhaps stem from our repeated references (in *Images*) to the work of de Soto and his colleagues on a general psychological bias towards the complete linear ordering as a conceptual good figure. In particular, we argued that sociologists have been more biased than the individuals they have studied, in their tendency to represent occupations as being ranked in a linear ordering. A further consequence of these perceptual biases is the prediction (confirmed by Alexander, 1972) that the closer observers themselves are to the bottom of a status ordering, the smaller is the spread of their status judgements about positions in that ordering. People at the bottom see a shorter scale of social status than the subjective scale seen by people at the top. These 'psychologistic' principles have recently been examined for their sociological implications by Lindenbergh (1977). He argues the existence of a cumulative pattern of effects, such that the lower one is placed on a rank order (i.e. the less power and resources one has), then the fewer categories (or social classes) one is likely to distinguish on the rank order. Granting this, the low 'objective' position leads to cognitive distortions (false consciousness), which inhibit any actions being taken to break out of the 'objectively' low position. While we do not take over Lindenberg's conclusions *holus bolus,* his independent discovery of the sociological implications of de Soto's work is encouraging.

Now a sin of omission, which fortunately turns out to be merely venial. We devoted some space in *Images* to a discussion of the differing social positions occupied by physicians in communist as opposed to capitalist countries. Our point was that the calculation of profile correlations between different countries' prestige hierarchies (a conventional sociological method) can be insensitive to important differences, because these differences tend to be overlaid by many basic agreements about such things as skilled jobs being better than unskilled jobs. Several colleagues have granted this methodological point, but have wondered that we failed to mention the work of Marie Haug, on comparative aspects of deprofessionalisation, and what she calls 'the revolt of the client'. Haug (1976) points to the effects upon the amount of deference accorded to primary care physicians, of such factors as the age and educational level of patients, in different places and at different time periods, the largely female personnel in primary medical practice in the USSR, and the fact that British general practitioners have shifted from individual practice, with fees being paid for services, to being all but salaried employees of the state, operating mostly in group practices (often from health centres), and functioning to a large extent as gatekeepers to non-medical benefits. Haug's findings square very well with our view that occupational status is in an important sense 'negotiated', both in social interaction, and at the institutional level.

The fourth chapter of *Images* concentrated upon evaluative judgements of occupations. We used rather simple techniques of ranking and of rating in 'marks out of 100' in order to collect such data, and it has been suggested that we might have done better to use the 'magnitude estimation' type of instructions as introduced to sociology by Hamblin. This data collection method supposedly generates evaluative measurements which are on a ratio scale. We chose not to follow Hamblin's example, partly because we wished to replicate the traditional sociological technique for prestige measurement, and partly because we found it difficult to agree with Hamblin's theoretical position that judgements of social status are nothing but responses to objectively defined stimuli, such as levels of income, or amounts of education. It is all the more interesting then, that Baker (1977) has used the Hamblin approach, and has reached conclusions similar to certain of ours. Baker focuses particularly on the so-called 'aggregation problem'. He argues (as we do) for the averaging of *parameters* derived from the fitting of specified models to to individual-level arrays of data, rather than for the traditional technique of separately averaging the scores given to single stimuli, and then fitting a model to the set of aggregated data points. This latter method can only give valid results when there is very high consensus between subjects; and, as the empirical evidence reported by Baker and by ourselves shows, such consensus is lacking. Baker shows, among other things, that improper aggregation tends to produce inflated values for certain correlation coefficients. He also notes that there is no strong theory predicting the existence of high consensus about the criteria for status evaluation — to the contrary indeed, symbolic interactionists and conflict theorists argue precisely the reverse.

We have received somewhat mixed reactions to our treatment of rank orderings as 'directional data'. On one hand, there have been congratulations for our importation into sociology of a method which solves the aggregation problem in an attractive way. On the other hand, it has been assumed that since a procedure very similar to one-way analysis of variance exists for directional data, there must also exist directional analogies to the analysis of covariance and to two-, threee-, or higher-way analysis of variance. Sociologists who have made this assumption have chided us for failing to use (for example) two-way analysis of covariance for some of the analysis in Chapter 4 of *Images*. Unfortunately, the assumption is incorrect. Directional data can be subjected to statistical analysis by a technique which is closely analogous to one-way analysis of variance, but this is a coincidence. The statistical theory for the multivariate analysis of directional data is by no means well-developed by comparison with that for the linear model. (See T4.7 for details.)

One of our original aims was to show the existence of socially patterned differences in the ways people interpret, think about, and make comparisons between occupations. We have succeeded in the modest aim of showing that such differences do indeed exist, and this is by no means trivial, for it provides a set of counterexamples to the conventional sociological wisdom in this field. What we have not done is to give a complete account of the social processes by which such differences in occupational cognition and evaluation might arise. We have provided what may turn out to be suggestive hints, in noting the associations between summary indices of occupational thinking and such factors as the educational level of the respondent, the degree to which he works with other people as opposed to working with data or things, his age, and more generally the pattern of his life history. We have also drawn attention to the role of historical, political and institutional factors in determining the overall social status level of occupations. Finally we have drawn attention to the seemingly general social-psychological principles which influence the descriptive and evaluative judgements of people who are situated higher or lower in some hierarchy of inequality.

Many of our colleagues would like us to combine these fragmentary insights and tentative conclusions into a fully-fledged structural equation model of the kind brought into the sociological literature by Blalock and Duncan. Such a model would use arrow diagrams to show the causal effects of one series of variables upon sundry indices of occupational cognition and evaluation. We resist such premature formalisation for a number of technical and theoretical reasons. First, we feel that this theoretical tradition tends to shape theory-development into a confirmatory, rather than into an exploratory mode, and we would rather pursue further exploration at present. Second, the structural equations tradition emphasises the importance of reliably measured exogenous variables (the 'uncaused causers' necessary in such models). Since measures of cognitive structure are difficult to measure at all (though none the less important for that), structural equations modellers tend to see them as being dependent variables at the end of some more or less complex causal chain. There seem to be tendencies in the technical substructure of this kind of formalisation which perpetuate the theoretical view that 'subjective' aspects of social structure are merely epiphenomena of the more palpable 'objective' aspects. As will be apparent from the first two chapters of *Images,* we would wish to avoid this viewpoint. A third reason for our not embarking upon path analysis is technical and statistical. For reasons discussed at length in Chapter 4 of *Images* we preferred to treat evaluative orderings of any set of occupations as *directions* over a two-or three-dimensional cognitive map. This procedure has a number of theoretical and technical advantages, but as we have remarked earlier in this chapter, the computation of partial correlations and partial regression coefficients is not a well-defined operation with directional data.

One of the more obvious hallmarks of our research both in *Images* and in the present book, has been the metaphor of a cognitive map, and the associated use of multidimensional scaling methods. Some readers may view such techniques as being merely a new kind of factor analysis, of little substantive relevance for sociological theory. Naturally, we disagree with such a pessimistic view. Those scaling models which contain parameters for individual differences (in particular, the INDSCAL-related models), now make it possible for sociologists to operationalise their intuitive notions about different social groups' perceptions of the 'same' social facts. Another useful point is the already-mentioned technique for scaling rank orders into the form of direction data, thus 'metricising' what were originally ordinal data, achieving a degree of data reduction, and also obtaining what we have called 'appropriate aggregation. Like any other technique, multidimensional scaling can be used well or ill. Factor analysis (a special case of multidimensional scaling) has suffered in reputation, not only for technical reasons, but also because of the speculative interpretations that social scientists have made of their factor analytic results.

We would argue that our own uses of multidimensional scaling methods are free of most technical difficulties. More important, we have taken great care to incorporate the verbalisations that our subjects made while being interviewed, directly into the interpretations made of our scaling results. Thus our interpretation of the 'horseshoe' configuration in Chapter 3 of *Images* is objective rather than speculative. In the same way, the scaling and hierarchical clustering analyses that are reported in Chapters 2 and 3 of the present book are given meaning by using the verbal descriptions that the subjects themselves had provided for their own clusters of occupational titles. By our general method, it is possible to investigate, rather than merely to guess at, the semantic characteristics of an overall cognitive map.

It will be apparent that the present book has been concerned with the problem of how one might represent occupational images. Many of the semantic representations we have given have been in the form of cognitive maps in the form of a continuous two-or three-dimensional Euclidean space, or alternatively in the form of strict hierarchies. Neither of these is wholly satisfactory. For example, we have found the strictly hierarchical representation to be a useful way of capturing the notion of higher-level organising concepts in occupational thinking, but we are very conscious of the oversimplifications this entails. As Glass (1975) notes:

> Though language meaning is tantalisingly hierarchical, it is just cross-referential enough to vitiate an attempt to capture meaning in strict hierarchies. (p.61)

This book consists of detailed empirical analysis, rather than the modelling or simulation enterprises in which the point made by Glass would be of crucial relevance. The early chapters deal with how subjects treat occupationally relevant stimuli in unconstrained and in hierarchically organised clustering tasks. We paid considerable attention to the strategies our subjects used in carrying out the sorting tasks, and also to their comments and their verbal descriptions of the clusters. Perhaps one of the more striking findings was that the content of a sorting often tells a completely different story from the verbal descriptions used by the subjects at the time. Some people, for example, claimed that social class had no place in their thinking and then proceeded to use it liberally. The various chapters of this book have focused, in different ways, upon finding out what higher-level organising categories of though were being used by our subjects. Social class of course is viewed by sociologists as a prototypical generalising concept. The chapters describing the sortings data showed that when men are given some quite complex and different tasks to carry out with occupational titles, they come up with a wide range of sociological distinctions. Overt social class imagery is comparatively infrequent, but terms such as 'skill', 'qualifications', 'training', 'pay', and various aspects of status appear to be the everyday versions of what sociologists would conflate into 'social class'. However, a careful textual analysis of our data on subjects' verbalisations shows that people use these class-related concepts in rather strictly delimited contexts, and at different levels of semantic generality. Chapter 4 shows that even where social class terminology is used, it tends to be restricted to saying that a given occupation belongs in a given social class. Such 'belongingness' judgements tell little about the cognitive structure concerned, except that social class membership is used as an attribute of occupations. We pursue the topic into the realm of 'belief systems' in Chapter 5, where the sentence-frame data show that considerable individual differences exist. Some representations of individual belief systems very clearly make use of social class as an organising concept, while others ignore the possibility, even when it is obviously an available one.

Further research in occupational cognition and evaluation might proceed in a number of directions. We note that the choice of units and levels of analysis will be important. For example, our own interests are in the images of occupations in the heads of individual persons. Sociologists whose interests are in measuring the social status levels of individuals would be foolhardy to confine their concerns to the prestige aspects of occupations.

1. Data already gathered on the perception of occupations should be re-analysed in the light of recent technical and theoretical advances of the kind discussed in our books. Our own data are publicly available, as are those of some other scholars.

2. There should be further research for correlates of individual differences in occupational thinking. We confined our own investigation to men, even though there are good reasons to expect sex differences. More generally, we have been dissatisfied with our failure to make a tractable 'variable' out of the theoretically appealing notion of 'occupational life history'. At the time we planned our research, we were unaware of Kohn and Schooler's (1973) work on the effects of job experiences upon psychological functioning, but future research might well combine our approach with his.

3. We should like to see direct replication of many aspects of our study. In particular, we are not satisfied that we managed to obtain a sufficient number of subjects from a truly working-class background. We should also wish to arrange sampling procedures in such a way that explicit age-constrasts were built into the design of the investigation. An extension of our basic research design to a quite different culture (for example to a rapidly urbanising and industrialising country such as Nigeria) would be of great interest.

4. We have many worries about the degree to which our research has (like too much sociology) become centred upon the characteristics of individual persons, and has therefore tended to ignore properly collective representations, and the emergent processes of social interaction. While our treatment of language and meaning in Chapter 4 of this book goes some way toward a treatment of how talk emerges from the social interaction between inter-viewer and respondent, we have hardly begun to tackle this important area. In future research, we should like to see explored the possibilities of 'group

interviews' in various formats. A number of subjects would be seated in each other's presence, and be asked to come to agreement about answers to a series of questions about occupational descriptions and evaluations. The focus of interest would be upon analysis of audio-tape and video-tape recordings of these discussions. Such an approach could easily be extended to include real or simulated situations of conflict, such as occur in industrial relations.

5. We have reported our analyses of the content of subjects' verbalisations in Chapter 4 of this book. This adds one more to the small number of applications of the *General Inquirer* system for computer-aided content analysis. One very promising line of further research would be the use of some kind of content analysis upon transcriptions of discourse involving occupations. The panel game *What's my Line?* is an intriguing example, as are the official transcripts of official and semi-official proceedings. Such transcripts are available in large numbers, and even though they have had indications of paralinguistic phenomena edited out, they furnish many examples of the situations in which appeals to occupationally-based expertise are or are not made, and they also show more general aspects of occupational imagery.

6. A final direction for further research would be the design of a computer system which could 'understand' occupational titles and occupational predicates — 'understand' in the sense that it could respond to the input of conventional English sentences by outputting sensible replies. We have already given the example of Quillian's scheme for representing 'semantic memory' in his Teachable Language Comprehender. Quillian's approach attempts to model what might be called 'cold' cognition, but so far as we are concerned with modelling the occupational ideologies held by individuals and by social groups, it will be necessary to include evaluative processes and 'hot' cognition in our model. Abelson's (1973) on simulating right-wing political ideology may be relevant to this enterprise, though the purposiveness that his model imputes to the actors represented in the belief system may have no counterpart in our representation of an occupational ideology. Other difficulties present themselves as well, since it is not immediately clear how one would represent cognitive biases of the kind shown to exist by Lindenberg and ourselves.

We should like to close this book with some general reflections on methodology and the incorporation of subjective in sociology.

Sociology is a fragmented discipline, as full of fads now as it was when Sorokin wrote thirty years ago. Much of our work can be fairly construed as a critique of what has passed for positivism in sociology — the design and analysis of large-scale sample surveys of national populations. We find ourselves unsympathetic to the way in which such studies atomise the subject matter of sociology. We also find ourselves embarrassed by their crude methods for quantification, and by the way in which meaning is systematically excised from quantified data, to be replaced by the sociologist's speculations upon aggregated versions of those data. Those who would include the beliefs and values held by social actors as essential parts of sociological theories are obliged to treat subjective meanings seriously, whether or not they follow the methods we have developed in this book. Thus we nail our colours, not to the use of multidimensional scaling programmes (as unfriendly critics might suggest), but to the proper place of language and meaning in accounts of social behaviour.

Notes

Chapter 1

1. Neisser (1967:281), for instance, points out that Freud's notion of 'cathexis' explicitly involves the arousal of something which already exists. This and similar preconceptions enter centrally into Parsons' account of the 'unit act'.

2. A similar point is made by Tagiuri (1969:397) in the context of person perception.

3. A readable and lively introduction to many central issues in artificial intelligence will be found in Minsky and Papert 1972.

4. The inclusion of plans (Miller, Galanter and Pribram 1960) is justified on the grounds that it has been shown that associations, attributes and plans are homogeneously representable as data (Newell 1968) and that their inclusion makes the *purposive* characteristics of images quite explicit.

5. For example, Chomsky's (1965) transformational grammer, Colby's (Tesler *et al.* 1968, Colby 1973), neurotic belief system model, Abelson's (1965, 1973) political ideology model, Quillian's (1968) semantic networks and Anderson and Bower's (1973) associative-memory model.

6. To some extent this problem can be circumvented by the use of a number of three-way scaling models, including factor analysis (Tucker 1963), canonical decomposition (Carroll and Chang 1969) models, and Procrustean individual differences scaling (Borg and Lingoes 1976).

7. The most telling test-bed for the analysis of human communication occurs in the development of natural language question-answering systems in artificial intelligence. Here it is evident that the semantic interpreter (aided by syntactic and pragmatic elements) performs a primary role. Despite the important and serious differences separating Winograd, Shank and Wilks, their systems are primarily semantically-based. See Schank and Colby (eds) 1973, sections 2.5.

8. The only systematic source, referred to by opponent and supporter alike, is the influential paper by Katz and Fodor (1963), which is written entirely with the assumption that 'semantics takes over the explanation of the speaker's ability to produce and understand new sentences *at the point where grammar leaves off*' (pp. 172-3, emphasis added).

9. We are here using the 'High *v.* Low Educational Requirements' factor (I:66-7) as a surrogate for the social class contrast.

10. Occupations in Quadrants C and D were matched most closely by U.K. Census Socio-Economic Groups (SEGs) 8, 9 and 11 (Foremen and Supervisors, manual, Skilled manual workers; Unskilled manual workers).

11. Occupations in Quadrants A and B were matched by SEGs 3 and 4 (Professional workers, self employed; Professional workers, employers).

12. The Final Report of the Project (referenced as SSRC Grant HR 1883/2) contains much of this information, and was lodged in the British Library, Boston Spa, in 1976. It is available through inter-library loan.

Chapter 2

1. 'Group', 'cluster', 'class', and 'category' are used interchangeably to refer to a subset of the subject's partition and 'element' and 'object' refer to the constituent members. The terms 'grouping', 'sorting' 'categorisation' and 'classification' are used as synonyms of the partition itself.

2. This is Arabie and Boorman's '1-NT/1+2' measure, a 'strong' normalisation based upon dividing the pairbonds value by the arithmetic mean of the height of the two constituent sortings $1/NT-1+2 = $ pairbonds/ $(h(P) + h(Q))$.

3. A similar problem arises in deciding on the most appropriate stopping-point for specifying blocks of structurally equivalent individuals in blockmodels of social networks (White *et al.* 1976).

4. Both connectedness and diameter solutions were used in the analysis, but since the solutions were virtually identical structurally, only the one (the connectedness) solution is reported here.

Chapter 3

1. But not in cultural authroplogy, where folk taxonomies have been collected for some time. The most similar parallel, however, occurs in psycholinguistics in the work of Fillenbaum and Rapoport (1971). They instruct subjects to form a similarity graph, which may or may not be a hierarchy. However, they do not analyse the intact individual graphs.

2. An explanation of the choice of occupation names is given in our first volume (pp. 66-9) and in fuller detail in the third, Chapter 2. The titles used in this task and their abbreviations are as follows:

1	Church of Scotland Minister	(MIN)
2	Comprehensive School Teacher	(CST)
3	Qualified Actuary	(QA)
4	Chartered Accountant	(CA)
5	Male Psychiatric Nurse	(MPN)
6	Ambulance Driver	(AD)
7	Building Site Labourer	(BSL)
8	Machine Tool Operator	(MTO)
9	Country Solicitor	(SOL)
10	Civil Servant (Executive Grade)	(CSE)
11	Commercial Traveller	(CT)
12	Policeman	(PM)
13	Carpenter	(C)
14	Lorry Driver	(LD)
15	Railway Porter	(RP)
16	Barman	(BM)

3. Up to the seventh level, the minimum and maximum HCS trees are (ordinally)equivalent. Beyond this level, the only difference, apart from trivial inversions in the order of chaining, is the location of Commercial Traveller. In view of its ambiguous position this occupation will be ignored in the following discussion.

4. The content (or entries) of a theme differ slightly from branch to branch, and even within a sub-tree. Thus, 'business profession' is only used in this sub-tree, and 'caring profession' is only used in sub-tree (iv). A full specification of this and other themes will be found in U3. 12.

5. Following each key term in this and other themes is the category specification (content tags) in the Harvard IV-3 Content Analysis Dictionary: see U4.3.

6. cf: 'Skill' in this sense is defined as 'Practical knowledge in combination with ability; cleverness, expertise' by the Oxford English Dictionary, and 'Skilled' is defined by the Concise Oxford Dictionary (1975) as '. . . (of worker) highly trained or experienced'.

Chapter 4

1. No entirely accurate or acceptable set of rules for lemmatisation (reducing inflected words to root form) has yet been developed. The numbers here are based upon the rather crude, but surprisingly serviceable, suffix-chopping procedures in the WORDS system (Iker 1974, 1976).

2. There is an extended debate about the precise form of the law and its synthetic nature (cf Mandelbrot 1966, and Herdan 1966: 438 *et seq.* for a highly critical view). In any event, the differences are too refined to affect analysis here.

3. Further detailed information can be obtained from Stone *et al.* (1966) on the original Harvard Dictionary, from Kelly and Stone (1975) and Coxon and Trappes—Lomax (1977) on the Harvard IV Dictionary, and from Dunphy *et al.* (1975) on the Sydney version.

4. Kelly and Stone (1975) point out that the number of word senses distinguished tends to vary with the size of the Dictionary.

5. Kelly (1970) and Kelly and Stone (1975) provide a full account of the disambiguation and lemmatisation procedures used by the Inquirer III system.

6. In fact, the Dictionary can be thought of in two ways – like a conventional dictionary (in which a word is divided into its distinct meanings, each of which is then defined by its semantic categories) or as a thesaurus (in which categories are specified by the word-senses which instantiate it).

7. I am very grateful to Mr Chris Baker of the Department of Industrial Relations, University College, Cardiff, for permission to use his Oakdale and Powell Duffryn material in this way, and to Dr Bob Towler of the Department of Sociology, University of Leeds, for permission to use the first set of letters of the *Honest to God* correspondence.

8. This is an entirely pragmatic decision, but a reasonable one. With the exception of major parts of speech such as verbs (which normally represent just over one fifth of words appearing in a text) nearly all tag percentages are between 0 and 5%. Fuller tag-tally information is presented un U4.7.

9. This also suggests a simpler hybrid task: to begin by asking the subject simply to form groups (as in the free-sorting task) and then go on to merge them successively into a single group,

10. Bernstein also expected to find the pronominal use of 'one' to be a characteristic of middle-class usage, since it often reflects the *differentiation* of one's own experience from the subject of discourse, and would therefore

be an instance of elaborated coding. But he did not find such use. In our data, there are eleven instances of the use of 'one' in this way, and all but one of these are in unimpeachably middle-class mouths. The Harvard IV disambiguation rules recognise this pronominal use as ONE2, but it turns out to be very hard to specify; many identifications are incorrect.

11. This corresponds fairly closely to Hawkins' (1977:155-67) distinction between 'Tentative' and Non-tentative (Factual, Naming) contexts.

12. Our thanks to Mary McPherson, who first brought this point to our attention.

13. A remark I attribute (I think correctly) to Professor Patrick Meredith of Leeds University, but originally made in the context of intelligence test scores.

Chapter 5

1. Word-association experiments usually consist of presenting a stimulus word to the subject, who then responds with the first word he thinks of. Evidence of cultural prescription, or preference at least, in association is given in the fact that the distribution of the associates of any one word is very markedly skew — i.e. although a wide range of words can be, and is associated with a given concept, the associates tend either to be very frequent indeed, or very idiosyncratic and rare. Moreover, there is evidence of culturally similar organisation of associates given by recall experiments where subjects are asked to recall lists of previously presented, randomised, words — randomised to remove any organising principles. In such studies it is found that regularly repeated grouping of words occurs in terms of superordinate concepts (e.g. blacksmith, baker, printer as 'occupations' among other words in the list such as muskrat, pumpkin, Gerald). There is additional evidence that such clustering is hierarchically structured and based upon semantic principles contained in Miller's rather striking work on the 'subjective lexicon'.

2. Whilst attributes and associations are distinct ways of representing the topology of semantic space, they are not necessarily different when implemented in computer programmes. In list-processing languages, which have been developed to deal with just these sorts of problems, the basic data structure is a *string* or a *list* — a *list* is simply an ordered sequence of elements (e.g. words, symbols, etc.); a string is a list whose elements are not themselves lists. It is the *list structure* which is the most important, for in a list structure the elements themselves may be lists. One particular form of a list structure is the binary tree, which is basically a list structure made up of elements of ordered pairs, either member of which may itself be an ordered pair. In this way, a complex branching structure can be built up. List structures lend themselves readily to the representation of associational data of the sort we have been discussing.

3. As it turned out, the descriptions from CODOT (which is intended to identify the requirements and duties of occupations) appeared rather unlikely to arise in any natural discourse. The material derived from previous interviews varied in type and amount, depending on what tasks were being carried out in the interview.

4. Sentence frame data are like semantic differential data in their formal structure, but the methods of analysis developed for sentence frames are quite different from the factor analytic techniques used by Osgood.

5. The technical details of parametric mapping are discussed in Appendix U5.1 (to our third volume, forthcoming).

6. The INDSCAL model is discussed in T3.12, and the details of this particular analysis are given in Y5.7.

7. Comparisons between configurations obtained with PARAMAP, INDSCAL and MINISSA are made in U5.2.

8. The INDSCAL model is discussed in T3.12.

9. Assignments of individuals to quadrants is shown in U5.3, and analysis of variance tables are shown in U5.4.

10. D'Andrade (1976), who is the first author we know of to use the logical implications presentation, adopts rather a weak definition of the implication/submission relationship, in that he allows up to three exceptions to occupy what ought to be the 'empty cell', before he considers a relationship to be not an implication. Throughout this chapter, we used a strong definition for the implication/submission relationship. However, D'Andrade's practice has a certain intuitive appeal, in the sense that people often seem to have mental rules for which thay make one or two exceptions.

11. Tabular representations for all the belief systems referred to in this chapter are given in U5.5. It should be noted that all the diagrammatic representations of belief systems shown in this chapter have been to some degree simplified. The complete information is given in the tabular presentations.

List of Computer Program Abbreviations

1. *Acronyms of multidimensional scaling models* used in this volume and computer programs implementing them (Edinburgh-Cardiff MDS (X) Programs): documentation available from Program Library Unit, University of Edinburgh.

HICLUS (or HCS)
:   *Hierarchical Clustering Schemes*; analysis of a square symmetric data matrix using a non-metric inclusional clustering model (Johnson 1967).
    Originator: S.C. Johnson, Bell Laboratories
    (Sections 2.4, 2.5, 3.4)

INDSCAL
:   *Individual Differences Scaling*; by a weighted Euclidean distance model (Carroll and Chang 1969).
    Originator: J.D. Carrol, Bell Laboratories
    (Section 5.3)

IDIOSCAL
:   *Individual Differences in Orientation Scaling*; analysis of sets of square symmetric (three-way) data matrices by a distance model, allowing idiosyncratic rotation and weighting of reference axes (Carroll and Wish 1975).
    Originator: J.D. Carroll, Bell Laboratories
    (Section 5.3)

MINISSA
:   *Smallest Space Analysis*, of a square symmetric data matrix using a non-metric distance model (Roskam 197
    Originator: E.E. Roskam, Nijmegen University
    (Sections 2.3, 2.5, 3.3, 3.4, 5.2)

PARAMAP
:   *Parametric Mapping*; analysis of a rectangular row conditional matrix, finding a configuration such that the data are related to the solution by a function which is as smooth and continuous as possible (Shepard and Carroll 1966).
    Originators: R.N. Shepard, Stanford University and J.D. Carroll, Bell Laboratories
    (Section 5.2)

2. Other Program Packages

INQR (or Inquirer III)	*The General Inquirer, III* (Edinburgh version). A series of linked programs for the content analysis of natural language text, using the Harvard IV Psycho-Sociological dictionary. The Edinburgh version is documented in Coxon and Trappes-Lomax (1977), Program Library Unit, Edinburgh. *Originators*: Canonical version: P.J. Stone, Harvard University; Australian Version: D. Dunphy, University of New South Wales; British version: A.P.M. Coxon, University of Wales (Sections 3.5, 4.2, 4.3, 4.4, 4.5)
COCOA (CONCOR) (Concordance)	*Count and Concordance generation on Atlas.* A program to carry out a number of text-processing operations, centred chiefly upon the production of concordances (Berry-Rogghe and Crawford 1973). *Originators*: G.L.M. Berry-Rogghe, Atlas Computer Laboratory, and T.D. Crawford, University College, Cardiff (Sections 3.5, 4.1, 4.2)
WORDS	A system library of subroutines from which the user selects a sequence of programs. Designed primarily for the analysis of the associative structure in natural text (Iker 1974). *Originator*: H.P. Iker, University of Rochester, N.Y. (Sections 4.1, 4.3)

Technical Appendixes (in Third Book)

References

Abelson, R.P., and J.D. Carroll (1965). 'Computer simulation of individual belief systems', *Am. Beh. Scientist, 8,* 24-30.

Abelson, R.P. (1973). 'The structure of belief systems', in R.C. Shank and K.M. Colby (eds), *Computer models of thought and language.* San Francisco W.H. Freeman, 287-339.

Alexander, C.N. (1972). 'Status perceptions', *Am. Sociol. Rev., 37,* 767-73.

Amarel, S. (1968). 'On representations of problems of reasoning about actions', in D. Michie (ed.) *Machine intelligence, III.* Edinburgh: University Press.

Anderson, A.B. (1969). 'Structural assumptions of semantic space; a nonmetric multidimensional scaling analysis', Working Paper 21, Institute for the Study of Social Change, Purdue University.

Anderson, J.R., and G.H. Bower (1973). *Human associative memory.* London: John Wiley.

Anglin, J.A. (1970). *The growth of word meaning.* London: MIT Press.

Arabie, P., and S.A. Boorman (1973). 'Multidimensional scaling of measures of distance between partitions', *Journ. Math. Psychol., 10,* 148-203.

Arnold, D.O. (1974). 'Dimensional sampling: an approach for studying a small number of cases', *The American Sociologist, 5,* 147-50.

Atkinson, J.W. (1958). *Motives in fantasy, action and society: a method of assessment and study.* Princeton: Van Nostrand.

Baker, P.M. (1977). 'The use of psycho physical methods in the study of social status: a replication and some theoretical problems', *Social Forces, 55,* 898-920.

Bannister, D., and J. Mair (1969). *The evaluation of personal constructs.* London: Academic Press.

Barnes, B., and J. Law (1976). 'Whatever should be done with indexical expressions ?', *Theory and Society, 3,* 223-37.

Batstone, E. (1974). 'Organizational size and class imagery', in M.I.A. Bulmer (ed.), *Working class images of society.* London: Routledge.

Berlin, B., D.E. Breedlove and P.H. Raven (1968). 'Covert categories and folk taxonomies', *Am. Anthrop., 70,* 290-9.

Bernstein, B. (1958). 'Some sociological determinants of perception. An inquiry into sub-cultural differences', *Brit. Journ. Sociol., 9,* 159-74 (reprinted in Fishman 1968).

——(1972a). Elaborated and restricted codes: their social origins and some consequences', in Gumperz and Hymes 1972.

——(1972b). 'A sociolinguistic approach to socialization', in Gumperz and Hymes 1972.

References

——(1962). 'Social class, linguistic codes and grammatical elements', *Language and Speech, 5,* 221-40.

——(1967).'Elaborated and restricted codes: an outline', *Sociol. Inquiry* (1967) 36, (2). Reprinted in Lieberson 1967.

——(ed.) (1973). *Class, Codes and Control, vol 2: Applied studies towards a sociology of language.* London: Routledge.

Berry-Rogghe, G.L.M., and T.D. Crawford (1973). *COCOA Manual: A word count and concordance generator.* Didcot and Cardiff: Atlas Laboratory and University College.

Boorman, S.A., and P. Arabie (1972). 'Structural measures and the method of sorting', in R.N. Shepard *et al., Multidimensional scaling: theory and applications in the behavioral sciences,* vol.1. London: Seminar Press.

Boorman, S.A., and D.C. Oliver (1973). 'Metrics on spaces of finite trees', *Journ. Math. Psychol., 10,* 26-59

Borg, I., and J.C. Lingoes (1976). 'A direct transformational approach to multidimensional analysis of three-way data matrices', Ann Arbor: Michigan Mathematical Psychology Program, Technical Report MMPP 76-1.

Bower, G.H., M.C. Clark, A.M. Lesgold and D. Wingenz (1969). 'Hierarchical retrieval schemes in recall of categorized word lists', *Journ. Verb. Learning and Verb. Beh., 8,* 323-43.

Boyd, J.P. (1971). 'Componential analysis and the substitution property', in P. Kay (ed.), *Explorations in mathematical anthropology.* London: MIT Press.

Brown, R.W. (1958). 'Is a boulder sweet or sour ?', *Contemp. Psychol, 3,* 113-15.

Buchler, I.R., and H.A. Selby (1968). *Kinship and social organization* New York: Macmillan.

Bulmer, M.I.A. (ed.) (1975). *Working class images of society.* London: Routledge & Kegan Paul.

Burling, R. (1964). 'Cognition and componential analysis: God's truth or hocus-pocus ?', *Am.Anthrop., 66,* 20-8.

Burton, M.L. (1972). 'Semantic dimensions of occupation names', in A.K. Romney, R.N. Shepard and S. B. Nerlove (eds), *Multidimensional scaling: vol. II applications.* Seminar Press, 55-71.

——(1975). 'Dissimilarity measures for unconstrained sorting data', *Multiv. Beh. Res., 10,* 409-24.

Burton, M.L., and A.K. Romney (1975). 'A multidimensional representation of role terms', *Am.Ethnologist, 2,* 397-407.

Bynner, J., and D. Romney (1972). 'A method for overcoming the problem of concept-scale interaction in semantic differential research', *Br.J.Psychol., 63,* 229-34.

Caplow, T. (1954). *The sociology of work.* Minneapolis: University of Minnesota Press.

Carroll, J.B. (1959). Review of Osgood, Suci and Tannenbaum, *The measurement of meaning* in *Language, 35,* 58-77.

Carroll, J.D. (1976). 'Spatial, non-spatial and hybrid models for scaling', *Psychometrika, 41,* 439-63.

Carroll, J.D., and J.J. Chang (1969). 'Analysis of individual differences in multidimensional scaling via an N-way generalization of "Eckart-Young" decomposition', *Psychometrika, 33*, 283-319.

Carroll, J.D. and M. Wish (1975). 'Models and methods for three-way multidimensional scaling', in R.C. Atkinson, D.H. Krantz and P. Suppes (eds.), *Contemporary developments in mathematical psychology*. San Francisco: Freeman.

Cicourel, A.V. (1973). *Cognitive sociology*. Harmondsworth: Penguin.

Colby, K.M. (1973). 'Simulations of belief systems', in Schank and Colby (eds) (1973).

Coombs, C.H. (1964). *A theory of data*. New York: Wiley.

Coxon, A.P.M. (1971). 'Occupational attributes: constructs and structure', *Sociology, 5*, 335-54.

——(1972). 'Reply to Jones', *Sociology, 6*, 453-5.

Coxon, A.P.M., and C.L. Jones (1974a). 'Occupational similarities: some subjective aspects of social stratification', *Quality and Quantity, 8*, 139-57.

——(1974b). 'Problems in the selection of occupational titles *Sociological Review', 22*, 369-84.

—— (eds) (1975). *Social mobility*. Harmondsworth: Penguin.

——(1976). 'Final Report: Occupational Cognition: Representational aspects of occupational titles and sociological aspects of subjective occupational structures (SSRC Grant 1883/2)', mimeo, Boston Spa: National Library.

——(1979). 'Images and predication: the use of subjective occupational hierarchies', *Quality and Quantity, 12*.

Coxon, A.P.M., and H.R.N. Trappes-Lomax (1977). *Inquirer III (Edinburgh version), user's guide*. Edinburgh: Program Library Unit.

D'Andrade, R.G. (1971). 'A propositional analysis of U.S. American beliefs about illness', paper presented at Mathematical Social Science Board Workshop on natural decision making processes, Palo Alto, California.

——(1976). 'A propositional analysis of U.S. American beliefs about illness', in K.H. Basso and H.A. Selby (eds), *Meaning in Anthropology*. Albuquerque: University of New Mexico Press.

D'Andrade, R.G., N.R., Quinn, S.B. Nerlove and A.K. Romney (1972). 'Categories of disease in American-English and Mexican-Spanish', in R.N. Shepard *et al.* (eds.) (1972), vol.II.

Dawkins, R. (1976). 'Hierarchical organisation: a candidate principle for ethology', in P.P.G. Bateson and R.A. Hinde (eds), *Growing points in ethology*. Cambridge: University Press.

Deese, J. (1962). 'On the structure of associative meaning', *Psychol. Rev., 69*, 161-75.

——(1965). *The structure of associations in language and thought*. Baltimore: Johns Hopkins Press.

——(1969). 'Conceptual categories in the study of content', in Gerbner *et al.* 1969.

———(1970). *Psycholinguistics.* Boston: Allyn & Bacon.

De Soto, C., and F. Albrecht (1968). 'Cognition and social orderings', in R.P. Abelson *et al.* (eds), *Theories of cognitive consistency.* Chicago: Rand McNally.

Doeringer, P.B., and M.J. Piore (1971). *Internal labour markets and manpower analysis.* Lexington: Heath.

Dunphy, D.C., C.G. Bullard and E.E.M. Crossing (1975). 'Validation of the General Inquirer Harvard IV Dictionary', Sydney: Department of Behavioural Sciences, University of New South Wales, mimeo.

Edwards, A.D. (1976). *Language in culture and class.* London: Heinemann.

Fillenbaum, S., and A. Rapoport (1971). *Structures in the subjective lexicon.* London: Academic Press.

Fishman, J.A. (ed.) (1968). *Readings in the sociology of language.* The Hague: Mouton.

Frederiksen, N., and H. Gulliksen (eds) (1964). *Contributions to mathematical psychology.* New York: Holt, Rinehart & Winston.

Galtung, J. (1966). 'Rank and social integration: a multidimensional approach', in J. Berger *et al.* (1966), *Sociological theories in process,* vol. 1. Boston: Houghton-Mifflin.

Garfinkel, H. (1967). *Studies in ethnomethodology.* Englewood Cliffs: Prentice-Hall.

Gerbner, G., O.R. Holsti, K. Krippendorff, W.J. Paisley and P.J. Stone (eds) (1969). *The analysis of communication content.* London: Wiley.

Glass, E.L. (1975). 'Implication as an alternative to set inclusion as the semantic primitive', in T. Storer and D. Winter (eds), *Formal aspects of cognitive processes.* New York: Springer Verlag.

Gleitman, L.R., and H. Gleitman (1970). *Phrase and paraphrase: some innovative uses of language.* New York: Norton.

Goldthorpe, J.H. (1972). In a 'discussion' of the use of occupational prestige scales in mobility studies. *Social Science Information, 11* (5) 382.

———(1974). 'Social inequality and social integration in modern Britain', in D. Wedderburn (ed.), *Poverty, inequality and class structure.* Cambridge: University Press.

Goldthorpe, J.H. and K. Hope (1972), 'Occupational grading and occupational prestige', in K. Hope (ed.), *The analysis of social mobility.* Oxford: Clarendon Press.

———(1974). *The social grading of occupations.* Oxford: Clarendon Press.

Goldthorpe, J.H. *et al.* (1969). *The affluent worker in the class structure.* Cambridge: University Press.

Gordon, D.M. (1972). *Theories of poverty and underemployment; orthodox, radical and dual labour market perspectives.* Lexington: Heath.

Green, R.F., and M.R. Goldfried (1965). 'On the bipolarity of semantic space', *Psychol. Monographs, 79,* 1-31.

Gulliksen, H. (1958). 'How to make meaning more meaningful', *Contemp. Psychol 3,* 115-18.

Gumperz, J.J. (1972). Introduction, in Gumperz and Hymes 1972.

Gumperz, J.J., and D. Hymes (eds) (1972). *Directions in sociolinguistics.*
New York: Holt, Rinehart.

Gusfield, J.R., and M. Schwartz (1963). 'The meanings of occupational
prestige: reconsideration of the NORC scale', *Am.Sociol. Rev., 28,* 265-77.

Hall, J., and D.C. Jones (1950). 'The social grading of occupations', *Brit. Journ.
Sociol., 1,* 31-55.

Haug, M.R. (1976). 'The erosion of professional authority: a cross-cultural
inquiry in the case of the physician', *Health and Society, Millbank
Memorial Fund Quarterly, 54,* 83-104.

Hawkins, P. (1973). 'The influence of sex, social class and pause location in
hesitation of seven year old children', in Bernstein 1973.

——(1977). *Social class, the nominal group and verbal strategies.* London:
Routledge & Kegan Paul.

Heise, D.R. (1969). 'Some methodological issues in semantic differential
research', *Psych. Bull., 72,* 406-22.

Herdan, G. (1966). *The advanced theory of language as choice and chance.*
New York: Springer Verlag.

Howes, D. (1957). 'On the relation between the probability of a word in an
association and in general linguistic usage', *J. Abnormal and Soc. Psychol.,
54,* 75-85.

Hymes, D.H. (1964). 'Discussion of Burling's paper' (Burling 1964),
Am. Anthrop., 66, 116-69.

Iker, H.P. (1974). 'WORDS: a computer system for the analysis of content',
Beh. Res. Methods and Instrum., 6, 430-8.

——(1976), 'WORDS system manual', Rochester: University Medical Center,
mimeo.

Johnson, S.C. (1967). 'Hierarchical clustering schemes', *Psychometrika,* 32, 241-5

——(1968). 'Metric clustering', Murray Hill: Bell Laboratories, mimeo.

Jones, C.L. (1972). 'Critical note: on occupational attributes', *Sociology, 6,*
451-2.

Jones, R.A., and R.D. Ashmore (1973). 'The structure of intergroup perception:
categories and dimensions in views of ethnic groups and adjectives used in
stereotype research', *Journ. Pers. and Soc. Psychol,. 25,* 428-38.

Katz, J.J., and J.A. Fodor (1963). 'The structure of a semantic theory',
*Language, 39,*170-210.

Kay, Paul (1971). 'Taxonomy and semantic contrast', *Language, 47,* 866-87.

Kelly, E.F. (1970). 'A dictionary-based approach to lexical disambiguation',
unpublished Ph.D. thesis, Harvard University.

Kelly, E., and P.J. Stone (1975). *Computer recognition of English word senses.*
Amsterdam: North-Holland.

Kelly, G.A. (1955). *The psychology of personal constructs.* New York: Norton.

Kemeny, J.G., and J.L. Snell (1972). *Mathematical models in the social
sciences.* London: MIT Press.

Kendall, M.G. (1962). *Rank correlation methods.* London: Griffin, 3rd ed.

Kiss, G.R. (1971). *Recursive concept analysis.* MRC Speech and Communication Unit Reports.

Kiss, G.R. *et al.* (1972). *An associative thesaurus of English* (microfilm version). London: EP Group of Companies, Microfilm Division.

Koestler, A. (1972). 'Beyond atomism and holism – the concept of the holon', in T. Shanin (ed.), *The rules of the game: cross disciplinary essays in models in scholarly thought.* London: Tavistock.

Kohn, M.L., and G. Schooler (1973). 'Occupational experience and psychological functioning: an assessment of reciprocal effects', *Am.Socio. Rev., 38,* 97-118.

Labov, W., and J. Waletzky (1967). 'Narrative analysis: oral versions of personal experience', in J. Helm (ed.), *Essays on verbal and visual arts* (Proc. Annual Spring Meeting of the American Ethological Society).

Landecker, W. (1960). 'Class boundaries', *Am.Sociol. Rev., 25,* 868-77.

Leary, E.F. (1957) *Interpersonal diagnosis of personality.* New York: Ronald Press.

Lenski, G. (1954). 'Status crystallization: a non-vertical dimension of social status', *Am. Sociol. Rev., 19,* 405-13.

Levy, P. (1972). 'Concept-scale interaction: in semantic differential research: solutions in search of a problem', *Br.J. Psychol., 63,* 235-6.

Lieberson, S. (ed.) (1967). *Explorations in sociolinguistics.* The Hague: Mouton.

Lindenbergh, S. (1977). 'The direction of ordering and its relation to social phenomena', *Zeitschrift für Soziologie, 6,* 203-21.

Lindzey, G. and E. Aronson (1968). *The Handbook of Social Psychology.* Reading, Mass: Addison-Wesley.

Lockwood, D. (1966). 'Sources of variation in working class images of society', *Sociol. Rev., 14,* 249-67.

Lumby, M.E. (1976). 'Code switching and sexual orientation: a test of Bernstein's sociolinguistic theory', *Journ. Homosexuality, 1,* 383-99.

Lyons, J. (1968). *Introduction to theoretical linguistics.* Cambridge: University Press.

Macaulay, R.K.S. (1976). 'Social class and language in Glasgow', *Lang.Soc., 5,* 173-88.

Mandelbrot, B. (1966). 'Information theory and psycholinguistics: a theory of word frequencies', in P.F. Lazarsfeld and N.W. Henry, *Readings in mathematical social science.* Chicago: Science Research Associates.

Mandler, G. (1957). 'Organization and memory', in K.W. Spence and J.T. Spence (eds), *The psychology of learning and motivation,* vol. 1. New York: Academic Press.

Martin, F.M. (1954). Some subjective aspects of social stratification. In D.V. Glass (ed.), *Social Mobility in Britain.* London: Routledge.

Miller, G.A. (1956). 'A magical number seven plus or minus two: some limits of our capacity for processing information', *Psychol. Rev., 63,* 81-97.

——(1967). 'Psycholinguistic approaches to the study of communication',

in D.L. Arm (ed.), *Journeys in science.* Albuquerque: University of
New Mexico Press.
———(1969). A psychological method to investigate verbal concepts.
J. Math. Psychol., 6, 196.
———(1972). 'English verbs of motion: a case study in semantics and
lexical memory', in A.W. Melton and E. Marlin (eds), *Coding process in
human memory.* Washington: Winston.
Miller, G.A., and N. Chomsky (1963). 'Finitary models of language users', in
R.D. Luce, R.R. Bush and E. Galanter (eds), *Handbook of mathematical
psychology,* vol. II. New York: John Wiley.
Miller, G.A., E. Galanter and K.H. Pribram (1960). *Plans and the structure of
behavior.* New York: Holt, Rinehart and Winston.
Minsky, M., and S. Papert (1972). 'Progress report on artificial intelligence',
Cambridge, Mass.: MIT Artifical Intelligence Laboratory.
Mirkin, B.G. (1975). 'On the problem of reconciling partitions', in H.M.
Blalock *et al* (eds), *Quantitative Sociology.* New York: Academic Press.
Moore, W., and M. Tumin (1949). 'Some social functions of ignorance',
Am.Sociol. Rev., 14, 787-95.
Mosteller, F. (1968). 'Data analysis, including statistics', in Lindzey and
Aronson 1968 (vol.2).
Neisser, U. (1967). *Cognitive Psychology.* New York: Appleton-Century-Crofts.
Newell, A. (1968). 'On the analysis of human problem solving protocols',
Proc. Conf. Calc et Form. Paris: C.N.R.S.
Nosanchuk, T.A. (1972). 'A note on the use of the correlation coefficient
for assessing the similarity of occupation rankings', *Canad. Rev. Soc. and
Anth., 9,* 357-65.
Osgood, C.E. (1970). 'Interpersonal verbs and interpersonal behaviour', in
Cowan, J.A. (ed.), *Studies in thought and language.* Tucson: University of
Arizona Press.
Osgood, C.E., G.J. Suci and P.H. Tannenbaum (1957). *The measurement of
meaning.* Urbana: University of Illinois Press.
Osgood, C.E., W.H. May and M.S. Miron (1975). *Cross-cultural universals of
affective meaning.* Urbana: University of Illinois Press.
Ossowski, S. (1963). *Class structure in the social consciousness.* London:
Routledge & Kegan Paul.
Parsons, T., and E.A. Shils (1962). *Toward a general theory of action:
theoretical foundations for the social sciences.* New York: Harper.
Perfetti, C.A. (1972). 'Psychosemantics: some cognitive aspects of structural
meaning', *Psych. Bull., 78,* 241-59.
Posner, M.I. (1973). *Cognition: an introduction.* Brighton: Scott, Foresman.
Quillian, M.R. (1968). 'Semantic memory', in M. Minsky (ed), *Semantic
information processing.* Cambridge, Mass: MIT Press.
———(1969). 'The teachable language comprehender: a simulation program
and theory of language', *Comm. Assn. for Computing Machinery, 12*
(Aug), 459-76.

Rainwater, L. (1974). *What money buys: Inequality and the social meanings of income.* New York: Basic Books.

Reiss, A.J. (1961). *Occupations and social status.* Glencoe: Free Press.

Robinson, J.P., R. Athanasiou and K. Head (1969). *Measures of occupational attitudes and occupational characteristics.* Survey Research Centre: University of Michigan.

Roskam, E.C. Ch.1. (1975). A documentation of MINISSA(N). Nijmegen: Department of Psychology, Report 75-MA-15.

Schank, R.C., and K.M. Colby (eds) (1973). *Computer models of thought and language.* San Francisco: W.H. Freeman.

Scott, W.A. (1969). 'The structure of natural cognitions', *J. Personality and Social Psychol., 12,* 261-78.

Shanin, T. (ed.) (1972). *The rules of the game: cross-disciplinary essays on models in scholarly thought.* London: Tavistock.

Shepard, R.N., and J.D. Carroll (1966). Parametric representation of nonlinear data structure', in P.R. Krishnaiah (ed.) *Multivariate Analysis.* New York: Academic Press.

Shepard, R.N., A.K. Romney and S.B. Nerlove (eds.) (1972). *Multidimensional scaling: theory and applications in the behavioral sciences,* vol. 1. New York: Academic Press.

Sherif, M., and C.J. Hovland (1953). 'Judgmental phenomena and scales of attitide measurements: placement of items with individual choice of number categories', *J. Abnorm. and Soc. Psychol., 48,* 135-41.

Silverman, S.F. (1966). 'An ethnographic approach to social stratification: prestige in a central Indian community', *Am.Anthrop., 68,* 899-921.

Simon, H.A. (1969). *Sciences of the artificial.* Cambridge, Mass.: MIT Press.

Smith, E.E., E.J. Shoben and L.J. Rips (1974). 'Structure and process in semantic memory: a featural model for semantic decisions', *Psychol. Rev., 81,* 214-41.

Snider, J.G., and C.E. Osgood (eds) (1969). *Semantic differential technique.* Chicago: Aldine.

Stone, P.J., D.C. Dunphy, M.S. Smith and D.M. Ogilvie (1966). *The general inquirer: a computer approach to content analysis.* Cambridge, Mass.: MIT Press.

Tagiuri, R. (1969). 'Person perception', in Lindzey and Aronson 1968 (Vol 3).

Tesler, L., H. Enea and K.M. Colby (1968). 'A directed graph representation for computer simulation of belief systems', *Math. Biosc., 2,* 19-40.

Thompson, E.P. (1968). *The making of the English working class.* Harmondsworth: Penguin Books.

Thorne, J.P. (1972). 'Models for grammars', in Shanin 1972.

Towler, R.C., and A.P.M. Coxon (1979). *The fate of the Anglican ministry.* London: Macmillan

Transgaard, H. (1972). 'A cognitive system approach to methodology: an outline', *Quality and Quantity, 6,* 139-51.

Tucker, L.R. (1964). 'The extension of factor analysis to three-dimensional matrices', in Frederiksen and Gulliksen 1964.

Tyler, S.A. (ed.) (1969). *Cognitive anthropology.* New York: Holt, Rinehart.

Warner, W.L. *et al.* (1964). *Democracy in Jonesville: a study in quality and inequality.* New York: Harper Torchbooks.

Warr, P.B., and J.S. Smith, (1970). 'Combining information about people: comparisons between six models', *J. Pers. Soc. Psychol, 16*, (1) 55-65.

Wesolowski, W., and K.M. Slomczynski (1977). *Investigations on class structure and social stratification in Poland, 1945-1975.* Warsaw: Inst. of Philosophy and Sociology of the Polish Academy of Sciences.

Westergaard, J., and H. Resler (1975). *Class in a capitalist society: a study of contemporary Britain.* London: Heinemann.

White, H.C., S.A. Boorman and R.L. Breiger (1976). 'Social structure from multiple networks, I: Blockmodels of roles and positions', *Am. Journ. Sociol., 81,* 730-80.

Wilson, B.R. (1966). *Religion in secular society.* London: Watts.

Wilson, D. (1969). 'Forms of hierarchy: a selected bibliography', *Gen. Systems, 15,* 3-15.

Wish, M., and J.D. Carroll (1974). 'Applications of individual differences scaling to studies of human perception and judgment', in Carterette (ed.), *Handbook of perception.* New York: Academic Press.

Yntema, D.B., and W.S. Torgerson (1961). 'Man-computer cooperation in decisions requiring common-sense', *IRE Transactions in electronics,* HFE-*2,* 20-6.

Young, T.R. (1971). 'The cybernetics of stratification: prestige and the flow of information', *Sociology and Social Research, 55* (3) (Apr) 269-84.

Name Index

Subject Index

Aggregation, 184, 187-8; *see also* INDSCAL

Belief systems: about occupations, 130; averaged, 179; causal imagery in, 162; differences between, 136; *see also* Cognition, Logical relations among beliefs, Sentence frame

Category formation, 101, 110
Chaining, 106
Chains of inference, 175
Chapter summaries, 53-5, 89-92, 127-9, 181-3
Class, social, xi, 8, 35, 95-6, 108, 182, 189; assignment of occupations, 128, 144; boundaries, 50, 55; categories, 42, 54, 114-16, 127, 162; differential, 111, 114; images, imagery, 51, 55, 85, 119, 189; language, 119-27; naming, 29, 181; reference in hierarchies, 124-7; reference in sentence frame implications, 161; terminology, 29, 48-9, 60, 68, 77, 80, 84, 91, 98, 120-4; *see also* Status, Registrar General's classification of occupations, Images
Classification of the occupational world, 18
Cognition, 1, 104; and evaluation, 184; and memory, 132; occupational, 1, 4, 187, 190; of social ordering, 15; *see also* Belief systems
Cognitive: maps, 189; operations, 104; organisation, 56, 154
Collective representations, 190
Collectivities, language of, 98; *see also* Kind of people
Connotative meaning, 39
Consensus on the content of groupings, 54, 71
Content analysis, 98, 102; categories, 101; *see also* General Inquirer, Harvard IV-3 Dictionary
Contrast, in occupational beliefs, 102, 171, 180-7; negative, 164-7, 178; pairs, 154; positive, 163-6, 172;

relation, 136, 140, 157, 175, 181; *see also* Equivalence, Implication
Co-occurrence data, 37
Cumulative scale, 173

Data collection, methods of: free sorting, 14-18; hierarchy construction, 58-62; sentence frame substitution, 138-9, 143-4
Deprofessionalisation, 186
Differences in occupational beliefs, 152; *see also* Belief systems
Directed graphs, 133
Directional data, 187-9
Disambiguation, 99, 100; *see also* Harvard IV-3 Dictionary

Equivalence in occupational beliefs, 170, 180; *see also* Contrast, Implication
Ethnosemantics, 13
Evaluation of jobs, 25, 40-1, 45, 48-54, 70, 86, 131; *see also* Status

Factor analysis, 188
Free sortings: context of, 152, 181; comparison of, 26; data, 33-53, 73-80; distance between, 27-36; height of, 22, 53-6; method of, 14-18, 58, 62, 110, 136

Gamma coefficients, 152
General Inquirer (Inquirer III) system of content analysis, 99, 102, 191; *see also* Harvard IV-3 Dictionary
Generality of judgement, 50, 56, 58, 106-8, 109, 175; *see also* Belief systems, Hierarchies
Generative aspects of logical implications, 169
Glossing, 74
Grouping, *see* Free sortings, Social class

Harvard IV-3 Psycho-sociological Dictionary, 99, 100, 101, 112, 116; *see also* General Inquirer